To Simon,

Merry Christmas (98)

All my love

Suexxx

THE
JIMMY HILL
STORY

MY AUTOBIOGRAPHY

Also by Jimmy Hill

Striking for Soccer
Improve your Soccer
Football Crazy

THE JIMMY HILL STORY

MY AUTOBIOGRAPHY

Jimmy Hill

Good luck!

Jimmy Hill

Hodder & Stoughton

Copyright © Jimmy Hill 1998

First published in Great Britain in 1998 by
Hodder & Stoughton
A division of Hodder Headline PLC

The right of Jimmy Hill to be identified as the Author of
the Work has been asserted by him in accordance with the
Copyright, Designs and Patents Act 1988.

10 9 8 7 6 5 4 3 2

A CIP catalogue record for this title
is available from the British Library

ISBN: 0 340 71248 1

Typeset by Hewer Text Ltd, Edinburgh
Printed and bound in Great Britain by
Clays Ltd, St Ives plc

Hodder and Stoughton
A division of Hodder Headline PLC
338 Euston Road
London NW1 3BH

CONTENTS

ACKNOWLEDGEMENTS

First and foremost I must thank my late father for having kept religiously all the press cuttings and articles since I first began my professional career in 1949. They were invaluable in helping to clarify details, dates and other information.

I would like to thank Data General Limited for letting us use their equipment to produce the manuscript for the book. Jim Estey (bless him!) was our lifeline to being on-line and was always prepared, whatever hour of the day or night, to trouble-shoot over the telephone should things suddenly go berserk. At one point we were thinking of putting him on BT's 'Friends and Family'! I now know what 'computer illiterate' means.

Canon (UK) Limited must get a mention, too. They have supported unstintingly a charity golf day organised in my name for SPARKS over the last few years, raising over £100,000, for which I give them heartfelt thanks. They also put an end to trips to our village library to use the photocopier by letting us have one here at home, which was used every day.

I thank my publisher, Roddy Bloomfield, and editor, Marion Paull, who never queried my judgement and who patiently sat through dummy runs of stories and anecdotes when we first discussed the book.

Last but not least, I thank my wife, Bryony, for her loyalty, patience and electric fingers, who typed my handwritten scrawl uncomplainingly at whatever time of the day or night when presented with a draft. For her editing skills, her spelling and suggestions and, although she did tend to hit the sherry bottle on a few occasions, for putting up with me.

1

MARRIAGE MISGUIDANCE... OR EAT, DRINK AND REMARRY

I HAVE enjoyed more than my share of happiness in life; whether it's deserved or otherwise is for others to judge. I consider myself very lucky so far in living up to my father's measurement of satisfaction and contentment – always having enough in my pocket to buy my friends a drink. In addition, in my youth I was blessed with athleticism and dogged stamina, and was bright enough to win a scholarship. That combination of physical talent and reasonable intelligence produced a fascinating life, the foundation of which was sporting and most of the fulfilment was, too. One sadness was to lose my brother and sister, in different ways, so early. Another arose from failing to remain married to Gloria, my first wife, and accordingly causing unhappiness to her and our three children, Duncan, Alison and Graham. It's easy to say that I fell in love with someone else because that's what happened and I can endeavour to ease the pain by pointing out that had I not divorced and married Heather, then two further equally attractive and lovable human beings, Joanna and Jamie, would never have been born. I am indeed a lucky man, because four of these children have produced ten fit and healthy grandchildren between them so far –

and Jamie's not even started yet. To make one mistake is perhaps forgivable, to repeat it not so.

However, at the height of Coventry's success in reaching the first division, during our celebration tour of the West Indies I met and fell in love yet again, with Veronica, of gentler temperament than Heather. That encounter eventually brought about a second divorce. I could try and conjure up excuses for my waywardness, but that would now be unforgivable as Heather was a victim of that indiscriminate disease, cancer, and died a few years ago.

Veronica and I lived together through a frenetic period in my life in the seventies, starting in a small flat in Hampstead on the Heath and ending up, via Notting Hill, in the Cotswolds with fifty acres, three cottages and twenty-four loose boxes. Having had two failed marriages, I thought perhaps the answer to permanence and peace was to remain single. This philosophy seemed to be working until a chance meeting with Bryony, who had been my secretary in the Notting Hill days, led to my final romance. It has lasted more than twenty years so far and seven years ago I married for the third time and Bryony for the first. I am doing my damnedest to make it last at least to extra time and hopefully penalties.

I am not proud of that record but in some kind of mitigation I could plead that all those lovely people involved, for my sake I guess, are on the friendliest of terms and seem to have forgiven me for any unhappiness for which I was responsible.

I could claim that I was always too busy looking for the solution to the problems of others to solve my own, but that's not a convincing argument. Whoever made us also created this appetite in many men, and plenty of women, too, to explore the delights of love and lust, I'm afraid, with more than one partner. In contrast, Gloria and I were brought up to believe that sex outside marriage was sinful and as a result of this upbringing and our own inexperience we did not find it a simple matter to adapt to a satisfactory sexual relationship. Virgins on our wedding night, afterwards it emerged we both learned so much more the second time around. Happily, Gloria fell in love again and has since remarried.

In looking back, I would recommend young people not to be over anxious to marry too soon. As I've found to my cost, it is not a simple matter to form a permanent partnership, however attractive and promising the situation may appear at the time.

1991 was quite a year. Bryony and I had been married for only six months when it was discovered that I had cancer of the bowel.

During the early summer months I had experienced some rectal bleeding while on holiday in France. This did not concern me unduly as I had already had some benign polyps removed a few years before; I simply thought that they had recurred. After some telephone calls and a great deal of assistance from the microfilm department at the old Westminster Hospital, we managed to hunt down the surgeon who had performed the original operation, Dr Ron Zeegan, and I was subsequently booked in for what should have been a routine colonoscopy examination.

Bryony drove me to the hospital in London, returning four hours later as instructed to take me home since I was not allowed to drive after the anaesthetic. I waited in the day-care room, impatient to leave, but Bryony did not come to collect me. What I did not know was that Dr Zeegan had asked to see her privately but had been delayed with another patient. Eventually, more than an hour later, a nurse came and asked me to follow her to a side room, where my wife sat with Dr Zeegan. It was obvious she had been crying; she told me, 'You have cancer of the colon, but the good news is they think it is operable.'

After the initial shock, as far as we were concerned, the disease was simply an irritating nuisance and it was the only time the dreaded 'C' word was ever mentioned at home or away. A few days later, I saw Professor Chris Wastell who was to operate. He didn't mince his words. Assessing the slender chance of avoiding a permanent colostomy at 20–1, he insisted it was imperative to act quickly. He reckoned he could remove the cancerous area, but because it was situated so close to my anus, there was a likelihood

3

that he would not be able to rejoin the bowel. Not very encouraging, I thought, although outsiders with longer odds sometimes come romping home. On consulting my diary I saw that on the date he suggested England were playing.

'I can't make it during the day, Prof, but I can come in late when the programme's over, if that's all right with you.' And so it was. I booked myself into the Westminster Hospital at one o'clock in the morning after 'Match of the Day'.

The operation lasted nearly five hours. As I came round from the anaesthetic I saw Bryony's face.

'Prof's done it!' she said, with a beaming smile. My surgeon's exceptional skill had brought home a 20–1 shot and in time he would be able to put everything back in its place.

The nursing staff were marvellous and kept my presence as quiet as possible so no one, not even my colleagues at the BBC, knew where I was or why. The hospital went to enormous lengths to hide my files since they had experienced problems in the past with public figures, including the odd MP, the House of Commons being just across the way. Apparently gentlemen of the press had been known to don white surgical coats and stethoscopes in order to gain access to wards and read confidential information, which they subsequently released in their newspapers.

For several days I was in the intensive care unit and then thankfully I was put into a room by myself. I was wired from every imaginable orifice, unable to move, but happy to be alive. On the ward was a delightful young student nurse from Ireland called John. I remember when the day came to change my dressing for the first time; he was all fingers and thumbs and very nervous. Having eventually managed to apply the fresh dressing, within seconds it fell apart. He was cross with himself and embarrassed. I said to him, 'Come on, John. Let's have another go,' and together we succeeded in applying a second dressing, with me holding and John securing.

A couple of days later, during a routine visit, having checked my temperature and pulse, John proceeded to fill in a mass of information on the clipboard at the foot of my bed. He was muttering under his breath and I asked if there was a problem. He looked at me, pushing the hair back off his eyes, and said in the most wonderful soft Irish accent, 'Oh Jimmy, if I'd known there was so much paperwork involved in nursing, I would have stuck to fish farming back home!'

The other nurses became good friends, too, popping in frequently to check I was comfortable. The jolly cleaning lady came in every morning with her brush and mop to sweep and tidy, singing away to herself and always smiling. One morning I gave her a bit of advice. I had noticed that every day or two a hospital official checked for dust above the basin by running his finger along the tiles. I mentioned this to her and later on when the official arrived and checked my room, the dust had gone. We laughed about it and it became a standing joke between us.

One particular visit sticks in my memory. Soon after I had been moved from the intensive care unit, there was a knock and the attractive wife of a neighbour poked her head round the door. Giggling, she tumbled into the room, followed by an equally pretty friend, both having clearly enjoyed a splendid lunch. Tripping over the safety cone in the corridor outside my room where the floor was wet, they picked it up, entered and offered it to me as a present. Two minutes later, to my horror, Prof arrived with the usual posse of students. The two girls could hardly stand up and in fits of giggles fiddled with my tubes and wires – luckily one of them was a fully trained nurse so I was in no real danger – but poor old Prof just didn't know where to look. One of the students caught my eye and choked back a snort, immediately setting off the others. How Prof managed to keep a straight face and maintain decorum in the circumstances in front of his students, I shall never know!

In spite of the success of the surgery, during which Prof had also removed an affected lymph node, it was necessary to undergo a series of radiotherapy and chemotherapy sessions for good measure, the former on a daily basis and the latter once a fortnight. For convenience I travelled by train from

Gatwick early every morning to avoid the rush, and the nurses would slip me in quickly and discreetly so that my presence remained a secret. I didn't suffer much discomfort internally, only a little burning from the radiotherapy, but yes, in case you are wondering, I did lose my hair, though not from my head!

The other inconvenience was harder to tackle. Without wanting to offend sensitive souls any further, as I have already explained, the location of my problem was such that, as it was going to take some time to heal, certain parts of my anatomy were put on hold. Although ultimately I would return to being a complete human being again, I had to learn to cope with a temporary colostomy. Believe it or not, as a mere male, I am not necessarily the most practical person in the world and I found it to be quite a palaver. Euphemistically, Bryony and I named the active piece of my equipment 'Horace', the intestine to which it would be rejoined eventually 'Doris', and the dormant area 'Boris', all sharing the family name 'Morris'. It was a secret code, because I'm afraid Horace had a mind of his own and a tendency to make extremely loud, embarrassing, rude noises totally unprompted, anywhere and any time.

After twelve days in hospital, and armed with plenty of knowledgeable and sympathetic advice from the stoma nurse, I went home.

You soon get used to a new way of life, and I did my best to carry on exactly as I had done before the operation. Little things simply took longer – like having a bath and getting dressed in the morning – but I quickly learned the rules and mostly remembered what not to do. For instance, if you are in a hurry to leave for an important Football League meeting in London, do not, repeat *do not*, put on any body lotion as the bag will not stick! Useful advice in retrospect! I continued to play golf and tennis, without inflicting my problem on the rest of the world. Interestingly, at a golf club where I played regularly, I observed I was not the only one similarly afflicted.

Once, on a flight back from Kenya, disaster struck. We had been invited to take part in a charity golf tournament at the recently opened Windsor Golf and Country Club in Nairobi to raise money to build a wire fence to protect the rhino population. The competition was an interesting one, nicknamed the 'Rhino Charge': each player was allowed to play the number of shots his handicap allowed, and when they had been used up he was to place a flag with his name on it at the exact spot where they ran out. If he had completed the eighteen holes with shots in hand, he would continue from the first tee until such time as he had to stop. There was a considerable amount of water on the course and we could spot more than one flag floating where some unfortunate player's ball had ended its days. It was great fun and a competition with a difference. The resident professional generously issued Bryony with her first official handicap certificate and she is now a proud member of the Windsor Golf and Country Club, Nairobi.

However, on the journey home, whether or not it was due to the air pressure in the cabin we shall never know, but with a long queue for the loo, an accident occurred. The stewardess, seeing my distress, kindly allowed me to go into the First Class section, but it was still too late. As we were walking through customs on arrival, the officer asked me to open my hand luggage. I clamped my hand firmly on the zip and offered undoubtedly as good a piece of advice as he had ever received in his life: 'I wouldn't open that if I was you!' He didn't!

The good news was that I was eventually going to be reconnected and functioning normally. The bad news was that I had developed an internal abscess which sometimes crops up with such an operation. This condition can't be treated with antibiotics and so we simply had to sit tight and wait for it to run its course. This took over eight months. However, almost a year to the day from the first operation I was back in the Westminster for Horace to be reintroduced to Doris and for Boris to come home from his holidays. Oh happy day!

Insofar as my professional career was concerned, I continued to work for the BBC without any interruption. Only once did I have an actual upset and this was prior to the FA Cup final at Wembley in 1992 when suddenly I felt unwell. Still no one was aware of my condition and just before going on air I had to rush out of the gantry, regaining my seat only moments before going on live. It was a narrow escape. Subsequently I was asked to stand in as presenter of 'Six-O-Six' on Radio 5 Live for three weeks. The first two programmes were fine, but on the Monday before the third show Doris and Horace were due to be remarried. Surgeons are wonderful. I was stitched up perfectly and able to cope with the verbal rigours of this popular football talk show on the following Saturday. I met a young lad two days later who asked, wide-eyed, 'Are you Jimmy Hill who was on "Six-O-Six" on Saturday?'

'Yes,' I replied.

'You do know a lot about football, don't you?'

I must admit I was extremely flattered. Unfortunately, it does not appear to be a vital qualification for a 'Six-O-Six' presenter these days.

After seven years now and regular annual check-ups, I am as fit as a flea. Very rarely did it get me down and anyway I knew I had to be cured as the marvellous surgeon who operated on me and monitored my progress has recently retired, and I don't want to have to train another one!

We had kept our secret ruthlessly, crushing any apparent breaches in the defences, but somehow or other one paper did get wind of the story and began to pester us. Despite several abortive telephone calls to my wife, two reporters turned up on our doorstep. Luckily I was in London that day and Bryony handled it in the way we had chosen to by saying nothing to them except, 'My husband has had a tummy operation, but he is fine now,' and left it at that, not denying or acknowledging their statements. Despite that, they remained outside all day.

When I was nearly home I telephoned Bryony to be told, 'The two reporters are still there waiting for you. Ring me when you reach the end of the lane and I'll come and open the gate so you can drive in and go straight inside.' This is what we did, but before I could make the front door the two reporters were at the gate and spoke to me. I was tired after the trip to London and annoyed at their persistent approach. I looked at them furiously and said, 'If I am suffering from the disease you say I am, do you think that your behaviour will help me recover from it? Think on that and print it if you dare!' We were never bothered again, and I had been granted an extension to a life which began in South London seventy years ago.

2

HOW IT ALL BEGAN

I T started in Peter Sellers' 'Gateway to the South', Balham, London, at five o'clock in the morning on 22 July 1928, in the downstairs bedroom at 57 Pentney Road, in those days not far from the bottom of the social ladder. We weren't free from snobbishness ourselves, and looked down our noses at the residents of Scholars Road, an adjacent street, whose gardens backed on to ours. Although it was only a two up two down, I can never remember an occasion when we did not have an auntie, or a grandmother, or even a lodger living with us. One paying guest used to write a column under the name of Professor McNaught for *The Boy's Own* paper. The Professor was a keen golfer and I used to keep him company at dawn as he played the nine holes carved out on Tooting Common, only a hundred yards up the road. As for family, my mother Alice had married during the First World War but sadly her husband was killed in the fighting. She was left with two young children, Wally and Rene, and it was some years later that she met my father; they married in 1926. My father had joined the Royal Marines in the First World War and in many ways I am the luckiest person in the world to be alive because he was torpedoed not once, but twice, first on SS *Cumbria* and the second time on the cruiser, HMS *Cornwallis*. Happily he survived, and on both occasions he was picked up by passing shipping.

The euphoric atmosphere that existed following the Armistice in 1918 was soon to evaporate. Those who had fought for King and country during the war faced yet another battle, to make a living. Many found that difficult, not least my father; work was hard to come by but finally he was employed delivering milk. There was nothing as posh as glass bottles in those days, but large churns out of which the milk was dispensed using measured half pint or pint metal ladles. He confided to me that some of his more enterprising, but less honest, mates used to make sure that their ladles had a sizeable dent or two in the bodywork. In the course of a day, the milk saved added up to something comparatively substantial in terms of profit for the milkman.

My uncle Sid, also employed by a dairy, earned himself a little on the side by taking bets from the customers on his rounds and before long he persuaded my father to follow suit. If only Dad had had less ambition and left it at that the family might have been far better off, but he decided after a while that it might be a better idea for him to take the bets himself. So for a period of time, which I can vaguely remember, we were pretty comfortable financially, but all good things come to an end and so they did for Dad and for the rest of the family.

The disaster occurred when a horse called April The Fifth won the Derby. The horse was owned by a popular actor of the time, Tom Walls, and it seemed that every housewife in Great Britain had had a little flutter on the animal, including most of those who had been on Dad's milk round. All that would have been fine had Dad stayed with his steady job on the milk trail. Unfortunately, because of the success of the mini bookmaking operation, he had abandoned his round and subsequently made a much healthier living from the punters. As a result of the speed of April The Fifth, the family's economy slowed down to a crawl. My father was on the dole for some considerable time before he was able to get work delivering bread for 'London's Greatest Bakers', A.B. Hemmings. The depot was alongside Blackheath. This necessitated Dad getting up in the middle of the night to get from Balham to London Bridge station, and from there to Blackheath,

11

walking across the common to the bakery. His day started before dawn and he was lucky if he managed to get back home by 7 p.m., all for the grand sum of £4 a week. In the circumstances, bearing in mind the country's state of deep depression, he was relieved to secure any kind of work at all.

When I was older, just before the outbreak of the Second World War in 1939, I used to help him on a Saturday. His round covered many of the roads which led down to the ground of Charlton Athletic Football Club and a few of the players lived on our round. What an enormous thrill it was for me to be serving two gods of football and I still treasure the autographs of the Oakes brothers on whose doors we knocked. From two o'clock onwards on Saturday afternoons I was green with envy as I saw the supporters streaming down the hill to watch their favourite team, then in the first division of the Football League. After the war, Dad left London's Greatest Bakers to become a store- man with the Mullard Radio Valve Company at Mitcham. So much closer to home and such a tranquil occupation, compara- tively, he thought he was already in heaven.

Looking back at the thirties, I was lucky to have an older brother and sister, both of whom played games well. My sister, Rene, was particularly talented. I had no doubt how it came about but she played for a local ladies' cricket club, the Redoubtables, whose ground was in Mitcham alongside Hackbridge station. I was very excited to be allowed to tag along and watch her and her team play. I have vague memories of standing with a small cricket bat in my hands on the edge of the field as various young ladies bowled balls at me, most of which I missed; a hit, though, produced irresistible approbation. Rene became rather more than a club cricketer such was her talent, and I can remember the bitter disappointment at home when, having been selected to tour Australia with an England XI, it became apparent the cost was out of the family's reach. In those days there was no such thing as sponsorship, and it was only wealthier young ladies who could afford to go.

Rene's boyfriend at the time was a young man named Edward

who ran a small garage, so all sorts of exciting cars and motor-cycles appeared outside our house. He was a Brentford supporter and sometimes took me to Griffin Park. Strange, wasn't it? Fulham was my club later, so I played for the first two league clubs I had been taken to as a child.

Tragically, Rene, my talented half-sister, was not too long for this world. Her enthusiasm for cars and motorcycles eventually ended her young life. Whilst riding her motorcycle one day, only half a mile from home, she was in collision with a lorry and was severely injured. Although she lingered for some months after the accident, she never really stood a chance. I can imagine my parents' distress when, as a seventeen year old, I bought a motorcycle myself and travelled daily, in all weathers, to and from the City.

My mother's side of the family seemed cursed. When my brother was conscripted in the last war and became a Royal Engineer, it was not expected that, with his particular skills, he would be in the firing line or in any special danger. Wally was working in Basra on lofty cranes when in July 1942 a jib broke and he fell from a considerable height, dying on the way to hospital. Fate does not appear to ration its devastating blows fairly and certainly not in my mother's case. I was at home when the telegram arrived from the War Office five days before my birth-day, saying that my brother had died following an accident while on His Majesty's service in Iraq. It was heartbreaking for my mother, who had lost her first husband in the First World War, then her only daughter, and now her elder son, wiping out three of those people so close to her. It left me an only child in a double sense. Whether such tragedies initiated in me a stronger and deeper determination to be successful in life, I can only guess. I know I always felt I wanted to do something for my mother and father, not only because of the difficult life they had led; after all, there were and still are plenty of families experiencing similar hardships, but they did not deserve such devastating misfortune.

At Cavendish Road School I made steady progress, particularly at games. I was in both the football and cricket teams at the age of eight, which was somewhat exceptional and probably gave an early indication that I might climb either or both those twin ladders to success in later years. I made my first mark in cricket in a match for the School First XI at that age. Playing against eleven year olds, I scored 31 not out, not an astronomical total, but because of my tender years I won a Jack Hobbs bat, awarded under a scheme promoted by London's *Star* newspaper. Later I learned that Johnny Haynes was in his school football team at the age of seven, which foretold his future in no uncertain terms.

Retrospectively, I and those like me owe an enormous debt to the teachers who freely gave of their spare time to coach us in a variety of games and other activities. They not only guided and encouraged us out of school hours, but in many cases laid the foundations for a successful professional career by sowing fertile seeds at the most potent time. It has been my hope now for some years that there would be a swing back to such a caring, unselfish attitude. I regret having to record that, although there are still some splendid exceptions, to date I have seen little sign of it. I can remember Mr Garnham who, in an effort to teach us to bowl on a length, would put a penny in a small circle on the perfect spot. After school we would bowl for hours, in an attempt to acquire consistency and the skill to torment batsmen. As other countries progressed with the provision of coaching facilities and trained personnel to encourage sporting skills, we seemed to have acquired a blinkered attitude to the teaching of games. We lived with the false belief that great players were born and could not be improved.

I was fanatical about sport: football, cricket, athletics, tennis or any competitive physical activity. On the other hand, I do not recall having over much interest in mental gymnastics. Thus it came as an enormous surprise to me, and a shock to the system, when the names of those who had passed the eleven plus exam were read out in the school hall. My name was among them; I didn't know whether to laugh or cry, not really understanding the implications, whereas Mum and Dad were extremely proud of their only son. For my part, I was also unaware of the extra strain it would put on their finances.

I was told we could choose any grammar school in the south London area. Don't ask me why the decision was mine and not my parents', but I selected Henry Thornton School in Clapham because my previous football hero at Cavendish Road School, Tommy Wright, had also won a scholarship and had chosen to go to Henry Thornton. I was due to start there after the summer holidays in September 1939. If you are my age, you won't need to be reminded that 3 September was the date when England declared war on Germany. Because of the threat of bombing, my parents, without my knowledge, had decided that I should be evacuated. A tearful Jimmy was spirited down to Pagham, a small village near Bognor in West Sussex, eventually moving across to Chichester, where for a period of six months, Henry Thornton School shared the classrooms with Chichester High School for Boys. From time to time my parents came down to see how I was faring and each time I burst into tears as they left, which upset them so much that at the end of six months I was despatched back to London.

There was another development that helped them to make that decision. Another reason they had put my name down to be evacuated was that they had been told there would be no local schooling in the event of a war. In spite of this, within six months the Henry Thornton School, Clapham, was re-opened to house the South West London Emergency School for Boys, enabling those grammar school lads who had stayed in London to receive an appropriate education. I stopped crying, joined the 88th London Company of the Boys' Brigade and was back in good time to see the first air raid and our Spitfires and Hurricanes defending the City from the Luftwaffe.

Every night for months on end during the air raids, eight of us would sleep in an Anderson shelter. The government generously dumped sheets of corrugated iron in our front garden leaving the family to dig a massive hole, fit in the segments and cover the lot with as much earth as we could make stick. Dad, innovative as

15

ever, had fashioned eight wooden bunk-type sleeping places long before the official ones arrived. The sirens would sound regularly around eight o'clock at night, before which we would play darts for pennies in the house. Not realising the seriousness of it all, my nerves were in somewhat better shape than those of my elders, especially Uncle Charlie, and in continually supplementing my pocket money, I had already turned professional.

Life carried on in London. Dad joined the Home Guard and caused great amusement the first time he put on his uniform. I don't know how many sizes too big it was for him, but it would have frightened the life out of the enemy, certainly if they had been tailors!

Away from the war, it was a time for learning; apart from French, German, mathematics, geography, history, religious knowledge and all the other subjects with which I was confronted, the Boys' Brigade added to the list. BB provided gymnastics, playing the cornet, learning first aid, drill classes and also the fundamentals of the Christian religion (Baptist branch). We certainly did not allow the Germans to prevent us from preparing for life.

On Saturday mornings I would play football for the school team at Rose Hill, Sutton, travelling home on public transport without taking a bath unless it was unavoidable. In the afternoon I would play my second game of the day, for the 88th London Company of the Boys' Brigade, on one of the local commons. On such days the bath around 5 p.m. was an event of maximum enjoyment and some necessity as it prepared me for the day's third major activity: the games evening at the local Baptist church. Playing table tennis, snooker, darts, etc. made sure that we were all completely exhausted by the time we went to bed. Sunday sometimes meant church parade in the morning, playing in the band on the way to and from the church, and Sunday evening always meant Bible class.

When the nightly raids started on London, they curbed some but not all of these activities. After all, we had regulation tin hats which would protect us from any falling shrapnel from the shells of the anti-aircraft guns, as we made our way from home to the church hall. Boys' Brigade activities were beneficial in many respects but they were time-consuming, which put pressure on those of us with homework to do. Nevertheless, after five years of this frenetic activity above and below ground, I was still in one piece. I was a sergeant in the BB, a reasonably accomplished player of the cornet, with a knowledge of first aid and elementary drill routines. The biggest miracle of all was that I managed to stagger through the matriculation examination, gaining a pass. I suppose I could have stayed on to take the higher school's examinations, and maybe after that go on to university, but if the thought entered my mind it soon found a way out. I was anxious to escape from studying, but uppermost in my mind was to repay my parents, by bringing some money into the house. I was cock-a-hoop; having dispensed with learning, I was about to enter the adult world and at the same time could congratulate myself on being a dutiful son.

For some reason that I can no longer remember, I wanted to work on a newspaper. Martin Isaacs, our goalkeeper at Henry Thornton School, had joined the *Daily Sketch* and later on, under the name of Martin Lee, was to sit in the press box and write favourably about his old team-mate. After a couple of interviews, the first job I was offered was as a clerk for the London and Lancashire Insurance Company, 7 Chancery Lane. I took it. The job itself was boring: initially there was a backlog of policy documents which had to be updated and I spent hours poring diligently over them but not getting any satisfaction. It became apparent that if I wanted to progress in the insurance world, I would have to begin studying for the various insurance examinations. Having escaped from homework, I was in no mood for further exams. Inevitably, therefore, when the opportunity arose, I joined a firm of stockbrokers, H.J. Garrett and Co. I found Stock Exchange life much more to my liking: I had always been reasonable at mathematics, so I was soon able to cope happily with the speed at which the Stock Exchange functioned. The amount of business done on one day varied greatly; sometimes

17

we would be working there until seven or eight in the evening, clearing up the aftermath of bargains that had been struck. Time flew by with breakneck speed, yet in contrast when business was slack, the office manager would say, 'Okay, no more today. See you in the morning!' and off we'd go. Such a logical approach enabled me to pursue my other life, BB and sport. I seemed to be doing well at work and was about to get to the 'Blue Button' stage – that's when a clerk was allowed access to the floor of the Stock Exchange itself and was able to witness and play a part in the business taking place. However, before this happened, I reached the age of eighteen and could find no way of avoiding National Service, which at that stage in the nation's history confronted every healthy young man.

I was posted to Bury St Edmunds, the headquarters of the Suffolk Regiment, for six weeks' basic training. As a result of my Boys' Brigade discipline it was less of a shock to me than it was to some. I was better off financially, too. I happened to own a cheap iron – trousers had to be pressed and ninepence was the price. By hitchhiking to and fro I managed to get home on five Sundays out of the six.

The next step was a move to the RASC at Cirencester to take a further six weeks' clerks course, whilst waiting to go before a War Office Selection Board to establish whether I was officer material. Since I played the cornet/trumpet, I had drawn attention to it in filling in a questionnaire, alongside my other skills and hobbies. My answers led to my getting in the football, cricket, athletics, table tennis and darts teams, but sadly not in the band. I'm afraid my Boys' Brigade cornet playing did not reach the standard required by the nineteen-year-old musical genius, Johnny Dankworth, the band's leader. I didn't even make the reserves.

I did make the football team almost immediately, playing in the Cirencester and District League on Saturday afternoons and earning the rest of the weekend off. At the end of the six weeks, I knew something about army office procedure and could touch type, but at only fifteen words a minute.

I was marched up in front of the CO who proposed a deal. If I gave up my ORI (Officer Rec. 1) grade I could stay on in the unit as a corporal (more money) and instruct on the same course I had just taken. Naturally, I would continue to play in the battalion football team (more weekends home). Having no real military ambitions, I jumped at the chance, instructed and played football for a year without missing one weekend at home. I also acted as MC at the extremely popular and crowded Thursday night hops, featuring the Dankworth band – my first break into showbusiness.

It was too good to be true and after twelve months I found myself transferred to Blackdown Garrison in Farnborough along with Derek Ufton, my pal.

'Do you know why you're here?' the CO asked, as I stood to attention in front of him.

'No, Sir!' I replied. 'Except that I understand that I'm to take charge of the Documents Office.'

'Ridiculous!' was the retort. 'You're here to play football, but see you do the other job as well.'

That surprised me, but nothing like so much as when I played my first match and found that Derek and I were the only two amateurs alongside nine professionals. Derek went on to play for Charlton and England and also keep wicket for Kent. Unlike me, though, he already had a toe in both those camps.

Those pros taught me how to play, i.e. that football is basically a passing game, the cornerstone on which all other more elaborate skills are based. After one handsome 5–0 win, I can remember thinking that I didn't dribble round anyone, and the realisation dawned that the ball travelled faster on its own. It's preferable that kids learn that lesson at nine, not nineteen.

After a month or two, I was asked by Ziggy Brown, our centre-half, if I would like to play a match or two with him for Folkestone Town in the Kent League. I travelled down by train, scored a goal in a comfortable win and was rewarded with a brown envelope containing £3 10 shillings to cover my expenses, exactly £1 2 shillings more than I was getting for serving His Majesty for a whole week – yet another hint of professional possibilities. On my second visit we also won and I scored again. The third time I wasn't so lucky – I ended up in Folkestone Hospital, a scything tackle by an opponent having torn a cartilage. The offending part was skilfully removed at the Cambridge Military Hospital, Aldershot, just in time for me to be pronounced fit to leave the army and face the world, with the cushion of a few weeks' paid demob leave.

The law of the land said that if I wished it, H.J. Garrett and Co. would be obliged to re-employ me for six months. However, they explained that the Stock Exchange was not at its most buoyant and if I could turn my hand to anything else, their advice was to do so.

I had heard a whisper that Ted Drake, then Reading's manager, had seen me play in an army match and was interested in offering me a trial. I had nothing to lose, and anyway I needed advice on rehabilitating my knee, just seven weeks after the operation. So I took the train to Reading one morning and knocked on the office door. I was welcomed royally, never mind nursing my knee, and within half an hour of arriving I was playing in a practice match – hadn't they ever heard of pre-season training?

I must have done something right because I was offered a prolonged trial, the club paying for my digs with Mr and Mrs Pointer on Donkin Hill. I played mostly in the third team. Wilf Chitty, who had played for Chelsea, was the team manager, also filling in occasionally when we were short. We competed in the Hampshire League and as often as not after a game stopped for a meal at the Criterion, Winchester. I can't remember much about the games, but I can remember how much I enjoyed tucking in to the feast provided by the restaurant, so much more sophisticated fare than life had produced hitherto.

I played a couple of games in the reserves towards the end of my time there and I remember one in particular against Brentford at Griffin Park. I was marked by a tough veteran, Vivian Woodward, who gave me an uncomfortable time. I fought back stubbornly and tried to give as good as I got. I must have impressed Jackie Gibbons, the Brentford manager, because there were two contrasting outcomes. First, Ted Drake told me he wasn't prepared to sign me as a pro and secondly, following one trial game for Brentford a week or two later, Jackie Gibbons said that he was – puzzling for a young lad, because Reading was in the third division and Brentford in the second. Who cared? I had got my chance.

3
BRENTFORD DAYS

FROM a position of desperately raw talent and minimal experience, I managed, by enthusiasm more than inherent skills, to win a place in Brentford's First XI and begin the climb to competence as a professional player. In the ecstasy of being offered a contract at the enormous sum of £7 per week and £5 out of season, I took the plunge and married my childhood sweetheart, Gloria. I tried to persuade our manager that £5 was not enough to live on in the summer and that I was just as good a player as I was in the winter, probably better; he put it up to £6. We started married life living upstairs at my mother's and father's in the house where I was born in Pentney Road, Balham, before the club found us a house in Whitton Manor Road, near Isleworth. We had the upper half, the lower half being occupied by Billy Dare, a pleasant young man with a lovely wife and quite a talent for scoring goals. He was a centre-forward, striker now, a pint-sized one, but exceedingly quick and strong with a trick or two to outwit taller defenders.

Bill did not own a car, whereas I was the proud owner of a dark blue Morris 10. One of the problems with the house in Whitton Manor Road was that the entrance to the garage was extremely tight. On mornings when we may have been just a minute or two behind schedule, the car was in grave danger of having its paintwork disturbed, as in haste I endeavoured to squeeze it out backwards on to the road. It was particularly frustrating if it was Bill who was late. More was to come. Believe it or not, merely by driving the car to the ground I was breaking a club rule: our manager, Jack Gibbons, had closed his eyes to my indiscretion originally because the journey from Balham on public transport was horrendous. I'd been told to park the car round the corner so that my crime was concealed; hence there was always a short walk to the tea hut, situated just inside the ground. The club provided this small luxury for the players before they started their training. First there, in the nature of things, would order and pay for the teas. In every other way Billy was a sweet man, but the electric pace and nimbleness which enabled him to reach numerous goalscoring chances first on the field evaporated entirely when it came to getting to the tea hut.

In terms of football skills and experience I had a very large L plate on my back, but as far as athleticism, strength and stamina were concerned, I could hold my own with more experienced players. That helped me to survive and learn quickly. There was no such thing as coaching in English football; everyone believed that great players, or even good players, were born and there was no way you could improve upon God-given talent. Brilliant players scoffed at the idea and lesser players dared not argue. So there I was, an unskilled, inexperienced professional in a business which I had to learn quickly if I wanted to survive.

The man who had taken a chance on me, Jack Gibbons, was better known as A.H. Gibbons, significantly an 'amateur' originally in a professional game. The A.H. came from this status while a pre-war Tottenham player. He was an intelligent, ambitious man, a former RAF officer, and not the usual stereotype of a football boss. Jack had just taken over from a successful but older style of manager, Harry Curtis, who had guided Brentford before the war and resolutely manoeuvred them into the first division, now the Premier League. He had a fine reputation but after the war Brentford had slipped to the second division and the board decided to make a change.

Jack Gibbons was different and in a hurry. My inexperience, especially in one department, was blindingly obvious. Although I measured six feet tall, I was not the best in the air. Heading was an art I had not acquired at grammar school nor in the army. I tended to wait for the ball to reach the ground before employing other skills. The manager, not surprisingly, had noticed this slight deficiency in my repertoire. Ignoring traditional beliefs, he thought that perhaps something could be done about it. Maybe promising footballers could be fast forwarded into better ones?

Our captain at that time was a reserved but inspirational man, Tom Manley; with a dry sense of humour and an equally entertaining left foot, he had played for Manchester United before the war. Imagine that! Even then, Manchester United in my mind certainly had a grandeur that Brentford lacked. Jack Gibbons had said to Tom, 'Jimmy's hopeless in the air. Take him over there, throw some balls at him and tell him, or show him, how you jump and head them!' I lived in awe of Captain Tom and this was the early sowing of seeds of a belief that coaching could help a player improve his skill, let alone tactical knowledge. Simplistic and basic as it all sounds now, it took the British game, chairmen, managers, coaches and players, some years to accept such philosophies and we still suffer as a result of it. Suffice it to say that later on, although in the air I was a long way from being a Tommy Lawton or an Alan Shearer, when I played as a striker I managed to head a valuable goal or two, including three in one game for Fulham. I even played some games for them as a central defender, not winning everything, but certainly winning my share and rewarding Jack Gibbons for his foresight and Tom Manley for the lessons which allowed me to climb to higher things.

My first official game as a pro for Brentford was in the reserves, away to Bournemouth. We lost 6–0: not the most encouraging debut! On the following Wednesday I retained the No. 9 shirt for my first home game at Griffin Park as a Brentford player. We won 6–0 and astonishingly I scored three of those goals. Excited as I was with such a dramatic swing in fortune, I did not look upon it as a passport to promotion to a second division league match. However, fate was offering a helping hand – the first team's results had been far from satisfactory. I am unable to remember any detail of what happened between Wednesday and 3 p.m. on the following Saturday except that at the appointed hour I was wearing the No. 9 Brentford strip kicking off against Leicester – the beginning of twelve years of fun, frustration, fantasy and fulfilment.

I slipped the ball gently to Kenny Coote, our inside-left, and ran forward in hope more than expectation. Kenny controlled it and played a short pass back to me as I moved out of the centre circle towards the Leicester City goal. Getting my head down, I can't remember going past any opponent until I got into a position on the edge of the Leicester penalty area, close enough to take a hopeful shot at goal. I was thoroughly excited by what was happening. I pulled my foot back and lashed at the ball, attempting to create the most impressive start to a footballer's career in the history of the game. Unfortunately, I barely made contact and the ball dribbled maybe a full yard and a half in the wrong direction and the fairytale quickly evaporated. Eventually we drew 0–0 so at least I could boast that I had played a part in earning a point for my team in my first game in the Football League.

The real excitement was to come later – would I be selected for the next match? We had been unable to score on our home ground despite my enthusiastic but raw efforts. The next match was away against Bradford Park Avenue. All through the week the big discussion point with anyone I could find to bore to death with the topic was would I be picked for the following Saturday? In those days we used to travel up on the train the evening before, so on Thursday the team sheet went up: twelve names, among them J. Hill, but in no particular order. It could mean that I had held on to my place. As I tried to sleep that Friday night, thoughts of what might happen the following afternoon kept rushing through my mind. I could think of nothing else. We were staying in a hotel next to the station and the incessant noise of the trains shunting up and down came through the windows alarmingly and annoyingly. The outcome was I didn't get a moment's sleep. I can remember vividly my panic at being awake hour upon hour upon hour with the anticipation of playing my second game for a professional football club. The ladder of Henry Thornton School, the unit team in the army, straight into Brentford's first team via Reading A team and reserves, was a steep one and my mind would not rest. Shrewdly, Jack Gibbons had pre-empted the effect such events would have on me, and the next day, to my bitter disappointment, I was made twelfth man. In those days there was no chance of a sub coming on, so in frustration I had to sit there for ninety minutes and watch the lucky chosen eleven battle it out against Bradford. It was a neat ploy by the manager and a basic lesson in man management. He realised what an impression it would have on me, with my temperament and enthusiasm, totally inexperienced, playing my first away match. When I next travelled away, I did sleep the night before the game, trains or no trains, and Preston, our opponents, offered £8000 for me.

I had an up-and-down season as an inside-forward; sometimes it would look as though I knew how to play the game and at other times I would appear to be a complete novice. It was fun, to be sure, but nerve-racking too. Again my athleticism enabled me to survive my shortcomings and continue to be selected by the manager. Jack Gibbons stood by me when things didn't work out, especially when a section of the Brentford crowd started to criticise me. There were times when I appeared to be slow, turning into an opponent and losing the ball, failing to see a team-mate in a good position to receive. I would attempt cross-field passes which I had seldom delivered in my life and sometimes failed miserably. It brought a few moans, and yet in the midst of these moans I would suddenly spring back to life and show a flash of skill which would calm down the critics until the next mistake. Altogether, it was a difficult baptism because, almost without exception, my colleagues in the team were far more experienced. I was indeed a learner. Nevertheless, on the bright side, before very long some quite pleasant things were written about me:

Clifford Webb, *Daily Herald*: **Brentford 1 – Sheffield United 0**
Man of the match was Jimmy Hill. He has a nice easy dribbling action, knows how to beat a man and how to make accurate passes. Quite a prospect, I would say.

News of the World: **Brentford 3 – Barnsley 0**
Hill, the Brentford inside-left, was the man of the match. His craft and methods make him stand out and he made ball control look easy while so many players found it difficult.

Harry Ditton, *News of the World*: **Brentford 2 – Hull City 1**
Hill wouldn't be out of place in an England team. It was a great move inspired by him that produced the first goal.

Needless to add, they described the good days – there were others.

One day, one of our players was injured and I was shuffled back from an attacking role as an inside-forward to a defensive one at wing-half. It meant that instead of playing with my back to the play, which tended to be the case for what we call a striker now, I found myself facing it. After that I began to be selected in that position, with Tony Harper, a stout defender, and Ron Greenwood completing the half-back line. I must say I found it so much easier and slowly but surely began to quieten the critics. Because of my innate attacking instincts, I tended to carry the ball forward and created danger for our enemies. This gradually turned the resident Griffin Park sourness into the sweet sound of encouragement and appreciation. It is of enormous benefit to a young player if a crowd will allow him time to survive the early days as he learns the job under pressure.

I began to respond to the applause which was exceedingly pleasant, as was playing alongside Ron, who became a good friend. With his experience he was able to help me tremendously in mastering the defensive arts, which were in short supply in my curriculum vitae. It was also Ron's influence which persuaded me to attend a Football Association coaching course at the National Recreation Centre, Lilleshall. I had never thought about it before, but it did seem to make sense to do everything I could to learn about the profession I had just entered. It also seemed to be a prudent provision for the future when I could no longer play; passing on such knowledge to others would be an added bonus. I put down my name for a course at Lilleshall for the forthcoming summer, as did other ambitious team-mates. Johnny Paton, an outside-left Brentford had acquired from Celtic, was among them. He was very bright, full of personality and fun, and will enter the scene later in another context. Our goalkeeper Ted Gaskell was older, more experienced and had already begun to visit local schools regularly for coaching sessions. Finally, Jack Goodwin completed our Brentford coaching posse, and come the summer off we went to Lilleshall to meet Walter Winterbottom, the man who, single-handed, was to revolutionise England's attitude to coaching. He succeeded in turning England from a relatively heathen football country in which footballers were supposedly born multi-talented into one in which it was accepted that it was possible to improve individual and collective skills, tactical knowledge and performance and achieve better results.

Acquiring the knowledge was one thing; being able to pass it on as a teacher was another. In that respect I did have an advantage from my earlier days, first in the experience I had gained in the Boys' Brigade as a sergeant and later in the army as a corporal. I was relaxed on my feet. Walter was an inspirational teacher; he had the personality, the enthusiasm and a new message of direction and hope which made sense. Many of us during that period were motivated to go out and preach his philosophies, including Vic Buckingham, Bill Nicholson, Malcolm Allison, Ron Greenwood and certainly myself. I recently caught a glimpse of a photograph of a squad of pupils at Lilleshall and there, standing at the back, was Bob Paisley. I don't know how much of Walter's philosophy rubbed off on Bob, but he went on to become the most successful manager, in terms of winning trophies, domestic football has seen, ahead even of Bill Shankly.

Within a short time I had earned my full badge and thus had set up the second string to my bow: a player and now a coach, which was to prove invaluable.

A year or two later I was back at Lilleshall as an instructor on the same course I had so enjoyed in my early days at Brentford. On Thursday evenings an impromptu camp concert was staged during which, if there was any talent in the entertainment field present, those possessing it did their best to enchant their colleagues. There is another word that, if I wasn't a gentleman, I could use about the nature of the audience, but let's just say they were not the easiest of gatherings to play to.

On the staff was a most talented footballer and extremely entertaining man, Southampton's George Curtis. In the days when there were few ball jugglers, George had magic boots. He had total control of the football with tricks to spare and was an extremely skilful and entertaining circus-like inside-forward. I knew that from one or two most frustrating afternoons spent trying to take the ball from him down at the Dell. But George had another talent – he could recite Kipling's poem 'If', and it had become a regular spot in the Thursday evening concert. After a year or three, some of us thought we might spice up George's performance. I suggested that while he was reciting, perhaps two or three of us could hum 'Land of Hope and Glory' gently in the background. The only problem was to make the music fit the poem, but after a few rehearsals we had it precisely timed. On the night, though, George inadvertently omitted two lines of the verse, which meant that he was getting to the end of the words before the hummers were able to catch up with him. As on the pitch, George was ahead of the game. So with the realisation that he was going to reach the goalline first, the slow double *piano* of the hummed voices in the background suddenly acquired a touch of panicky *accelerando*. By dint of exceptional fortune we reached the final chords almost together to tumultuous applause from the audience – at any rate, I think that's what it was!

Fun and games it may all have been but there was a serious thread leading to 1966 and England winning the World Cup for the first and only time.

At about that time, in 1951, our second division club was invited to play against the Dutch National XI. That in itself speaks volumes for the foresight of the Dutch FA, as well as registering their humble position in terms of world football during that period. Believe it or not we managed to draw 1–1 which would hardly be the case if those levels of teams were to play each other nowadays. It only goes to show just how far Holland has progressed since then.

The second most astonishing thing that stays in my mind was the quality of the food that we were offered. Six years after the war had ended, back home we were still rationed, having to surrender coupons in exchange for butter, clothes and other commodities. In contrast, here we were staying in a luxurious hotel in Amsterdam confronted by an array of food the like of which we had never seen in our lives before, let alone eaten. To a man, we came from families where the budget did not stretch to such luxuries even without a ration book and that quality of nourishment just wasn't available at any restaurant that we may have patronised in the UK. In truth, I have to admit, I was a touch sluggish for the first fifteen minutes at least, because of the enormous amount of food with which I could not resist stuffing myself the night before.

In my mind, Brentford in those days is inextricably linked with Johnny Paton, mentioned earlier, the outside-left who had come to Griffin Park via Celtic. Johnny had four things in his favour: a bright personality, an attractive wife and two young children. He was the first one to make me aware that there would come a time when I would no longer be able to earn a living playing football, and perhaps not coaching, and to raise the dreaded question, 'What then?' John had taken steps himself and paid for a correspondence course in salesmanship. Occasionally, when we were on a train or in a coach travelling to an away match, he would be reading his notes and would pass on little nuggets of knowledge to me, which began to open my mind to the possibilities. He didn't exactly talk me into it, but he did encourage me to begin thinking about life after football. Thus, we both wrote for jobs advertised in the London *Evening Standard* as trainee part-time salesmen for a company called Accessories Electrical Supplies. We went for interviews and couldn't believe our luck when we were taken on. No sooner had we finished training at Griffin Park than we were knocking on the abundance of factory doors which existed up and down the Great West Road, presenting cards asking to see managers, sales reps or anybody else prepared to give us the time of day. Electric light bulbs were our stock in trade, but Arnold Weinstock had little to worry about. Nevertheless, it was educational and kept us out of mischief and in touch with the real world, which we would have to rejoin sooner or later.

My interest in golf, having flickered into life during my time on trial at Reading, developed slowly at Brentford. We used to play on days off at Wyke Green Golf Club, not all that far from the ground, and occasionally at other clubs in the area. I don't know why we found ourselves playing at Hanwell Golf Club but I will not forget the day I holed out in one; I can't even remember at which hole, except it was about 150 yards or so par three downhill and I took a five iron. I can't claim that it was a very good golf shot: it was sliced and low and hit the corner of the green on the left, faded across the green and, to my absolute delight, went straight into the hole. An undeserved piece of luck, but one that caused about as much celebration as we could muster.

While still living in Balham, I searched for somewhere to play locally. A popular course for peripatetic golfers was Beckenham Place Park, not all that far away, twenty minutes or so by car. With three friends I used to play regularly on Sunday mornings, not at a normal teeing off time, but at six o'clock to avoid the rush. We would aim for 5.30 a.m. for a prompt start. By nine o'clock we were round and on the way home for a Sunday morning breakfast and a day with the family.

One day, on a day off from training, I was in the locker room at Beckenham when a voice asked, 'Anybody want a game?'

'Well, yes,' I replied, 'I'm here on my own.' The questioner was a man called Ossie Noble. We played a round together and from that chance meeting became friends and rather strange business colleagues.

Ossie was on the stage, a mime artist. It was a delight to see him entertain an audience without speaking, dressed as a dumb clown and creating laughter with solely visual humour. He was also an accomplished drummer. We played golf together regularly. In order to establish a good rhythm for his golf swing, Ossie was following advice. He had heard that the swing should adopt the pace and flow of the 'Blue Danube Waltz' – 'La da da da boom!' etc. and at the 'boom!' you hit the ball.

Ossie provided another example of the anxiety which footballers, other professional sportsmen and in his case those on the stage and in the theatre carried with them, fearing the day when they would no longer be able to earn a living through their particular talents. Ossie was always looking for ways in which he could establish a future, something that would earn him a living if his act lost its magic. As it happened, with the availability of television, music hall was soon to lose its attraction and many floundered. Ossie was haunted by the thought that one day the public might tire of his act and he would be unable to support his wife and lovely children.

One idea for prosperity came from having seen an advert in a newspaper for pies which were made in Scotland. The manufacturers wanted people to distribute them in London in large numbers for a commission. According to the advert, if they could be sold in reasonable quantities, the seller would become rich overnight. I took home the offer, made some calculations and quickly established that we would have to sell hundreds of pies before we made a fiver and an astronomical number to underwrite Ossie's ambition and our future. We left the pies alone.

What Ossie did, though, was to start the Immaculate Chimney Sweeping Company. I'm certain he had never swept a chimney in his life, but he was sold on the idea and purchased a vacuum machine which was supposed to suck the soot from a chimney. The main selling point of the exercise was that we could sweep a chimney without any of the soot escaping and soiling a room. The way in which this was avoided was to seal off the grate with a square steel plate bounded by sacking and sticky tape. It could be adjusted to fit most fireplaces so that when the soot did fall down as it was dislodged by normal sweep's brushes, it would not billow into the room. The name 'Immaculate' was fundamental in advertising the cleanliness of the service so that the visit of the chimney sweep would not become a mucky nightmare necessitating a subsequent spring clean. Ossie had the technology, what he needed were customers.

My cut was a shilling out of every seven shillings and sixpence, which was the cost of having a chimney swept by Ossie Noble, for each order I obtained for him. I went from door to door as close to his home in Streatham as I could get. I had the telephone number and the 'Immaculate' name printed on a series of slips of sticky paper and I would knock on a door and ask the unsuspecting lady of the house whether she wanted her chimney swept. If she said no, as most did, I would lick the back of the label and say, 'Well, you may need to at some time in the future. Put this in your telephone book and when you want a chimney sweep, the number will be nice and handy for you.' Of course, as the label was wet and sticky, something had to be done with it; it didn't always work but I did manage to offload quite a few. The outcome of all this was that after a time, Ossie began to get more orders than he and a friend, who sometimes helped him, could cope with and they had their hands full.

'How would you like to come and help me to fulfil these orders, Jimmy?' Ossie pleaded. 'Because I really am in trouble.'

Never one to refuse a chance to support the family, I got off my backside and joined him, equipped naturally with the essential white coat. The philosophy was that a chimney sweep in a pristine overall was incapable of blackening his reputation. A customer only had to look at the sparkling uniform to see how effective an invention the vacuum was. What was not known, of course, was that Ossie had a whole series of these garments. By the time we had finished sweeping chimneys for a day, we had each gone through about four or five coats, changing them as soon as they became soiled. Poor Mrs Noble's washing machine worked overtime.

Unhappily, I did my sweeping in the summer months and, even worse, I suffered from hay fever. Soot did not agree with me and brought on uncontrollable bouts of sneezing. Couple this with the moment when the brush became stuck, as it did from time to time, and let your imagination do the rest. Getting the brush to the top was partly technique but often brute force. It was an essential part of the process, as three out of four housewives would want to see the brush poking out of the stack to show the job was done. More often than not we accomplished it, but there were occasions when the chimney won the match and we shamefacedly had to admit defeat.

So there we were, the Immaculate Chimney Sweeping duo wanting to play golf much, much more than sweep chimneys but imprisoned by the constant rumblings of insecurity arising from the fear that one day our art would no longer feed the family: the nagging shared insecurity of showbusiness and professional sport.

All of a sudden, in only my second season as a full time pro, following what must have been much better performances, my name started to appear as a possibility for representative honours. Within a short space of time both Ron Greenwood and myself were selected for more than one FA XI, which at that time was looked upon as a potential stepping stone to the full international side. I played in one FA XI which included Cliff Holton of Arsenal and Tommy Harmer from Tottenham Hotspur, against an army team including Bobby Smith of Spurs and Tommy Taylor, who sadly died in the Manchester United air crash. We won 4–2. After that match, Bernard Joy, former Arsenal and England centre-half, wrote that I was the pick of the FA defence, a compliment to Ron Greenwood, bearing in mind how few matches I had played in my life, let alone as a professional, in a defensive position. Ron's guidance was quickly bearing fruit.

The most exciting happening to date was when, in November 1951, I was chosen by the London FA to play against a Berlin XI in the Olympic stadium, holding 80,000 people, in the German capital, the first representative match to be played between the English and German teams after the Second World War. It turned out to be a most enjoyable and emotional experience. Our half-back line consisted of Bill Nicholson, Ron Greenwood and myself, and with inside-forwards Eddie Baily and Jimmy Logie, it was overwhelming. I wondered what on earth I was doing in the team; some of those players were gods to me and only a short time ago I had paid to watch them.

As for the match, volatile journalist Desmond Hackett's report in the *Daily Express* was uncomplimentary. Cliff Holton was particularly abused for missing numerous open goals and goal-keeper Harry Brown was in the Hackett doghouse having let in a single goal which took longer to bump into the corner of the net than our kettle does to boil. However, Mr Hackett did write, 'The half-back line of Bill Nicholson, Ron Greenwood and Jimmy Hill is sound material for bigger games in the future.' We were presented with a leatherbound photograph album of the trip. One of the shots of the match itself showed James Hill bending down and picking up a German player from the stony area on the edge of the running track on to which I had previously knocked him, obviously doing my utmost to avoid provoking a Third World War.

It was a very happy period. Brentford were in the promotion race. I was being selected for representative teams and kind things were being written about me in the press. Altogether a far cry from the barracking I received from the crowd in the early days. John Arlott was kind enough to write:

Of those competitive footballers who are the rank and file of the game, one in fifty after a few seasons takes that extra step in development which makes him of international class. This season Jimmy Hill, the Brentford left-half, has done that. Strong, faster than the next man in reaction, movement and assessment of a situation, he has in striking degree the quality of determination. Without neglecting his defensive duties he varies his tireless prompting of attacks with solo rushes which are always likely to take the opposing goal by storm. He is a rapid, direct dribbler, hard to move off the ball, adroit in the use of the short or long pass and with an unquenchable enthusiasm for employing his powerful shot.

I suppose all things being equal, that wasn't a bad tribute from a respected journalist to someone who was still learning the business after two years in the job.

One extraordinary match at Griffin Park stands out in my memory; it was against Preston North End, who had the superlative Tom Finney playing at outside-right. The match was in some doubt as Griffin Park was looking more like the River Thames than a football pitch. Saturday morning came and the rain had not let up, but despite the inclement weather the magic of Finney had enticed a vast crowd of over 25,000 people, an excellent gate in those days. The maximum limit today is 12,000.

Three-quarters of an hour before kick-off, the referee announced that he would take the ball out and bounce it around the penalty spot; if it bounced, the game would go ahead. He emerged with his linesmen and Jack Gibbons and unceremoniously bounced the ball. They nearly lost it sinking into the mud – bounce was not a description which leapt into anyone's mind. For reasons known only to himself, the referee said the game would proceed. There was about a yard or so of decent grass fringing the pitch, that was all.

By half-time Brentford were three goals down, all of them having been constructed by Finney. The Master didn't deign to use the muddy parts of the ground but stayed fixed in his wing position until one of his colleagues managed to get the ball to him. Tom conjured up all three first-half goals by dribbling his way down to the corner flag, turning sharp left, bamboozling further

36

opponents on his way in towards the near post, and picking the precise moment to lay on three perfect goalscoring opportunities.

Try as we might we could not break the Tom Finney spell during the first half. Nevertheless, a stirring half-time talk from the Boss sent us back on to what was left of the pitch for the second half. George Sands wrote in the *Middlesex Chronicle* in his report of the game: 'In the second half, Jimmy Hill picked up the Brentford forward line and hurled them at goalkeeper Gooch, of Preston North End,' which was a flattering way of putting it. As it happened, Brentford did score two goals and closed the gap on Preston, but sure enough the inimitable Finney chose yet another moment in the game to lay on Preston's fourth, and that was that! I shall never forget the majestic performance of Tom Finney in overcoming conditions which would have sent many superstars I have known scuttling home to their mummies. I'd have given him his gong there and then.

4

OVER AT THE COTTAGE

I T was the temperament of our manager, Jack Gibbons, and the skill of a Southampton player, Frank Dudley, that caused Ron Greenwood and myself to ask to be put on the transfer list. It was around Christmas time and we were challenging for promotion, an ambition shared by our opponents.

I can remember the game at Griffin Park as if it was yesterday. In those days defenders often found themselves outnumbered: two against one was normal, three against one not all that exceptional. Ron, using his intelligence as well as his natural defensive ability, had become a master at holding up two players by not diving in at one when he was outnumbered; that merely created the simple opportunity for the ball to be slipped to the other. I had seen this ploy work many times, causing two players to dither and become indecisive, which allowed that fraction of time needed for another defender to get back into position. Frank Dudley had an eye for goal. He was pacey, strong and gangly with a penchant for doing the unexpected. During the game, he had been unusually quiet and Brentford were on their way to an important win. Southampton were not finished though. Dudley came in from an oblique angle. Ron was outnumbered two against one as another Southampton player lurked in the centre, waiting for Ron to close on Dudley who would then

38

make the telling pass. Ron stood his ground, as always not being drawn to the tackle and hoping to encourage fatal indecision. The strength of the ploy was that the attacking angle of approach was so oblique (as when Ian Wright hit the post in the 1997 World Cup qualifier in Rome) that if the goalkeeper was correctly positioned just on his post or just outside it, the target was a very, very narrow one. Thus although it may have looked more dangerous not to tackle, in effect Ron was causing the forward to shoot from a position where the odds were stacked against him. I had seen it work previously so many times. On this occasion, Frank Dudley with dead-eyed accuracy and a touch of good fortune – at the last moment the ball bounced a couple of feet to the right – managed somehow to squeeze the ball past Alf Jefferies into the Brentford net. Southampton spirits soared and to complete the misery, Dudley went on to score the winning goal. Brentford were seen to throw away a home match and with it, their hopes of promotion.

Jack Gibbons went berserk and laid into Ron Greenwood, my good friend and inspiration who had helped me survive as a defender, despite my inexperience. He really was brutal. Ron argued the case, emphasising the numerous other times when the same ruse had rescued the team, but I could see he was furious. It was a setback in what had so far been an exhilarating season, but excruciatingly damaging as it turned out. I could understand a certain loss of temper, but as I came to realise only too well later on as a manager, if you want to retain the confidence of the team, it's imperative you hit the right targets in moments of crisis. Players know who's to blame and they quickly find out a manager who doesn't, or who shows favouritism.

The result was that Ron asked to be put on the transfer list, and out of loyalty and a sense of justice I joined him. The incident brought about the end of my association with Brentford, which until then had been an extremely happy one. The strange conclusion was that my good friend Ron decided to make his peace with the club and remain at Griffin Park. Inadvertently, I had put myself out on a limb in strange territory. However, within a short time, thank goodness, Fulham FC, who apparently had been watching my performances, declared their hand and I made the short move from Griffin Park to Craven Cottage in a swap for Jimmy Bowie plus a £5000 transfer fee. Jimmy Bowie of Fulham was bought from Chelsea for £20,000. So, having been in the game for such a short time and still with a very big L on my back, I was proudly telling my friends that my value at that time was £25,000, about a million or more in today's currency.

Although the distance from Brentford's ground to Craven Cottage is only a few miles, when I arrived in March 1953 the change from one dressing-room to another was distinct: Brentford chasing promotion, Fulham threatened by relegation and the need to revitalise the playing staff. Among the senior players were Joe Bacuzzi, whom I had watched wide-eyed with admiration in the Fulham team as an eleven year old just before the war, and Jim Taylor, another boyhood hero of mine. The unforgettable Ronnie Rooke, my absolute favourite, had not long left Fulham for Arsenal, whilst Scotland's flame-haired Archie Macaulay had made the reverse trip. As for new blood, one highly publicised, expensive acquisition had been Charlie Mitten, for whom Fulham had paid Manchester United £17,000, a pretty sizeable transfer fee in those days.

Charlie and Neil Franklin, Stoke City and England's centre-half, had caused a sensation by accepting an offer to play in Bogota. They just opted out of the archaic retain-and-transfer system in this country as heroes or traitors, depending which side you took, but things didn't work out and both had come back. Charlie was indeed a character. He certainly wasn't short of footballing talent, nor was he short of confidence and in the upper range of cheekiness. He possessed the sweetest and most powerful left foot combined with the utmost nerve to beat opponents, tempting them to tackle and then fooling them with his trickery. He was capable of scoring with his powerful left foot in open play from almost anywhere in or outside the penalty area; as he played on the wing, most of these shots came from an oblique angle. Who better to be Fulham's penalty-taker, needing only to beat a goalkeeper from a mere twelve yards? Charlie was never a shrinking violet and confidence is obviously one of the chief attributes essential for success in taking a penalty. However, Charlie had encountered a setback – he had missed a penalty for us. At that time, Frank Osborne was in charge of the team and presided over Friday team talks in the boardroom itself. Frank would walk round the table in full flow, and sometimes, to make a point, he would lean or stretch across it, illustrating a tactic which merited discussion. At the end, he would conclude: 'Penalties. All right to take them, Charlie?' On the first occasion after Charlie's miss, not all that surprisingly, he replied, 'Yes, Frank, fine.' Taking into account such confidence, the unexpected outcome was that Charlie missed the next penalty kick and the charade occurred once more. Frank giving Charlie the opportunity to opt out, if his faith in his trusty left foot had weakened, ground out grudgingly the unavoidable phrase, 'All right for the penalty kicks, Charlie?' Without a hint of a pause, 'Fine, Frank,' once again came the answer. This scenario continued until Charlie had left Craven Cottage having missed certainly four if not five penalty kicks in a row, which must be a world record. Who else but Charlie would still have had the nerve to carry on taking them? Charlie never once backed down and no manager had the courage to stop him; after all he had the reputation of being a masterly taker of spot kicks, as history had unhappily failed to record.

The treatment room in those days was the smallest room in the Cottage, leading off the first-team dressing-room. Frank Penn, our trainer, part-time physiotherapist, psychiatrist and treater of injuries, operated from there. Every afternoon a queue would line up outside the dressing-room, awaiting attention. One day I turned up for treatment and I couldn't believe my eyes when I peered into the room itself; on the table was a Greyhound positioned under the heat lamp with our trainer massaging a joint on the dog's leg. Frank had a whimsical sense of humour and an extraordinary measure of patience. He looked up at my face, which must have been a picture of puzzlement. With the slyest of winks, he said, 'I think we'll have him fit for Saturday!' The dog, needless to say, was Charlie's who saw nothing untoward in his animal being first in the queue ahead of injured players.

My first match for Fulham was away to Blackpool. I managed to score a goal from a midfield position but we lost the game. My second was at home against Arsenal. I remember it particularly because Joe Mercer, a giant of a footballer in my eyes, was in the Arsenal team. To me, Joe was a superstar and a gentleman, an inspiration to play against. We drew 0–0 and I was elated, but elation was not enough to prevent the misery of Fulham's relegation to the second division. Having just left it with Brentford, I found myself back where I started.

However, change was beginning to stir at Craven Cottage. Old players were gradually filtered out and it turned out to be the beginning of the most successful period in Fulham's history. It didn't happen immediately because the outstanding talent that became available was far too young at that time: Bobby Robson, Bedford Jezzard and on the horizon, Johnny Haynes, were names that later would bring recognition, some glory and eventual promotion back to the first division. Four or five barren years of frustration were to be endured first, during which we exhausted an interesting collection of managers. Frank Osborne was the father figure and switched roles from general manager to team manager in emergencies, occasionally coming into the dressing-room side of the business, but it was the team managers who were found wanting and went. The first was Bill Dodgin, who had been Southampton's manager when Fulham had pipped them for promotion at the run-in by getting maximum points from eight matches, as the Saints found themselves unable to win a match. One of Bill's favourite expressions was, 'Friends are better than money', which wasn't bad propaganda to prevent players from pushing for higher wages when the annual argument came round. Bill had a year or two in which to win promotion; it didn't happen, so he went. I was sad because Bill was the main influence in acquiring my transfer from Brentford, and it was his initiative that had persuaded Frank Osborne to give the go-ahead for the signing.

Bill was replaced by another individualistic managerial talent, Dugald Livingstone. We were told that he had previously managed the Belgian national team with some success. He was a pleasant man but with a certain vagueness and not without a sense of humour, which one definitely needed as a player at Fulham, let alone a manager. The Dugald story that did the rounds was that when he went to Belgium the national side had a most successful season, winning all their matches for twelve months or more, and then all of a sudden the magic disappeared and they couldn't win a match. The explanation the cynics manufactured was that during that period, Dugald had learned to speak French. Thus the team was at last able to understand his instructions, the results being better when they hadn't.

Managers have their own peculiar ways of extracting inspirational performances from their teams. Dugald Livingstone was no exception. Such sermons took place either in the boardroom on Friday or in the dressing-room just before kick-off, or for away matches, perhaps in a suitable room in a hotel. I am not absolutely sure where Dugald's first team talk took place, but I can remember almost to a word the contents:

'In life and in football, lads, you get what you **expect**. It's a simple philosophy: if you **expect** to win a game of football, you're more than halfway there to winning it. Have confidence in yourselves, believe in yourselves and **expect** to beat your opponents. I can tell you, they're only ordinary fellows like yourselves wanting to win the game. Nothing special about them, nothing to worry anyone. They have the same doubts as you have. So, whatever you do, when you run out there on the field you must **expect** to beat these fellows. **Expect** to beat them, and you'll win.'

I must say, delivered in Dugald's pleasant, gentle Scottish brogue it was not an unattractive oration. Certainly it had its inspirational qualities and our manager had the personality and eloquence to put the words together in potent, encouraging fashion. A week or two afterwards we were playing Leeds

United in an away game at Elland Road, not the Leeds United they became under Don Revie, but none the less not easy opponents on their own turf. They also had Big Jack Charlton at centre-half and other players of reasonable stature. However, they were not thought to be invincible and we approached the game, if not with absolute confidence, certainly not without hope. In the hotel before the game, Dugald gave us his predictable team talk. 'You've got to **expect** to win this game,' he said, etc. etc. etc. By the time he had finished it was evident to us all that providing we did not limit our expectations, the result was a foregone conclusion. Accordingly, as per the scenario, we scored first – 1–0 up at Elland Road against Leeds United and a stirring start. Unfortunately, Leeds were working from a different script; they didn't take too kindly to being one goal behind and replied by scoring six goals against us. Thus the final result was: Leeds United 6 – Fulham 1.

Dressing-rooms following a loss or a poor performance are unhappy places. I leave it to your imagination to conjure up the atmosphere after losing so badly. Normally in such circumstances you hear a few curses, and occasionally players might tear into each other over an incident that may have led to a mistake which might have given away a goal. Mostly, though, it's silence: long, miserable silences, sometimes broken by a boot hitting the floor or a frustrated hand hammering against the dressing-room wall. Such was the case on this occasion, which brought about one of the longest silences ever experienced in football legend. It was broken only by our right-back, Tom Wilson, who mouthed, 'All that I can say is that some rotten f . . . . r in our team was **expecting** to lose this game today!' Dugald did not stay with us long.

Shortly after joining Fulham, I went to Wembley to see the Hungarians play in that extraordinary match in which they beat England 6–3 in November 1953. It was a revelation and I will never forget the experience. It was as if they were players from another planet, magnificently skilled, with perfect teamwork and like nothing I had ever seen before or could have imagined. I was so fascinated by it that I managed to get hold of the Hungarian coaching manual which explained the routines with which they had persevered in recent years in order to achieve the standard of excellence which I had seen but hardly believed. There were practices in the manual of which I had never dreamed and certainly couldn't accomplish but there were others, much simpler, which I felt certain could be employed beneficially in England. As it happened, Fulham were between managers around the time I acquired the book, and a long-time servant of the club, Eddie Perry, who had played at centre-forward before the war, had taken over temporarily pending a new appointment. I chatted to him one day about the Hungarian manual. Eddie, like most people, had been staggered by the quality of their play.

'You know, Ed, some of the practices that are recommended in this book might even help us,' I told him. Eddie thought about it for a day or two, and then shocked me.

'Would you like to organise the pre-season training along those lines?'

That was a very strange request, when you think that I was around twenty-seven and only a player myself. It's true, I was a qualified FA coach and had experience of coaching at lesser levels, but for a player to take charge of pre-season training with his playing colleagues was unusual to say the least. I talked to one or two of the team, who seemed not to be against it, so I planned the pre-season training schedule for Fulham FC for the 1955–56 season. Quite a lot of the practices were based on one- and two-touch training, used in small-team games to quicken up players' reactions and to give them the capacity to knock balls away when being threatened by opponents' tackles and thus to live ahead of the marking, as it were. To start with, the sessions went very well; some of the different, purely physical activities were more interesting than the boring laps that had previously been the pattern, and the players accepted them very well. They also used to enjoy attempting some of the strange and tricky skill practices and found that with sufficient perseverance at least some progress could be made. At the end of the straight physical

45

part of the activity and any special skill practices, it was usual to enjoy a small-sided game, a light-hearted but fiercely competitive end to the session. It worked for ten days or so and seemed to be going well.

Then one morning, having finished the formal fitness and skill sessions, I said, 'Okay, lads, we'll play fifteen minutes two touch and then we'll finish with one touch.' Unfortunately, our centre-half, Gordon Brice, with his Marines background, was more used to giving orders than taking them and he took exception to the fact that we still appeared to be involved in a restricted training activity as against being allowed the freedom of playing proper football.

'Okay, Gordon. If that's the way you feel, that's what we'll do,' I said. The outcome was I didn't train the players again.

There were only a few days to go before the start of the season and our first match was at home against Blackburn Rovers, who were tipped, as we were, as promotion candidates. We scored five goals against Blackburn on that day and played some of the best football I've played in. Would you believe that the team in its first seven matches scored five, four, three, two, two, six and three goals. Quite an extraordinary start to the season. I was convinced that this was as a result of the one- and two-touch training that we'd embraced following the Hungarian pattern. Strangely enough it didn't last. In the last ten games of that season, Fulham managed only seven goals. Despite that shattering comedown, I didn't lose faith and was convinced that the coaching had been of great value. Surely if we could achieve so much immediate improvement in such a brief time, what could be done over a period of months and years if we persevered with it? I did notice that after England's most successful run in qualifying for the 1998 World Cup finals, culminating in the 0–0 draw in Rome, Glenn Hoddle referred to the training that they had undertaken in the week before that particular match in Italy and he revealed that one- and two-touch training played a prominent part. Nothing new is there; except there was to Fulham players in 1955.

Coaching was something I enjoyed immensely and I was

delighted to have the opportunity to coach the Oxford University team. During my first year with them, the captain was Harry Joynt. Harry was an amiable, determined man who wasn't designed to be the greatest athlete in the world; he was strong and resolute, with some games-playing ability, but never destined to be a star. He was chosen as captain for his other qualities. I found the University players wide-eyed, cooperative and most willing to learn. I don't suppose they realised that I was on a learning curve too, because for the first time in my coaching life I was to be responsible for results; in this case, one result especially – winning the Varsity match against the deadly enemy, Cambridge. Influenced by the Hungarian approach, I based much of my coaching practices and philosophy on their beliefs.

Retrospectively, it's simple enough to see why the result turned out as it did. In the build-up, Oxford looked quite stylish with bouts of inter-passing which worked smoothly, but at other times they gave the ball away in the wrong places and suffered accordingly. Nevertheless, by the time the Varsity match arrived, we had achieved a good result or two but without consistency. The pattern was similar at Wembley against Cambridge, producing some pretty pretty football. Surprisingly, we led by two goals to nil at half-time. Dr Tommy Thompson, the inspiration behind and founder of Pegasus – a team of former Oxford and Cambridge players who won the Amateur Cup – also took a leading role in advising the Varsity side. Although it was the captain who had the power, Tommy was not averse to exercising whatever influence he could on aspects of team selection and performance. He ran around the dressing-room at half-time, offering advice to one and all, including words which may have cast the fear of losing indelibly in their minds. It was not easy for me to prepare the team for the onslaught which I knew would be forthcoming. Sad to relate, Cambridge scored three goals in the second half and won the match.

In the second year, I inherited an equally determined but more skilful captain, David Harrison, these days chairman of Corinthian-Casuals. We quickly struck up an excellent relationship and were determined to reverse the previous year's Varsity result. We obtained some good results in the early season matches playing against Spurs reserves, the army and the navy among others. I was still encouraging the players to play with style as well as with determination and method, and I felt the team was stronger than that of the previous year. The Varsity match came round again with all the excitement such a Wembley occasion engenders. The numbers attracted to Wembley were not of Cup final proportions, but they made as much noise as if it had been full. In the talented Cambridge XI, Keith Sanderson, Jackie Pretlove and David Millar were among those destined to move higher up the football ladder. As a result, Cambridge were favourites, but that did not prevent us from thinking we had a fair chance of winning on the day.

Results immediately leading up to Wembley had been encouraging, losing 2–1 in the last minute to a strong FA XI and beating the army 3–1 with goals from Dick Chadder and the fast-improving Robin Trimby. It was Trimby who scored in a 1–1 draw with Pegasus. Hopes were high for Wembley and the quality of the game was remarkably good. Cambridge with considerable flair scored twice in the first half hour, but Roberts reduced the arrears as Trimby's header rebounded from the bar. Cambridge went 3–1 up before Sweeney reduced the lead again. Despite fierce performances from David Harrison's team, Cambridge held out.

There was some compensation, however, when the game itself was praised for quality as well as drama and judged to be on a par with the best in the history of Varsity football. For me, though, it was very frustrating. Losing two Varsity matches was not good for the Hill ego nor the future prospects of someone who one day was going to earn his living as a manager. Before I had time to lick my wounds, an offer to coach came from a similar direction, but based rather nearer home. London University were looking for a suitable person and invited me to join them, despite my 2–0 losing ratio in Varsity football. Since their training ground was less than a mile away from my home in

Worcester Park, it seemed too good to be true. I was determined to improve on the past by finding the secret to winning games at that level. I developed a stable and friendly relationship with Wally Goss, the Tommy Thompson of London University football, and was also guided by the enthusiastic and helpful influence of Jim Clarkson, a teacher friend whose passion was football and striving to unravel its mysteries.

What I had seen at Oxford was that over-emphasis on a classic approach did not win matches at that level. Although improving the creativity of a team gave me most pleasure, it soon evaporated when the results did not match the beauty of the performance. Thus I changed my attitude at London University as a result of the two years I had spent with Oxford. I leaned more towards making life difficult for opponents by playing a tighter, tactical game and building the creative pattern around the strengths and weaknesses of the players at my disposal.

My week consisted of training four mornings at Craven Cottage, concluding with a communal bath; two afternoons a week with Oxford University, followed by a refreshing shower; and two evenings coaching Sutton United, where it was back to the bath before bedtime. In one way I was undoubtedly the cleanest player in the Football League! Most clubs have individual showers these days, less extravagant lower down the scale but a long way from Fulham in the fifties. If Albert, our groundsman, failed to get out of bed at 4.30 a.m. to light the boiler, Haynes, Robson, Hill and Co. shivered in lukewarm water as we searched for the Sunlight – soap, that is!

Around this time our Players' Union delegate, Norman Smith, whose task it was to collect the subs and attend meetings, decided to take up a career in accountancy, and as a result resigned from his Union responsibilities. Since I had done the job at Brentford I was made favourite to take over at Fulham. Needless to say there was not a queue but I was quite happy to help, not realising for one moment that it would mean anything more than a couple of meetings a year and collecting the subscriptions. At the time it didn't promise to be time-consuming or demanding but it turned out to be a decision which would change my life and thrust me into a public battle as a young man which would alter the face of football as well as my own future.

There were some rumblings of discontent stirring in the Players' Union at that time. Cliff Lloyd was the secretary and Jimmy Guthrie, ex-Portsmouth, was chairman of the Union. Jimmy managed to present the case for change pretty well publicly: he spent time in Fleet Street churning up interest among the scribes, campaigning by underlining the total unfairness of the situation in which professional players found themselves. He spoke articulately at meetings in a forceful Scottish accent and was, as far as I could gather, a popular figure among the players. I had little knowledge of what went on behind the scenes, but picked up some of the flavour of the battle that was to be fought before long in conversations with players from London clubs. Through coaching I mixed with, among others, Ken Armstrong and Derek Saunders of Chelsea, Phil Woosnam of Leyton Orient, Malcolm Allison of West Ham, and of course my old Brentford friend, Ron Greenwood, who eventually moved via Chelsea and a championship medal to Fulham. The feeling of unrest was beginning to ferment. The war had been over for ten years and the crowds that had flocked to the grounds in the aftermath had not diminished. It was not exceptional for a second division match to pull in 30,000 people, nearly all standing, but it didn't seem to spoil their enjoyment. Such figures are in stark contrast to Fulham's average gate which hovered around 4500 during my ten-year chairmanship forty years later.

I'm often asked the question, 'Where did all the money go?' The answer is not a simple one; I'm quite sure the directors did not stow it away into their own bank accounts, but neither did they spend much of it on improving their grounds. I think there was just no need to raise the prices; football was very cheap, and was clearly the working man's sport. Any surplus income could be used to strengthen the playing staff. No one seemed to worry. In the carefree aftermath of the war, fans lapped up the entertainment and the happier times in which they lived. Football was simply part of that post-war euphoria. The players enjoyed an above-average wage but hardly sufficient to quieten underlying fears about how they would manage when they passed the dreaded thirty mark. Nevertheless, they still looked upon it as a joy and a privilege, caught up in the excitement of being a professional player. In their sixties at least now, those ex-pros must look upon the current scene with a mixture of disbelief and envy.

So much for the general mood at the time. Fulham were going nowhere fast and were not to make any progress for a year or two. I was moving up the coaching ladder and was now on the FA coaching staff at Lilleshall for the regular annual courses. I had also gained valuable experience by coaching Oxford and then London Universities. As those two strands of my life moved slowly forward, my Union activities were suddenly beginning to take over. They were in stark contrast to the happy-go-lucky fellowship existing among the contrasting characters to be found in the Fulham dressing-room.

Robin Lawler came to us from the green fields of Ireland. He was a stylish international player, playing at left-back or left-half but in a far more constructive way than was normal in those days. Next to Jean, a passionate Fulham supporter who eventually became Mrs Lawler, Robin loved a Guinness. Not only did it soothe his nerves after a game, but Robin looked upon this pillar of Irish life as a necessary whistle-wetter the night beforehand. At home there was no problem, but in a hotel before an away match he had some difficulty in persuading manager Frank Osborne that it would have a beneficial effect. While others chose Ovaltine, cocoa or just plain hot milk, Robin pleaded for just one Guinness. The request was granted; the dark liquid was despatched in a flash and almost before the empty glass hit the table came the plea, 'You know, Frank, a bird never flew on one wing . . .'

Robin was a master at inventing nicknames which stuck. Even Johnny Haynes, our young superstar, did not escape. John was prone to hand out the mother and father of all rollockings to anyone who fell short of his high standards and not the least to his good friend, Tosh Chamberlain, even though Tosh had been the biggest influence in persuading Johnny to join Fulham rather than Spurs. Yet however outspoken he was on the field, it would all immediately be forgotten once the game was over, and the smile would come back to John's face and consequently to the faces of lesser brethren. Robin manufactured the perfect sobriquet for John: 'The Little Nark'. Even when he reached the heights as England's captain, at Craven Cottage he was known simply as 'Narky'. In one game Tosh had made more than the usual number of errors and each time his best friend had remonstrated as only he could. Suddenly, enough was enough. Tosh fought back using every naughty word in his extensive vocabulary. On hearing this the referee warned, 'Mind your language, Chamberlain!'

'But he's on my side!' came the retort, to which there was no reply.

Bedford Jezzard also played for England and later, following serious injury, became manager of the club. Beddy was an outstanding athlete, the quickest player on the staff and extremely well muscled. Sometimes human beings built that way tend to pile on the pounds if they miss training for a brief period. A slight puffiness around Beddy's cheeks was enough for Robin to find, again, the nickname that stuck. Thus Bedford Jezzard became 'Pud', and to his old team-mates 'Pud' he remains to this day.

Bobby Robson, who became the England manager following his outstanding achievements at Ipswich, and went on to manage successfully in Holland, Portugal and Spain, was only nineteen. Young men in that eighteen to twenty group were conscripted into HM Forces for two years. Bobby was found to have a problem which saved him from this fate worse than death: one ear did not function properly. After having been examined by an army doctor, the blemish was discovered in this otherwise perfect specimen. Thus Bobby was not given the opportunity to serve King and country as a national serviceman and Robin struck gold yet again; 'Cloth Ears' went on to an illustrious playing career and even greater success as a manager.

Gordon Brice, our centre-half, who had been a captain in the Marines, was known simply as 'Whizzo'; Arthur Stevens, with his dark hair and a wonderfully prominent Spanish nose, not surprisingly inherited the nickname 'Pablo'; Trevor Chamberlain became 'Tosh'; John Chenhall, a purchase from Arsenal, who had a face like Johnny Weissmuller and a chest to match, became 'Garth'. Tom Wilson was known as 'The Whip' because one of his many superstitions was to slap his backside jockey fashion with an imaginary whip for luck as he ran out on to the pitch. I did not escape, and to the public and press I became known as 'The Rabbi', although not really in the dressing-room. In one game when George Cohen, our right-back, was bringing the ball out of our penalty area, I made a run towards the touchline screaming for a pass. As George hesitated, a lone voice came from the crowd: 'Why don't you give the Rabbi the ball when he asks for it, Cohen?'

On away trips, Saturday mornings tended to drag by. We would fritter the time away meandering round local stores looking for anything in the least likely to make the clock tick more swiftly, though we were hardly financially equipped to break any shopping records. One amusing way to pass the time, which cost nothing and which Jezzard, Haynes and Hill pursued with glee, was to stand around in the ladies' hat departments of the town's larger stores. We would position ourselves strategically in jury fashion directly behind the mirror as the prospective purchaser sought to find that multi-flattering masterpiece of millinery. It was difficult for the object of our scrutiny to ignore a shake of the heads in unison or three beaming smiles and thumbs up. Matters became more complicated when there was a split vote, but I'm pleased to say our efforts were nearly always appreciated and brought kick-off time that much closer – Pud, Little Nark and the Rabbi, fashion consultants.

I firmly believe that it was as a result of that dressing-room spirit of fun and friendship that Fulham eventually achieved success before the end of the fifties. Remembering that experience, I later did my best to foster the same kind of happy camaraderie at Coventry City when I became their manager.

5

WEST INDIES INTERLUDE

By a complete accident I found myself going to heaven. Bedford Jezzard and Bobby Robson had been selected as members of an FA party to tour the West Indies, playing on various islands during the summer months of 1955. The accident that enabled me to enjoy this touch of sporting bliss was to a player, Eric Bell of Preston North End. He had originally been selected for the party but unfortunately broke his leg and a substitute had to be found. It was my luck that the FA chose me in Eric's place.

So one fine May evening, I joined my pals Beddy and Bobby at the FA headquarters in Lancaster Gate. We sat down to a splendid meal accompanied by a liberal amount of wine, which none of us was used to. We were also unused to the kind of journey that awaited us, seven or more hours in a Stratocruiser before landing in Bermuda, our first port of call. Stratocruisers had bunks for first-class passengers and the FA officials who were accompanying the tour, including Joe Richards, the Barnsley chairman, put themselves to bed while the players reclined as best they could beneath them. Unfortunately, I was not born to fly and I began to feel unwell. I am perfectly happy in aeroplanes provided they don't jump about but, as with boats too, if there is any movement that's more than gentle I am in trouble. I was as sick as it is possible to be and from the kindness of his heart one of the FA officials vacated his bunk and allowed me to sleep it off for the few remaining hours of the flight. It was not the most promising start to my representative career.

I awoke somewhat refreshed as we were landing in Bermuda and it seemed to me that heaven's portals had opened for us. The clear blue sky, bright sunshine and intense colours were quite sensational. We arrived at the Elbow Beach Hotel alongside the most beautifully coloured sea I could ever have imagined, fringed by bright, sparkling white sand. It seemed a long way from Brighton. We gloried in the sunshine, the ocean and the other heavenly delights Bermuda offered, but not forgetting the reason for our presence: we were to play two matches against a representative Bermuda XI.

The party's strongest team was chosen for the first match which, to our astonishment and relief, provided an overwhelming 11–1 victory. Those who had not been chosen for the first match, including yours truly, were included in the eleven for the second. Since there appeared to be little doubt about the result, the competition was to see if we could score more goals than the first-choice team. We managed it and won by fourteen goals to one.

We would have been astonishing human beings if we had not taken those victories as sanction to enjoy to the full the other pleasures Bermuda had to offer. We sang, we danced, we swam, we sailed and had the time of our lives. It was all over far too quickly, and before the week was up we were on another plane on the way to Jamaica. This time round I was very careful not to drink any alcohol whatsoever before flying and kept myself, as far as was possible in those circumstances, in good mental and physical condition. I was rewarded by an event-free flight, culminating in yet another unforgettable landing in Kingston.

Within minutes of touching down to the welcoming sound of a calypso band, we were awash with friendliness and rum punch, double and treble measures of each. On reflection, hospitable as it was, I suppose it was not the ideal way to greet a bunch of supposed athletes. Nevertheless, it seemed like a very good idea at the time, and we left the airport with the calypso rhythm running, or rather galloping, through our veins.

If Bermuda was very beautiful, Jamaica took our breath away. Although we bedded down in Kingston, a busy noisy capital, before long we were introduced to the delights of the north-coast resorts of Montego Bay and Ocho Rios. War-torn England and rationing seemed light years away from the sheer delight of this Caribbean paradise. We were hypnotised by the locations and a quality of life we were completely unused to for all kinds of reasons.

On the field the first-choice XI managed to win 7–0 in the opening match, again putting our minds at rest about the strength of the opposition on the island. The heat was intense and although the matches were played late in the day, it still felt like playing football in an oven. It was not overpowering because the skill difference enabled us to run our opponents round rather than chasing them.

The second eleven was chosen to play match number two and I was on the field once more. The rosy script appeared to be going according to plan as we took an early lead and gradually built it to 4–0. The crowd was quiet; it seemed to be a formality for us to score a few more goals before the ninety minutes were up. Then with only about twenty minutes to go, a Jamaican player shot from an oblique angle and scored. Ted Bennett, one of three or four amateur players in a party of full-time professionals, some-how managed to let the ball slip between the near post and his left hand; merry hell broke loose. Such was the noise they made you would have thought that the whole population of the island was cheering their team. Drums, musical instruments, horns, pipes, clapping, suddenly came to stereophonic life. It was an extra-ordinary kerfuffle. The effect was to fire up the home side to a degree that we had not thought possible. That goal sent their confidence soaring enabling them to produce previously dormant skills and the boot was firmly on the other foot. Within a minute or two they had scored a second, a fine goal, and at 4–2 we were in danger of losing our unbeaten record. They ran us ragged for the last twenty minutes but fortunately we managed to hang on to that 4–2 score. I had never felt as hot or exhausted in my life. Unfortunately, I made the mistake with a few other members of the team of gulping down pints of the wonderful fresh fruit juices which were offered to us in the dressing-room; they were irresistible as I had never been so dehydrated. It was heavenly nectar but a short time later we began to feel a devilish effect – brought about by ice-cold liquid on red-hot stomachs.

From Jamaica we moved on to Trinidad, the land of the master calypso writers. Whilst Bermuda and Jamaica had been rich in beauty we found that Trinidad was rich in oil and people, happy souls of all colours, shapes and sizes with a carefree spirit and a bubbling inner joy.

Included in the official itinerary was a reception hosted by the Trinidad FA where we expected to meet our opposite numbers. As a welcoming bonus, we were also greeted by a smiling collection of attractive young ladies so varied in colour and appearance that they may have represented every nationality in the world. Their sing-song, local dialect was akin to a Welsh accent and they were full of life, vitality and friendliness. As always, no one counted the number of rum punches that were taken on board. As I lay in my bed later that night, the thought crossed my mind how far all this was from 3.30 on a freezing January afternoon, trying to find a way round the uncompromising Bolton defence.

We managed to remain unbeaten in Trinidad but the tour was beginning to take its toll; what we did learn was that there was a difference between Trinidad time and British summer time. The evening of the discovery of this phenomenon was when we were invited by the Trinidad and Tobago FA to a reception and dinner at a local hotel. Fittingly attired, we arrived promptly at seven o'clock ready for pre-dinner cocktails. It must have been an hour and three-quarters before anyone from the Trinidad contingent pitched up and by that time we had consumed rather more alcohol than was good for us. Our own officials were showing some frayed tempers over the politeness of our friends in inviting us to spend the evening with them, and failing to make an appearance. Our leader, Joe Richards, was offended by what seemed to be an indignity. However, gradually our hosts trickled in not in the least bit ruffled by their considerable lateness, and by nine o'clock the party began in earnest.

A year later when I returned to Trinidad on a coaching appointment, I was shown once again that there was a formidable gap between British time and Trinidad time. When I arrived the second time around for a six-week coaching stint, I had no idea what to expect. The Trinidad FA had booked me into Madam de Montbrun's boarding house. The proprietress was a size that suggested healthy eating and a warmth of welcome no less grand. My fellow guests were from different West Indian islands and intensely proud of their own birthplace and noisily competitive in advertising each one's merits. I stayed neutral and pretended I came from nowhere.

I was given a list of the week's coaching appointments – two sessions, morning and evening, per day and one on Saturday morning. A chauffeur-driven car picked me up at 9.45 a.m. to take me to a local school playing field for my first session. Tracksuited, with a large net filled with footballs, I stood waiting. I could hardly fail to notice that the playing field was covered with cows, who would presumably move once we got the ten o'clock session under way. . . At 10.30, not one lad having appeared, I asked the driver whether we were in the right place. He assured me all was well and the class would be along shortly. I waited and waited as patiently as I could. The first boy appeared at 11.20 and by 11.40 I had a classful of people, the cattle having moved aside.

When the session was over I instructed the driver to take me to the headquarters of the FA. I was soon pointing out that I had hardly come thousands of miles to waste my time and their precious funds. The message went home. I'm not saying that afterwards my charges had ever heard the word 'punctuality', but we came to a kind of mutual understanding that there was 'Trinidad' time and 'Jimmy Hill's' time, the difference averaging one and a half hours. I also became accustomed to brothers and friends sharing boots – one would have the left and the other the right, but don't think for one moment that they didn't tackle with both!

By the time the six weeks were up I had coached young lads from almost every League and school in North Trinidad and on leaving attended a farewell party at each one. Every League had found some money for a 'thank-you' present to give to me. I revealed them with some considerable pride to the customs officer at London Airport. The gifts were not valuable and there was no duty to pay, but no one could put a price on the pleasure they had given me.

However, back to the first tour with the English FA and the final match in Curacao. The Dutch island was less of a tourist trap and appeared more businesslike in atmosphere than its British counterparts. That turned out to be the case on the field, too. Although the island's temperatures were not extreme, the skills of its footballers were a few degrees above those to which we had become acclimatised. Consequently we found ourselves in the last game of the tour trailing 1–0, with our unbeaten record in danger. My great pals Beddy and Bobby had not excelled up front. In fitness terms, the pace of the tour had begun to show and we were sagging somewhat in the heat. When Beddy missed another chance to equalise, I was upset. In retrospect, having been promoted to the Senior XI in our last match, professionally I did not wish to be part of the only defeat. I endeavoured to encourage my friend with some carefully chosen footballers' language, which did not land well at the receiving end. Beddy's reply in the same tongue ended with, 'If you think it's that easy, then bloody well come up and do it yourself!' A few minutes later, Beddy scored the equaliser, maintaining our unbeaten record.

'Well played, Pud!' I shouted – an ecstatic end to six weeks of paradise.

6

PFA BATTLES

M Y route to becoming the first unpaid chairman of the
Players' Union wasn't plotted. Originally, my limited
clerking skills made me a potential candidate for the basic
responsibility of collecting and recording subscriptions. At Brentford the Union delegate was transferred and I took his place for a
short time. When I arrived at Fulham, Norman Smith was the
incumbent delegate and it wasn't until Norman chose to study
accountancy that the task fell on my shoulders for the second
time. At my first AGM in 1955 I sat listening to pretty vitriolic
criticism of our paid chairman, Jimmy Guthrie. Some begrudged
his salary, others his loose-cannon methods. It was also clear that
the Football League leaders were not enamoured with him. I
stood up and defended Jimmy on that score – if our opponents
didn't like his performance, he must be doing well for the players.
As a result, Jimmy was elected for another year and I was also
elected to the eight man Committee of Management – a punishment for not keeping my mouth shut.

A year later the same pressure came from the floor and when
the time came for Jimmy's re-election, not one hand was raised in
favour. However, it followed that there was total support for my
suggestion that we should dispense with a paid chairman, giving
more responsibility to Cliff Lloyd, our paid secretary. The new

chairman was to be elected by the management committee from among its members at its next meeting. It turned out to be me, but proud as I was, I had not the least idea of the enormous difference it would make to my life, or to the lives of professional footballers, or that it would eventually lead to the sky-rocketing rewards now available to today's superstars. When the Darren Andertons and Ian Wrights of this world make scathing comments about my professional performances and opinions, I reflect quietly to myself, 'They don't know how lucky they are!' But I do not begrudge any player his earnings, however high, provided that the player individually and his team collectively are actually 'earning' that money.

As things stand the superclub players make huge salaries, whereas very few clubs outside the Premier League, and not all those in it, produce balance sheets in black ink. The reality is that many of those clubs will wither or die and, knowing what that side of it is like, my sympathy in most cases now is with the enthusiastic directors of those clubs. They not only carry the worrying responsibility of survival, but more often than not are abused for it.

Contrary to what some would like to believe, I've never changed my tune. Players should always have been free to be paid what they have earned, not in anticipation of what they might achieve. On that basis clubs would be able to survive and Great Britain would continue to afford more than twelve healthy and profitable clubs.

It's light years away from 1956 and the crisis which confronted me within weeks of being voted chairman of the Players' Union. Six Sunderland players were accused of receiving improper payments to induce transfers and as incentives to win matches. It sounds ridiculous these days that professional players could be treated like criminals for endeavouring to earn a better living for their families as a reward for their dexterity and achievements. It's true that archaic regulations imposed upon them had been breached, but in essence those regulations were outrageous in a country which had not long since fought for its freedom.

I was aware that, although not every club or player had been as brazen about their attitude to the system as Sunderland, payments over and above the stipulated amounts were being made. I had the idea that if I could get every player who had received a penny over the enforced maximums to sign to that effect, the Sunderland case would end in fiasco. The problem was there were only seven days left until the season ended, after which the players would disappear for three months. Nevertheless, we had a week, during which time I managed to collect 250 signatures from the 300 or so players I had been able to approach. The percentage was enough to convince the public that the system was iniquitous.

It was my responsibility, untrained as I was in legal matters, let alone as a QC, to defend the accused. That wasn't such an easy task! When Ken Chisholm, an extraordinary character who in later life I spotted winning snooker tournaments on ITV, was asked, 'Was there £750 in the brown paper parcel?' he replied, 'No, there was no brown paper parcel and if there had been, the amount was certainly not £750.' QED.

At that time I was also asked to defend players on disciplinary charges. With a sound knowledge of the laws of the game, I found I could make life difficult for referees presenting their case when a player had appealed against a sending-off. Dave Hickson of Everton and Swansea's Colin Webster were not the most innocent of forwards when it came to looking after themselves, but somehow I managed to cast doubt in the FA judges' minds about their absolute guilt and they were reprieved. Consequently, I was overwhelmed with requests from offending players to bring about miraculous 'not guilty' verdicts.

Another cry for help came from Mick Lynch in the Irish League for me to visit Dublin to meet a few of his comrades. He wanted them to consider forming a union among Irish professional players. As the result of an injury I was not fit to play, so I agreed to fly to Dublin one weekend and was met at the airport around 8.30 p.m. by a small group of current Irish players including Mick, my host for the two days. Rather than drive straight into town and my hotel, we adjourned to the airport bar for a quick drink so that we might get to know one another. The 'quick drink' and conversation lasted well beyond midnight, when a liquid guest was eventually deposited at his hotel.

The following morning I was chaperoned around town, an intimate tour of that incomparable city. Among the pleasures on offer, we visited the haunt of Brendan Behan and were lucky enough to find him in residence, only too ready to regale us with his charm and wit. As we wandered around Dublin during that day and evening, quite a number of young male locals acknowledged us with, 'I'll see you at the meeting, Mick!' Dublin is such a lively, friendly place I needed no such reminders of the real purpose of my visit. The historic meeting was due to take place late on Sunday afternoon and before then I wasn't allowed to waste a moment's enjoyment, including sufficient time being allotted to confirm that Guinness imbibed in Dublin is nectar compared with the equivalent overseas. Taking into account the above, it is as well to remember that, as well as being chairman of the Players' Union, I was also a current player, supposedly earning a living as a result of my talent and sobriety.

The meeting started amazingly on time, and after what was left of me was introduced to the gathering, I made a brief speech outlining the advantages to them of forming their own association, emphasising even more strongly the disadvantages of being without any protection whatsoever. The decision was taken to go ahead and Mick Lynch asked for volunteers to act as committee men. Half the room raised their hands. I explained that the English Union had eight on the committee and I suggested six would be about the right number.

'Okay,' said Mick. 'We'll vote for six among those who put up their hands and the rest can be delegates.' Throwing up that impressive word meant that the Professional Footballers Association of Ireland was formed with everyone having a title – nothing so prosaic as ordinary 'member'.

So much for defending players and spreading the word. After five years' service with Fulham FC I qualified for a testimonial/

benefit payment of £750 from the club. In those days it was taxed. However, if an outside body arranged a match, it was thought that tax could be avoided. Accordingly, our local host, Jack Baron of the Red Lion, formed a committee to organise a match. The takings less expenses were around £1100 and I was to be paid the maximum allowed under league rules, i.e. £750. Despite those efforts and an appeal, I had to meet a tax demand for nearly £300. During the same period, cricketers were taking benefits and successfully avoiding tax by the very same device. Denis Compton, qualifying for a double helping from both Arsenal and Middlesex, was taxed on his football earnings and not on the manna from heavenly Lord's. Perhaps England was a free country, but don't be misled that it was a fair one.

In 1960 I was already in my second two-year term as chairman of the Professional Footballers Association (PFA). I had persuaded the committee to dispense with the name Players' Union and give our title the somewhat superior status of a professional body of people – snobbish if you like but it did no harm to the cause we were fighting. The progress Fulham had been making in those two years with me now in a striking role was doing no harm in enabling me to present players' cases with added authority. We had narrowly missed promotion in 1958–59, yet reached the semi-final of the FA Cup and I had scored in every round. In the following season we finished runners-up to Sheffield Wednesday and gained promotion to the first division.

Off the field, it was rather more complicated. I was now thirty-two years old, but had enjoyed a wide range of activities which were to stand me in good stead for the battle which was to come. The PFA had staggered from one fruitless meeting with the League's representatives to another. Although they were involved in a team sport, the league clubs were never able to engender the slightest spirit of togetherness. I'm afraid that's still the case in the Football League although, lousy with television's lolly, the Premiership clubs have now publicly at least managed to avoid being seen to be in conflict. At one point Tom Claro, the Ministry of Labour Conciliation Officer, managed to identify twenty-two points of difference between the players and the Football League. It took us some time to sharpen our verbal weapons and find the formula to show the public the strength of the players' case. As the rules stood, clubs were restricted to paying their players a maximum wage of £20 a week in the winter, £17 in the summer. When a player signed a contract with a club, that club controlled his whole future playing career. Under the standard terms of the contract, he could not leave to join another club without his original club's consent. Even when the term of the contract ended, the club still had the option to prevent the player moving elsewhere. If he didn't want to re-sign, the club could retain his registration and were not obliged to pay him anything at all. The club could, however, transfer the player to another club whenever they wanted. If he refused to go, again they were not obliged to pay him anything at all. If the Football League had got its act together at any time during 1960 they could have settled for a £30 maximum wage and some reasonable adjustments to the contract in relation to the retain-and-transfer system. The players would have been delighted and would have forced the committee's hand to accept such a deal. It was, however, the ignorant bickering that went on at meetings plus the refusal of some chairmen to approve a concerted plan of action that kept the dispute in the headlines. The longer it continued the more the public, and our committee for that matter, began to understand the basic rights which were at stake. We were able to turn the arguments from being about money to being about two basic principles. The first was the freedom to earn as much as an employer was prepared to pay, and the second the freedom to leave an employer at the end (not in the middle) of a contract.

The players were not seeking, as Bosman did in the nineties, the right to leave a club at the end of a contract without a fee. They were happy with a system which, with the help of a neutral tribunal, assessed the figure at which a transfer should take place. Such a system worked smoothly for thirty years, excepting that human nature being what it is, no club ever thought it received too much or paid too little. What it did was to encourage clubs to continue to invest money in recruiting and training young players.

Going back a little, the first get-together for eighteen months was convened between the League and the PFA on 7 December 1959. It was an appalling meeting. The enemy listened in silence to our arguments without enthusiasm or contradiction, except to undertake to put our pleading before the clubs. Later we wrote inquiring what the outcome of that meeting had been. The answer was that the clubs had put matters back in the hands of their management committee. It didn't matter where the message came from; when it arrived it said simply that they insisted on the retain-and-transfer system and would not concede the abolition of the maximum wage. The sting in the tail was in advising us not to put these two items on the agenda at future meetings. On our other subsidiary requests, the outcome was no longer playing contracts, no legal representation at tribunals, no income for players from pools contracts, and no financial help towards a group insurance scheme. Not surprisingly, at our AGM early in 1960 the committee were empowered to take any steps they thought necessary to bring an end to these restrictive and unjust Football League rules.

Our first considered step in February 1960 was to refer what we had now declared to be a dispute to the Ministry of Labour. it meant that at least our life-and-death conflict would have a referee. With twenty-two points of difference – a significant number for a football dispute – it was not easy for the public to sympathise. Our basic demands as discussed with the Ministry were to establish proper negotiating machinery; abolish the maximum wage; establish the freedom to move at the end of a contract; and increase the minimum wage for players over the age of twenty, then £8. We soon agreed on the appointment of an independent chairman and under his stewardship we made some progress in tidying up the retain-and-transfer system and increasing, but not abolishing, the maximum wage.

On 8 November 1960, an Extraordinary General Meeting of the Football League was held for the management committee to report back to the clubs and for the League to come up with some concrete offers. In truth I was afraid they would recommend encouraging increases in the maximum wage and bonuses, which together with other concessions would result in overwhelming acceptance by the players with our two principles forgotten and cast aside.

I need not have worried. The Football League management committee or the clubs, or both, had completely misread the strength of the players' feelings and also those of the public. Their offer was pitiful. Never mind principles, which it ignored completely, it was as if no negotiations whatsoever had taken place. Far from placating the players, which was my fear, the League's offer had enraged them.

My message to our members was, 'Play your hearts out on Saturday and come to Monday's meeting and tell us what you think!' We had convened three players' meetings, at the Abercorn Rooms in London, the Imperial Hotel, Birmingham, and the Grand Hotel, Manchester. My next worry was that at such short notice our numbers might not represent to the public the depth of players' feelings. Again, I need not have worried – over two hundred players crowed the room in London, interested enough in their own profession to turn up. It had never happened before. The committee was given one month to negotiate the four fundamental points, including the two freedoms, and the players emphasised they would go to any lengths to establish them.

The meeting in the Midlands was smaller but even more determined to let the world know that enough was enough and gave the committee its unanimous support.

In Manchester, over two hundred players turned up, including Stanley Matthews. Stan had previously stated that he was against strike action and we all wondered if he would support the PFA and his fellow members in striking if all else failed. When we asked for a show of hands all eyes were on Stan, who raised his arm to cheers from all sides. Afterwards he said, 'I was torn between my principles and loyalty to fellow players. I have done well out of the game, but could I ignore the injustice to my colleagues? Rightly or wrongly I made my decision. Loyalty to the players won and my hand went up.'

On television and radio, Bobby Robson, Jimmy Greaves, Ronnie Allen, Don Howe, Tommy Docherty, Roy Bentley, Johnny Haynes, Bobby Charlton, Phil Woosnam, Tommy Harmer and so many other stars joined the campaign to win over the public. It was one thing for me to chant on my Union soapbox, it was quite another to hear so many heroes singing the same tune. It provoked immediate action. Tom Claro called the warring parties together on 22 November 1960 for three hours and forty-six minutes of lively discussion. A plan was discussed which would first be put to the management committee then back to the players on 5 December, and if agreed, would go before the league clubs on 9 December. All things agreed, the League was prepared to call an EGM to approve the changes. The players were to await events at three regional meetings beginning on 13 December.

On 2 December, Alan Hardaker, the League Secretary, announced a seven-point plan including an increase in the maximum wage, longer contracts and a joint committee of the League and the PFA with power to enforce decisions on clubs and players. We made our way to the Ministry of Labour on 6 December to be surprised to find different proposals from the ones Alan Hardaker had disclosed four days earlier. For some peculiar reason we were sworn to silence until after a League press conference on the following Friday, 9 December, which would immediately follow a meeting of all club chairmen. The League had recognised the value of good press relations and had reduced seven points to four with real money on the table:

1. £20 per week could become £30 by £2 annual raises if a player remained with his club. The sting was a transferred player dropped back to £20 per week.
2. Contracts could be for up to three years.
3. Signing-on fees would be £150 per year, with a tax-free testimonial after eight years' service.
4. A joint dispute committee to be formed.

It was obvious from the initial favourable reaction of Fleet Street that the League's ploy was working. Knowing the susceptibility of all of us to newspaper headlines, I felt that some of our members might be misled by the ultimate carrot of a fifty per cent rise and £30 a week and forget the principles for which we were striving. It was necessary for them to see the complete picture immediately. I called the Press Association inviting interested journalists to meet me in the Red Lion, just off Fleet Street, at 5.30 p.m.

As quickly and positively as I could, I told them the deal on offer was nothing like the settlement that the players had been seeking. There would still be a maximum wage and no guarantee of a player's right, at the end of a contract, to leave and join another club, subject to the payment of a proper fee. In the end, the League reneged on an agreement that had offered these freedoms, so how they would have operated one that didn't, heaven only knows.

Once again we had to test the players' feelings. Early signs were not good. The players of two clubs represented on our committee wanted to take the offer. News came in of directors and managers pressuring and threatening their players; players were concerned about their families in the event of a strike, and would the PFA support them? Wednesday, 13 December was the chosen date for the London meeting. Those players stood firm and passed a resolution to give the League one month's strike notice and for the committee to act as they thought necessary.

As I had expected, the PFA and its chairman were put under severe public pressure. Joe Richards, chairman of the Football League, led the way and others followed.

'Strikers' (strange – in football, it now means something quite different) 'will render a grave disservice to the game and will probably put out of employment large numbers of professional footballers. I congratulate Jimmy Hill,' said the Leyton Orient chairman. 'This could break the greatest game in the country!'

The widely respected Arthur Rowe, manager of Spurs, said, 'Strike? They must be barmy!'

Faced with this public pressure, I travelled to Manchester in trepidation. I missed the airport coach and caught the local bus into the city. Buried in a newspaper, I hardly raised my head until, looking up as we reached the centre, I saw the word 'STRIKE!' It seemed to be an omen. In fact, Manchester Corporation buses had a piece of matchbox with the inflammatory word along the back of the seat for top-deck smokers.

We spent the morning at the PFA offices devising ways and means of support for the players in the event of a strike. The Manchester papers carried quotes from chairmen, directors, managers and players, all against a strike. So were we; it was the last thing we wanted.

In the afternoon, the northern players at Belle Vue backed the London resolution 254 to 6 and passed another resolution deploring the personal attacks made on their chairman. The same resolution was backed by the Midlands players at the Imperial Hotel, Birmingham. We advised players to set up employment committees at each club, sounding out businessmen among their supporters who might believe in the players' case and provide temporary work. The Showbiz XI declined to help but the TV All Stars, including Pete Murray, Mike and Bernie Winters, Bernard Bresslaw and Honor Blackman's husband, Maurice Kauffman, were ready to play for us to raise money in the emergency.

At the end of the week the 'strike' vote was won handsomely 694 for 18 against. I had an underlying feeling of certainty that, if we convinced the world and particularly the Football League chairmen that we were prepared to go on strike we would never have to do it. So the message to players was clear: think strike, speak strike and prepare for a strike! On 16 December, Ted Hill, chairman of TVC, declared his support for the players. On 17 December, the Football League said that they intended to carry on the Football League programme using amateur players. On Monday, 19 December, the strike notices due to expire on 21 January 1961 were sent to the Football League. On 21 December, Bob Lord of Burnley pronounced publicly that he had changed his mind about the maximum wage and two or three other chairmen supported him.

On that day we met the League representatives with a seven-point package to put before the chairmen. On the two main issues, the package included a two-year £30 maximum wage and then no maximum, and last but not least, a clause which hinted at the second freedom: 'If a player refuses to re-sign for his club, the League has to help him to sign for another club.'

Those terms were published on 29 December 1960 and it was generally thought that the clubs would accept them as a basis of an agreement to end the strike. In fact, those terms were never put to the clubs at a meeting. Their reaction to it privately was so violent that their principals judged that they had better put something to them that they might accept. As a result, the following proposition was made on the main issues: no maximum from next season, the carrot, but no change whatsoever to the retain-and-transfer system, the stick.

The issue was far too big for the committee to decide itself so once again it was on our bikes round the regions to decide on the League's final offer, as it was represented. The big question was whether to withdraw the strike notices. My view was that the players would accept the offer fulfilling as it did one count, although closing the other door. Of course, it seemed a substantial victory but my feeling of disappointment overrode the elation.

The first meeting at St Pancras Town Hall rejected the offer on a vote of 3 to 1. Jimmy Greaves of Chelsea spoke for his fellow star players.

'Players on low wages backed those who were luckier and it's up to those better off to stick out to achieve the things that would benefit everyone.'

The space between the regional meetings gave us both thinking and decision-making time. If by the end of the week the players were divided or we had lost public support, we could accept the offer with the maximum wage gone for ever and make it clear that we would still campaign against the retain-and-transfer system. Since the 3 to 1 vote, our employers, not least Joe Richards, the League president, were not offering fatherly advice.

'I have told the players this was the last word,' he said, 'and there will be no more from us now. It seems we have wasted our time. I think the players are being very foolish. We shall not go to arbitration and if there is a strike we shall carry on the League as best we can. It is up to the clubs to tell their teams they have a lot of amateurs on their books and they could carry on.'

The Swansea manager, Trevor Morris, said, 'The players are showing a grave lack of intelligence.' He might at least have added, 'but a lot of guts.' Sir Stanley Rous, on behalf of the FA, offered to arbitrate, but the League had already turned its back on arbitration.

The Midlands meeting hit the headlines because of the apathy of the senior Aston Villa players. They wanted to accept the League's offer and made it clear that they were not prepared to strike. Fine, they were entitled to hold that view, but they hadn't the courage to attend the meeting and confirm what they had said publicly and Villa were represented by five reserve players.

As already described, the sinister nature of the system that the League was determined to carry on was that if a player refused terms at the end of a contract, his registration could be retained, he could not join another club and in the meantime he would not be paid. George Eastham had found himself in that situation at Newcastle for some months and had only recently got back on to the pitch and a payroll for Arsenal, having been transferred reluctantly. On George's behalf and indeed on behalf of every player, the PFA was examining the legal implications of New-castle's actions and the legality of the system. As matters turned out, it was very wise.

At a meeting on 9 January 1961 we asked whether the new proposals would ensure that an Eastham-type situation could not happen. We were told 'No'. Three days later the League secretary, Alan Hardaker, denied that any player could be kept out of the game without wages. Not only that, but it was made clear to us that they were not even prepared to accept a representative of the

PFA on a committee which would deal with disputes where a player was caught in the system without being paid. It was again a brutal 'No!' and it showed only too clearly then and later that our employers would go to any lengths to maintain this unjust system.

The Midlands players understood the principle involved and in smaller numbers, it's true, backed their committee unanimously, including the brave young lions from Villa.

As I travelled to our Manchester meeting I was aware of the number of our members who did not understand the principles involved in the negotiation, and who were quoted in the press as not supporting a strike. When I arrived and someone counted 344 players, I didn't know whether to laugh or cry. Did that mean fervent, increased support or were they there with fear of what a strike might mean uppermost in their minds? When they heard the facts they were overwhelmingly in favour of the resolution to support the strike notices. I've had a few original ideas in my time and luckily I've also recognised the brilliance of others' brain-waves. Ally MacLeod, the Blackburn Rovers winger, and later Scotland manager, suggested, 'Why don't we invite the press in to see us take the resolution?' We did just that. For a moment, fifty or so journalists were speechless, but resilient as they are, they recovered quickly. I asked the players, 'Is there anyone in the room who wouldn't strike?' The 'No!' could have come from the Kop at its loudest. As it was reported, 'It was fantastic to see the complete unanimity and determination of these young men who mean to get what they want – something you and I take for granted – the right of not being unfairly held to a contract after it has expired, and without pay.'

Alan Hardaker was protesting loudly that their proposal was not meant to mean that a player could be kept out of the game without wages, while his chairman was saying, 'This is our final offer, we shall budge no more. I am not budging on the issue of the transfer system, which will remain as long as there is a league competition in this country.'

We were asked by Tom Claro to suspend the strike notices

because it was not possible to arrange a meeting between the parties. We declined politely. I was not surprised, though, when someone changed someone's mind and we were invited to a meeting on Wednesday, 18 January 1961. If Mary Tudor had Calais written on her heart, that date's written on mine! Beforehand, it was bedlam. Ted Hill, chairman of the TUC, called on all union members to support the strike, not to attend any blackleg matches and to do everything possible to support the players and win a hundred per cent victory. Vernon Stokes, a director of Portsmouth, opposed blackleg matches and the idea was sinking fast. On the other hand, we knew that subject to finding forty-six pitches, we could provide *bona fide* fixtures for the pools companies. All that would be necessary would be an adaptation of club names so as not to infringe copyright. We tried to put crowd problems at the back of our minds, fearful of how many would turn out for Manchester United Rovers playing Manchester City Pirates on Wythenshawe recreation ground. Wisely, the pools promoters decided to wait and see. The supporters waited, too, wondering what else they might do on Saturday afternoon. The clubs paused in selling tickets and the nation held its breath – as I did!

The meeting started at 2.30 p.m. and at 6.20 p.m. the strike was off as a result of an agreed seven-point plan solely to facilitate a fair and legal formula to operate at the end of a player's contract. The vital clause was number seven, which said, 'If by 31 August he is still not transferred, the management committee of the Football League will, on the application of the player, deal with the matter.' The player in dispute would be paid throughout, although only a minimum wage of £15/14/13/12 per week, depending on which division, from 30 June to 31 July.

Two points arose: first, a player would still lose the difference between a minimum wage and his contract wage during the month of July. Secondly, the phrase 'deal with the matter' was key. It was understood to mean 'get the player moved' subject to a reasonable transfer fee being paid to his club.

As I sat reading the newspapers on 19 January I was a very

happy man. It seemed as if English football had turned the corner. No further need for players to go to Colombia or Italy, except on holiday, which they may now be able to afford, and the competition would surely raise the standard at home – five years later we won the World Cup.

However, there was mischief afoot. . . The press understood the agreement –

> John Camkin, *Daily Mail*: 'The players are granted the fundamental rights to change clubs at the end of a contract.'

> David Miller, *Daily Telegraph*: 'The players have been granted the right to change their clubs, the club the right to demand a transfer fee.'

> Clive Toye, *Daily Express*: 'The League conceded to the players THE RIGHT to leave their clubs, once their contract ended.'

Yet the league clubs received a letter saying, 'The new arrangement is not designed to make it easier for a player to leave a club, but to give both club and player protection whilst maintaining the club's right to retain.'

I went back to playing football again, much more fun than industrial disputes, having recovered from a series of frustrating injuries, although my right knee sadly was not long for this professional football world. On 5 March, the *Sunday Times* reported a game against Everton: 'Brightest spot of the match was the effort of bearded Jimmy Hill. Tireless and covering acres of ground he never gave up until two minutes from the end when, trying to force an equaliser, he received a nasty knock.' That 'knock' was a torn cartilage and ligament damage which meant it was my last game for Fulham as a professional player.

Supposedly, in the previous two months the League had been drafting new regulations along the lines of our agreement: an agreement clearly documented and witnessed by the whole nation. A meeting with them on 16 March completely destroyed such dreams of integrity. It became abundantly clear to our legal advisers, Tom Claro, Cliff Lloyd and myself, that the new regulations in no way incorporated what had been originally agreed on 18 January 1961. Not surprisingly, it was a stormy meeting. At its conclusion, the League's representatives agreed to take back the original agreement to the clubs and inform us of their reaction before our AGM on 27 March. In fact, they did not, but the players kept their cool and were prepared to wait patiently for the League to honour our agreement.

On 14 April the League clubs met and refused to adopt the principle of the agreement made on their behalf at the Ministry of Labour on 18 January, announcing 'Come what may, the Football League clubs will not alter the present retain-and-transfer system.'

One journalist wrote, 'The Football League, born in 1888, died of shame at high noon yesterday.' On 18 April, in the House of Commons, John Hare, the Minister of Labour, said in answer to a question about the disputed agreement, 'We have no doubt in our minds the PFA was right.' On 26 June he said, 'No final settlement has been reached because the AGM of the Football League decided not to implement the agreement in full.'

Personally, I was in a difficult position. It had been my belief that the chairman of the PFA should be a current player and unpaid and it had resulted in my appointment. It began to look as if my playing days were over and I would have to earn a living somehow and, according to my own conviction, resign as chairman. On the other hand, I was loath to give up the battle on behalf of the players, especially with the League seeming to have got away with outrageous duplicity. As it happened, I had been offered a partnership by Bagenal Harvey to join him in his sports agency business. We were in the middle of negotiating terms and as far as the business was concerned it would not have been a problem to continue as PFA chairman, if the members wished it, certainly until we had implemented the 18 January agreement by overcoming the League's deviousness.

That deviousness was confirmed at a meeting of the Football League clubs on 3 June 1961 when they rejected the main point of the deal regarding the retain-and-transfer system, provisionally agreed by the League with the PFA. At that time I was in Canada on a promotional tour, appearing on television and radio endeavouring to encourage spectators to watch teams such as Montreal Concordia and others as they strove to popularise soccer. The first thing to do on my return to the United Kingdom was to call an urgent meeting of the players to discuss what course of action we should take following the developments that had taken place. Secondly, I had to get rid of the troublesome cartilage which had caused me to end my season in March.

Fulham's attitude to my operation was interesting. I had been given a free transfer following the injury that I sustained in the Everton match. In fact, at the end of the season I was not in a position to play football as a result of that injury. I think the club had been suspicious of the fact that I had not been available to play for them as often as they or I would have liked over the previous eighteen months. Retrospectively, I suppose, I can forgive them for believing that my union activities were not helping me fulfil my professional obligations with Fulham. As it was, life would have been so much easier for me during that period if I had been fit to play forty-two games a season. The niggling injuries were a far bigger embarrassment to me than to the club.

However, when it was reported in a newspaper that I had had a cartilage removed, Frank Osborne, our general manager, quickly arrived as a visitor at the hospital. He was at great pains to point out that Fulham would pay for the operation to restore my fitness. The Fulham chairman and board had envisaged the publicity that would have arisen had I been left to fend for myself, having been injured in the service of Fulham Football Club. What Bill Tucker, former international rugby player and current orthopaedic surgeon, found vindicated me entirely from any accusation of malingering; in fact, he was amazed at what I had been able to accomplish with the knee in such an appalling condition. I learned later that Fulham had an insurance policy on their leading players, including myself. Thus should I be unfit to continue playing professionally, they could claim £10,000 compensation. Finally, that's what happened. Not a bad profit when you consider

I had been bought for £5000 plus Jimmy Bowie, and later on, Fulham had re-signed Jimmy for nothing. They had eight good years, 277 games and forty-one goals, plus a £5000 profit to boot.

However, my problem was insignificant compared to the PFA's task of finding some means of forcing the Football League to keep its word in relation to the agreement that had been made between their representatives and the PFA on 18 January 1961. Meantime, the lifting of the maximum wage was having an effect. Four out of every five league players had negotiated better contracts of some kind. A fifth found they couldn't improve on the last season's terms. I knew of one particular player who was much worse off than his counterparts at the start of the season. That was a chap who had been given a free transfer by Fulham FC and had not recovered from his injury sufficiently to play for any club, let alone one in the first division, i.e. me.

We held three regional meetings in July and the mood of the players was mixed, but it was decided by a large majority that the best tactics would be to refer the dispute to the Ministry of Labour and in the meantime continue to attempt to negotiate with the Football League to put into practice the agreement that had been reached in January.

The PFA committee decided that since it seemed as if we would not win the second targeted freedom in fair fight, perhaps we might succeed legally. So Cliff Lloyd and I arranged a meeting with leading Counsel in London. Although George Eastham was happily dancing round defenders at Highbury and elsewhere, the legacy of Newcastle's treatment of him remained. Since the league chairmen had steadfastly clung to the remnants of the retain-and-transfer system, however brutally and unfairly, perhaps a spike of honest-to-goodness law up their backsides might steer them away from it.

We talked at extensive length to the QC and after a couple of hours I posed the question, 'What chance would George have if we funded the case?' He thought for a moment. 'About fifty fifty,' was his reply. We walked from the law courts into the Fleet Street sunshine mulling it over.

'We might never get another chance like this,' I said, persuasively, expecting Cliff, who was the most careful gentleman, to say, 'No fear, think of the cost!' Instead it was, 'Why not, we've got to win somehow!' Three years later the Eastham case was fought retrospectively, funded by the PFA, and the second basic freedom was cast in immovable legal stone and had to be accepted, even by the Football League management committee.

George Eastham was back on Arsenal's transfer list, open to offer from any club in the country (he went to Stoke City). I was able to survive financially during this uncertain period by writing a weekly column for the *News of the World*. Living in Albion Street, Bayswater, at the time, I kept fit by running in Hyde Park. Four or five clubs approached me to sign for them, including Queens Park Rangers where Alec Stock was pressing persuasively for my signature. Alec was prepared to take me on a year's contract, even though there was no guarantee yet that my knee would stand up to a professional season.

PFA matters continued to keep me busy. One of our members had got himself into an absolute pickle with his club. His name was Jimmy Greaves, the club was Milan, the problem was a contract to play for them for three years. Jimmy had decided that he had had enough of Italian football and didn't want to return to Milan. He explained to me how difficult he had found it to adapt to the kind of life he was expected to lead, so different from that of a professional footballer in this country. Jimmy had decided to leave England before the maximum wage was abolished and it was clear that he regretted that decision. I was able to persuade him that he should not just walk out but should at least give it another try.

Later Walter Winterbottom, England's team manager, explained over a coffee how disadvantageous it was from England's point of view to have a player overseas, playing in a different environment. I listened carefully.

Jimmy was contracted at that time to write for the *People* newspaper, but was not practically speaking the best person in the world to provide the copy. They sought my help. A combination of these happenings resulted in my catching an aeroplane to Milan together with Jimmy's wife, Irene. I had two, or more honestly, three objects in mind: to make sure that Jimmy would and could fulfil his obligation to the *People*, and to improve his relationship with the Milan club, so that he would find it easier to settle down and produce his best football. At the same time, I hoped that they would see and understand the difficulties of an Englishman playing abroad. The third tranche was the hidden agenda; perhaps Milan could be persuaded that it would be better for them to negotiate a sizeable fee for Jimmy than to continue to select a player who was not able to produce his best form. I knew Walter Winterbottom would be extremely pleased with that outcome and it would not be difficult to find the right club for him in England. So the hidden agenda was not necessarily an objective, but if it had come about I would not have lost any sleep over it.

Since the players went into training from Thursday onwards, I busied myself looking after Irene, although I did watch Milan's training sessions under the fearsome Signor Rocca. There was a tennis court alongside the training ground and at the end of a session interested players tended to pick up rackets and have a knock-up. Jimmy was keen to play and persuaded me to don borrowed kit and partner him against two Inter Milan players. Jimmy was desperate to win the game but he wasn't the most talented tennis player in the world. At football he could give me at least fifteen points a game, but at tennis the situation was reversed. Jim, though, was passionately keen that we should beat his Italian team-mates, especially with the rest of them looking on. He was an extravagant tennis player and had a tendency to go for difficult, sometimes impossible, shots. In football he could accomplish such miracles, in tennis he couldn't.

'Jim,' I pleaded, 'please just get the ball over the net and leave it to me to find the moment to hit a winner.' It really was hard work. We fell behind, we fought back; we fell behind, we fought back again. Finally, bad light saved us and we salvaged a draw, seven games all. The reputation of Great Britain in Milan had been preserved.

The Italians couldn't really understand why I was there in the first place, but they treated me with respect, knowing my background and that I was a friend of Jimmy's. Came the Sunday, the day of the match, I was being driven not by a member of the Ferrari family or team, but by a man who obviously thought he was. At frantic speed he drove me to Venice, where Milan were playing in the afternoon. He was courteous and kind, very interested in sport, and we built up a warm relationship in spite of his broken English. I sat next to him during the game. The longer it went on, the more uneasy I became. I had a funny feeling that things weren't going to happen the way we wanted. Jimmy didn't get that many touches early on and the Milan side were pretty well under pressure; they were certainly not producing the kind of stylish football expected of them. It wasn't helped when, after maybe fifteen minutes, a Venetian player challenged Jimmy and kneed him in the thigh, accidentally I believe. It caused a dead leg. It's not a major injury but it's very uncomfortable and restricts movement somewhat. It would have been in Jimmy's best interests if he had left the field. Whether it was his decision, or the trainer's, or the manager's, I don't know, but Jimmy stayed on for the whole of the game making a negligible contribution. It was inevitable that the home team were going to score. Sure enough, they did just that ten minutes or so from the end and Milan, the favourites, the powerful team from the big city with superstars to spare, had lost the game.

I had previously been invited to travel back by train with the team, but it was a very different journey from the one I had undertaken with my kind Italian friend in the car. Nobody spoke to me, and all I could see were miserable faces. It was as if I had been responsible for losing the game. I could understand their disappointment, but even small tokens of Italian charm and hospitality vanished completely on the journey and the day ended in abject misery. I returned to England on the Monday, fortunately having been able to transmit a reasonably respectable 'Greaves' column for the *People* that Sunday.

At least two parts of the mission had been accomplished, with an honourable away draw on the tennis court as a bonus. The hat-trick was not long in coming – Jimmy Greaves came home.

7

START OF THE
COVENTRY YEARS

WHILE this was going on, yet another opportunity was lurking on the horizon. Jim Laker, the Surrey and England cricketer, introduced me to Derrick Robins, Coventry City's chairman, at a Lord's Taverners' function, and we exchanged ideas on the way to run a football club.

Soon after, I was invited to Derrick Robins' house in Leamington alongside the cricket ground. The occasion was warm, Derrick referring to his wife as 'Mum'. The lunch was impeccably appetising, the wine of a much higher quality than I had been used to, and the subjects varied from the potential of a football club in the city of Coventry to Derrick's enthusiasm for the game of cricket, and not the least his intention to turn Coventry City Football Club into something worthwhile. The question was put, might I like to become the manager?

At the end of the afternoon, I promised to think it over during the coming week and was invited to their home match on the following Saturday, a Cup-tie against non-league King's Lynn from East Anglia. For a number of reasons it was thought prudent to keep my intended visit to Highfield Road a secret. A ticket for the far stand arrived in the post, not the stand in which the directors' box was situated. When Saturday came round, I sneaked into my seat, tucked my collar up round my ears and pulled a trilby hat well down over my forehead in the hopes that few people would notice me. It's not all that easy with a nationally known chin and here and there came acknowledgements and stifled gasps of surprise that I should be at Highfield Road, the reason not easy for them to detect.

Astonishingly, Coventry City lost at home to King's Lynn, which was a major shock to everyone concerned and increased the drama surrounding and the pressure on the club during that weekend. Strangely, taking or not taking the job had nothing to do with the potential that I may or may not have seen at the ground itself, nor even the football team. Certainly, it was not to do with the very poor result in that particular match. I have come to believe since that most probably I took it because I could not resist a strong urge to test whatever capacity I had to get results as a manager of a football club, and Coventry was the first opportunity to present itself.

Other doubtful thoughts had entered my mind concerning the intended partnership with Bagenal Harvey and what it would mean to spend the next few years of my life as a sports agent. With hindsight, it might seem easy to judge my joining Bagenal Harvey as inopportune because it might seem inevitable that other alternatives would have arisen in a variety of interesting fields. On the other hand, not many people would turn down a partnership in a rapidly expanding business involved in sport where the financial rewards in the years to come could be of substantial proportions. Yet, the little voice inside me kept nagging away to test my ability to coach a football team to success.

Negotiations with Bagenal were continuing. One letter from him referred to the fact that I was still coaching London University at Motspur Park on one or two afternoons a week. He queried whether I would want to continue to do that once I was employed in the partnership. There was a feeling of underlying unease in my mind when I read the letter. The university appointment wasn't vastly demanding and obviously not enormously profitable either. It easily slipped into the category of a not particularly time-consuming hobby and perhaps I didn't exactly warm to the idea of a partnership controlling twenty-four hours a day of my life. Perhaps it was something else. The letter was written in such a way that it seemed to be closing the door between football and myself. Whatever it was, I made my decision and telephoned a shocked Derrick Robins to tell him that I had decided to take the job as manager of Coventry City Football Club. Derrick had assumed that Coventry's appalling performance against King's Lynn in eliminating themselves from the Cup would have been enough to deter even the most determined potential manager from the obviously huge task that confronted him. Bagenal was disappointed at the news but the relationship continued as I continued to be a client.

I had made it clear to Derrick that if I took the job I would want to appoint my own coaching staff. As a result, it would be necessary for him to dispense with the services not only of Billy Frith, the manager, but also the entire present coaching staff. It was ruthless and I am quite sure that some decent people were hurt by it. On the other hand, getting results in a football club requires the utmost determination, knowledge and perseverance. More than anything else, it requires loyalty: total, undivided loyalty from those who are working with you. From time to time, even the most successful clubs hit a bad patch and it's during those times that a manager needs to know who his friends are. In order to bring an end to such a spell at the earliest possible moment, brutal frankness is needed, as well as unswerving support, to overcome the destructive demons who have you on the football rack. I had written a book not long since published, entitled *Striking for Soccer*, including the following words:

> You all know how frequently managers are fired. One of the reasons for this is that they themselves are never able to appoint the staff they want. Would you, going into the job for the first time, say, 'Well, it's very nice of you to appoint me. Now I want to sack four of your most loyal servants.' This is obviously the courageous thing to do, but in doing it you would risk losing the sympathy and cooperation of the rest.

I stuck by my convictions and manager Bill Frith, head trainer Alf Wood, who had been at the club for twenty-five years, his assistant Ted Roberts, with twenty years' service, and chief scout Arthur Jepson, a similarly long-time servant, were all to leave the club, three of them immediately, and one shortly afterwards.

I started single-handed without any recognised staff but with the help of one part-timer, Arthur Cox, who later made his own mark in the game as manager of Derby County and Newcastle United and coincidentally now helps Kevin Keegan at Fulham.

Alf Wood let the world know he was going with an indelicate but powerful quote: 'We're the victims of results. We have been trying to teach cart-horses to be footballers.' Such was the atmosphere at Highfield Road and the early days were turbulent, if exciting.

The first problem was to pick a team to play at home against Northampton Town on the following Saturday. We held a practice match on Wednesday morning, and I picked my first league eleven, dropping Brian Hill from the No. 9 position, in which he had played against King's Lynn, and telling him that when he came back into the side it would be to stay, but positively not as a striker. As it turned out, I was spot on because Brian became a first-class defensive wing-half in the team that eventually won promotion to the first division.

Came the great day, my first league match as a manager, and the players put up a stern fight. We won 1–0 and I could not complain about their endeavour. However, Northampton were clearly the better side despite losing full-back Tony Claypole, who broke his leg early on in the game. Typically Northampton's manager, Dave Bowen, who must have been more than doubly disappointed at the outcome, offered some advice to me as a new manager on the following Monday morning in the *Daily Herald*. 'Don't listen to anyone,' he wrote. 'Have faith in what you believe and don't let anyone try to talk or force you out of it. Good luck, Jimmy, and don't forget the advice of Brother Dave!' It was excellent advice and I valued it and stuck to it. It also said so much for the knowledge and charity of that delightful Welshman.

However, further controversy was just around the corner. Eight days after taking over as manager, I held a press conference and announced that a ten-year ban on players talking to the press would be lifted at Coventry City. I was very happy for our players to break their lengthy, enforced and unreasonable silence. You will not be surprised to learn that within a day or two, my old antagonist, Alan Hardaker, had written a letter to the club asking us to explain what we meant by this action. Chairman Derrick Robins wrote back to the League saying that the board supported its manager in his decision to allow his players the freedom to talk to the press. On another tack, he pointed out that they'd also given sanction for me to continue writing regular articles in the *Daily Express*. We didn't hear any more from the League, so in a very short space of time, yet another freedom had been achieved for twenty or so professional footballers and their manager.

On a much more pleasant note, we broke new ground in another way. We decided to invite youngsters under sixteen to a 'Pop and Crisp' party on Boxing Day to be held underneath the main stand after the match. We thought maybe a hundred or so young ones would turn up for the glass of pop and packet of crisps which were on offer, and the lure of players' autographs plus the goodies proved magnetic. We overcame Newport County 2–0 in the match, which provided a stimulating overture. The players had been told that it would be necessary for them to stay on for half an hour to fulfil our commitment to the young people of Coventry. It didn't take us long to realise we were going to be overwhelmed. We counted over 500 kids in the queue and it took over two hours for the players to do their duty. Cooperative as they were, there was a limit to their patience, so every time a player's glass emptied it was filled in the hope that no one would notice the time slipping by.

The party was a major success. The news spread, and such a simple, inexpensive idea created enormous fun for those who turned up, and, even more important, it conveyed the message that something dramatic was beginning to happen at Coventry City FC. Suddenly, it was a 'come in' club. We had made a start with young people to show them that we needed them and that they had a part to play in enabling us to achieve our ambitions. The 'Pop and Crisp' party was the first of a number of ideas which we launched to make our supporters feel an integral part of the club.

In January 1962, the first anniversary of the end of the maximum wage was coming round and I marked it in two vastly different ways. The first was to announce that the club would promote a competition between sixteen junior soccer leagues; each league would select a representative team of under eighteens. Those teams would play off behind closed doors at Highfield Road on Sundays and the best eleven players of the series would be chosen to play a game against Coventry City's first team. The second was to marry for the second time. On 18 January 1962 I married Christine Harding (as it was reported in the local paper, but she was always known as Heather). There was no honeymoon, it had to be business as usual as we were away to Notts County on the following Saturday afternoon. We lost 2–0 and there was disappointment and drama on another front.

The Council of the Football Association, of which I have been a member from time to time, though hardly at that point in my life, has made many decisions over the years in the interests of football. Some have been controversial; I would judge a respectable proportion to have been wise decisions, but an unfortunate number have not. I have never been in any doubt that the worst decision the Council has made in the history of the Football Association was to choose Dennis Follows ahead of Walter Winterbottom to be the Secretary of the Association. Previously Dennis Follows had been Honorary Treasurer of the FA and was, professionally, Secretary of the Airline Pilots' Association. At the time I said I cried for the future of English football. I meant no disrespect to Dennis Follows. He was a decent man with reasonable talents in a number of directions. In other circumstances I might not have reacted so fiercely against his appointment. However, the FA had in its ranks a man ideally qualified for

With Mum and Dad.

Brentford – new career, new overcoat.

Henry Thornton School First Xl – yesterday's three, three, five formation. I'm number ten.

Above: Walter Winterbottom – a smiling revolutionary.

Left: Full marks for determination, rather less for style!

Below: Ambitious young innocents – with Ron Greenwood at Brentford.

Admiring Ron Greenwood's resolute tackle. We were playing for an FA Xl against a Berlin Xl, in Berlin, in 1951. It was the first representative game between our two countries since the end of the Second World War.

Under manager Dugald Livingstone (*far left*), this Fulham team 'expected' to win – sometimes!

Frank Osborne of Fulham – stylish dresser, scratch golfer and shrewd businessman.

Charlie Mitten – the sweetest left foot to fail from the penalty spot.

Pud and the Little Nark, also known as Bedford Jezzard and Johnny Haynes.

Cloth Ears, alias Bobby Robson.

An improvement in heading technique.

Early days at Craven Cottage.

Working for the PFA, ready to take on the world.

Two freedoms, or strike! Addressing a players' meeting in Manchester with Cliff Lloyd *(on my left)*.

Just feel the quality! Jimmy Greaves and Terry Paine display the fur-lined benefits of no maximum wage.

Getting on with the Saturday job at Craven Cottage.

A trio of freedom fighters – with Gordon Banks and George Eastham.

Try putting current prices on this Internationals Club team. Back row: *(left to right)* JH, Derek Ufton, Wally Barnes, Ron Springett, Ronnie Burgess, Pat Saward, Bill McGarry, Bedford Jezzard, Eddie Low. Front row: *(left to right)* Stanley Matthews, Nat Lofthouse, Jimmy Scoular, Graham Leggatt.

the position; he had been inspirational to those who had benefited and been motivated by his influence and personality; he was a highly efficient administrator blessed with great charm and powers of persuasion to lead others. Sir Stanley Rous had influenced the world of football and to follow him England was in need of a man of similar stature; a man who also had the capacity to revolutionise attitudes to the professional game and within it. The FA councillors made the odd poor decision in the brief period I served it, but nothing to compare with that farce. By fifty votes to twenty, Follows was voted in instead of Winterbottom.

Walter at that time was manager of the England team, but it was inevitable, following that rebuff, that he was not going to keep the position for long. Soon after, an offer came from the Sports Council for him to be its Director and football was to lose its most persuasive disciple. Walter moved from a sport where his influence had already been immense and would surely have grown even greater to a job which would enable him to spread his talents over many sports. It wasn't so much what the Sports Council might gain which worried me but what football would lose. I just could not understand how the Council could reject a man who had commanded nothing but respect and admiration for himself and the Football Association. Even as I write, there are ninety councillors and not one of them has earned his living as a full-time professional player – the group whose skill provides the Association's vast income.

But back to work and although we were more than holding our own in the third division, it was evident that we did not have the necessary talent to move up the League.

One evening, Derrick Robins invited me over and during the course of dinner mentioned to me that his company, Banbury Buildings, was about to make a share issue, giving one share for every share possessed by a current holder. Significantly, as majority shareholder he would make a substantial profit. He didn't want to put me under any pressure, but, if I agreed, he would be prepared to donate £30,000 to the club to buy players and accelerate our climb to the top. He explained his worry that if I accepted the offer and the team wasn't successful, such failure could well result in the end of our relationship and I would disappear over the horizon. I asked him for time to think about it and responded pretty quickly. I wasn't in any way frightened of the responsibility of spending that amount of money, but the thought had occurred to me that if we were to announce the gift to the club immediately the price of any player we might be looking at would inflate and we would not get value for money. Accordingly, I said, 'Thank you, Derrick, I will accept the money, provided that no public announcement is made until such time as we have spent it.'

'Done!' he replied, and off I went with my shopping basket.

The first of the signings was Terry Bly from Peterborough for £12,000. Terry was an eminent goalscorer who had caused problems for us when playing against Coventry and he was to be the linchpin of our initial on-the-field campaign for success.

I have never believed it is possible to win matches consistently unless you have attacking players with prolific enough goalscoring records. That sounds fundamentally too simple to be true, but goalscoring is not a habit which can be manufactured in a player who lacks the capacity. Teams short of players with healthy records are always destined to struggle, putting an enormous strain on the defence. A desperate feeling arises that if they should lose a goal, they will have terrible trouble in reaping anything from the ninety minutes. The fee for Terry was a large slice of the £30,000 but I saw him as vital to our success. The remaining £18,000 had to go a long way so we were looking for players from less expensive sources and Northern Ireland seemed as good a place as any to pick up a couple of talented players at bargain prices, keen enough to improve and further their ambitions. I already knew Mick Lynch from the early Players' Union days. He had played all those strange games they play in the Emerald Isle as well as football and had been over for a trial himself. Mick was almost the finished article, but not quite. My attention was drawn by him to Willy Humphries, a right-winger, and Hubert Barr, a goalscoring striker, who played for Ards and Linfield respectively. Willy Humphries had already crossed the Irish Sea to play for Leeds United but he had not settled in what seemed to him a strange environment. However, with Derrick's help it wasn't that difficult to make both young men feel welcome and wanted, and to communicate to them how desperate we both were to create a winning team at Coventry. In the end we got our men, Willy for £4500 and Hubert for £8000.

On the way back on the aeroplane, having completed the signings, I mentioned to Derrick that John Sillett might be available from Chelsea for a small fee.

'Well, why don't we go to Stamford Bridge from London Airport and see if we can get him?' was the reply. Derrick was a dynamic supporter and influence, so there was never any time like the present to leap into action. He was determined to acquire the nucleus of a side which would bring to the city of Coventry some of the excitement which had been missing for so many years. We caught a taxi straight from the airport to Chelsea. Tommy Docherty, then manager, was rebuilding his team and happily produced John for our inspection. John was excited at the prospect of first-team football again, and of getting away from Chelsea as the Doc and he weren't bosom pals. What seemed a pretty low fee, £4000, was the asking price, but in the end we whittled it down to £2600 – quite a bargain as it turned out a few years later.

For the time being, we still had to persuade John's wife to move out of London. Unfortunately, she was confined to bed having dislocated a cartilage – a strange twist for a player's wife to have a cartilage problem! So off we went, the chairman and I, to the Sillett residence, located behind the ugly gasometers between Chelsea football ground and Wandsworth Bridge. I couldn't believe the status of the house in which John Sillett, a Chelsea player, was living. Although Mrs Sillett was worried about travelling to the unknown Midlands, I was able to reassure her that the houses we offered to our players at Coventry were like palaces compared with this inauspicious dwelling. We hoped that she would think it over while we went out to lunch. Derrick, John and I enjoyed a splendid meal and, with a burst of inspiration, the chairman persuaded the restaurant to prepare lunch which we could take back for Mrs Sillett. Whether that was the final straw which convinced her, I don't know, but it did lead to John joining us for the princely sum of £2600.

There was one further obstacle to surmount. John had promised his elder brother, Peter, he would not make a move from Chelsea without his blessing. Messages were sent out to Peter to join us in a club on the King's Road, thankfully open in the early evening. On Peter's arrival we duly celebrated the transfer with a bottle or two of champagne, there appearing to be no negative vibes coming from that direction. For personal reasons, which will emerge later, that transfer was going to have a significant effect on my life, and on John's too!

The prospective team still looked unbalanced as we needed an outside-left. Brighton were prepared to sell Bobby Laverick for £2500. I had once seen him play for Everton and telephoned Johnny Carey, Everton's manager, for an opinion. John thought that I should be comfortable paying £2500 for him because in the past he had been assessed much more expensively. Last, but not least, Jimmy Whitehouse had had a recent tiff with his club, Reading. Harry Johnston was the manager and such a pleasant person I find it hard to believe that anyone would have a disagreement with him. Later it turned out that it was the chairman whom Jimmy had upset; but whatever had happened I was extremely thankful that we were able to sign Jimmy Whitehouse for a few hundred pounds as compensatory payment for a benefit that he would lose if he left Reading. So, our shopping basket was full and we were in a position to announce to the world that those purchases had been funded by the generosity of our chairman, Derrick Robins. Publicly I said, 'It was a fantastic gift from a man who loves football.' I was only too glad to say that, because Derrick's generosity meant that I had a much better chance of being a successful manager.

Soon after, I took on a Hungarian coach, Janos Gerdov; not necessarily to work in tactical areas, especially in relation to the first team, but to introduce our players, particularly the young ones, to the kind of valuable skill practices and attitude I had previously been made aware of through the Hungarian manual.

8

CONSOLIDATING AT HIGHFIELD ROAD

S EASON 1962–63 did not start too well. There were some extremely exciting games but we tended to throw away points by making silly defensive mistakes. One thing which quickly became evident was that Johnny Carey's opinion of Bobby Laverick was out of date. He played a few games and I saw flashes of ability, but not enough to compensate for an apparent lack of passion. Fortunately, we had a young Welsh outside-left, Ronnie Rees, only eighteen years old, on our staff. His predecessor went more quickly than he arrived and Ronnie was thrust into league action sooner than he should have been. Nevertheless, from the outset he didn't let anyone down, his enthusiastic approach making up for lack of experience. Once Ronnie settled into league football he was a considerable asset. With confidence, his natural skill blossomed and he became an outstanding player, soon being selected for Wales. I had taken decisive, impetuous action over Laverick and fortune had blessed it by producing Ronnie Rees.

Often since then I have spotted managers making an expensive purchase and the player going on to perform badly in the team. Because of the high outlay, the manager will persevere, trying to prove his purchase a sound one, to the detriment of the rest of the team and the results. I was lucky to learn that lesson early and did not forget it. To make a mistake in the transfer market is inevitable; to compound that mistake by continuing to play the chosen one in the first team is unforgivable.

Our new group of players was making steady, but not extraordinary, progress in the third division with nine points after the first nine games. We had moved up the table to within striking distance of the leaders, Peterborough, coming up to Christmas. Someone suggested we should have a club song for the supporters to sing and perhaps even to inspire the team to better performances at times of emotional drought. John Camkin, a journalist writing for the *News Chronicle* and later for the *Daily Mail*, had become a director of our club. John also commentated for Anglia Television and on Sunday evenings would occasionally call at our house in Kenilworth on his way back home. One such evening around nine o'clock we were enjoying a gin and tonic together when he raised again the question of finding and choosing a club song. A glass or two or three later, we agreed on the emotional, lilting melody of the 'Eton Boating Song' and between us we began to compose a few words as well as rendering them to each other. Whatever his poetic talents, John's strength was not in his voice! So it fell to me to do most of the singing and we shared the other inspirational contributions. The outcome was the Sky Blue song which can still be heard from the seats at Highfield Road and elsewhere in the Premier League. I imagine it will still be sung and heard long after John and I have departed this life. John died sadly after a long illness in June 1998. The supporters seemed to like it, especially as the results were getting rosier. It was extremely moving to hear them at full throttle when we were winning and even more so when the team was down. Unlike some of the more raucous terrace chants and songs, the Sky Blue song has a special hymn-like quality which can produce tears as well as smiles of joy.

That Christmas the cast in the pantomime at the Coventry Theatre included Sid James and Frankie Howerd. They were kind enough to attend the press conference when the players sang the following words to launch the Sky Blue song:

Let's all sing together,
Play up, Sky Blues!
While we sing together
We shall never lose!
Proud, Posh or Pompey
Saddlers or anyone
They can't defeat us
We'll fight 'til the game is won!

Later on, bandleader Ted Heath recorded a jived up version arranging the music himself. It sold extremely well in the shops and added another unusual string to the bow of the enthusiastic, cheeky, up-and-coming Midlands football club.

Not all of our eventual heroes came expensively, including Ernie Machin. Ernie had been recommended by a scout from the Lancashire area, Alf Walton. Alf was keen on the young man and was pressuring me, hinting that other clubs would be signing him if we didn't get there quickly. So one Saturday when we were without a match, I travelled up to Nelson in Lancashire, met Alf Walton and watched Ernie Machin play. Ernie didn't have a great game on that day; he looked extremely slow, but nevertheless when he was in possession of the ball he hardly wasted a pass. He didn't seem to be an outstanding athlete, nor did he have the confidence or the luck to do something special which would crystallise positive thoughts and encourage me to take a chance on signing him. Afterwards he came up with his mother and father and we were introduced. It was rather strange; I said later that the real reason I took him on was because I liked the look in his eyes, a remark which caused mischievous ones to question my choice of words – eyes not being the normal place where one looks to find footballing talent. Ernie did have a bright eye and he said, 'If you give me a chance, I won't let you down.' I gambled on that determination, as well as on what I had seen in the game. I had heard remarks from people to the effect that it wasn't an outstanding game for Ernie and that he was capable of far better performances.

Obviously, in the circumstances, I wasn't going to pay a huge transfer fee for him and I said to the chairman of Nelson, 'Look, the boy's a good lad and I'd like to give him a chance and we haven't got many inspirational purchases in mind at Coventry. Suppose I offered you £50 for his transfer; would that be okay?' To my absolute amazement he agreed. For decency's sake, I added that if Ernie did do well and earned a first-team game, we'd bump it up to £200. Ernie signed for us and turned out to be a star, a great passer of the ball, extremely determined and full of craft and subtlety. He was never going to be a Greyhound, but he became quick enough. During the summer we put him in the hands of a sprint coach back in Lancashire and when he returned to Coventry we also arranged special sprint training. We didn't turn a tortoise into a hare but we did enable a most determined sixteen year old with far more than his share of natural ability to become one of the eleven players who eventually put City into the Premier League.

Whether it was the song, the new signings, the coaching or a combination of all those things, I don't know, but in the League the team's fortunes were gradually improving and by Christmas, having taken three points out of four from league leaders Peterborough, we were only four points behind them. Our successful run in the FA Cup alongside an unbeaten league spell alerted the nation to something special taking place in Coventry.

If you remember 1963, you will know that it was the year of the Big Freeze. No one in the footballing world will forget it, because games were snowed or frozen off for a period of at least six weeks. Drawn away, Coventry had beaten Millwall at the second attempt in the Cup – no mean achievement – and waited for the draw for the third round. It was away to Lincoln City; not the easiest pick from the hat but nonetheless not an impossible task. As a result of the interminable freeze and the extra thinking time it gave us, we made a couple of late New Year's resolutions regarding our pitch. As things stood, there was a fall of fifteen feet from one corner flag to its opposite number at the far end, which obviously was not ideal for any third division club, let alone one which harboured our ambitions. We resolved to remove the slope at the end of the season, which was achieved for £15,000. The second resolution, which took a little longer, was to install underground water pipes, a method Dutch farmers used during the winter to facilitate growth. Eventually, in 1980, we accomplished it, enabling games to be played on our perfect surface while other more sophisticated clubs had to postpone matches when at the mercy of the elements.

Domestically, another first occurred when my wife, Heather, gave birth to a baby girl, Joanna, in the early hours of the morning on 6 January. Derrick Robins kept my nerves at bay, staying up with me at his Kenilworth home playing snooker until the baby was born. It was a significant sign of a close relationship between the chairman and his manager, which I have come to believe implicitly is the mainstay of any successful professional football club.

Willy Humphries, our £4500 mini genius from Ards, was voted Player of the Year by the supporters and the freeze went on. . . and on. . . and on. The Lincoln City v Coventry City Cup-tie was put off for the sixth time on 29 January. We attempted to beat the weather by arranging a friendly match with West Bromwich Albion at Highfield Road on 13 January, but in the end it became impossible. Such was the hold that Jack Frost had on the country, not only Coventry City, but every club in Great Britain was struggling to find a pitch on which they could play a game of football. Someone telephoned me and suggested using Shamrock Rovers' ground in Dublin, because they had not experienced anything like the bad weather which was occurring in England and their turf was in perfect condition. I thanked him for the opportunity and said that I would do what I could to find another team who would play against us. I rang Joe Mercer at Aston Villa and invited him to play a friendly against us and so keep his players in touch with the game of football. Joe didn't seem too keen on the idea but said that he would ring me back. When the call came through, Joe reported that he had talked it over with one or two of his players and they decided against it because of the possibility of injury. I tried again with another manager; why not Matt Busby of Manchester United? Matt was welcoming and certainly more adventurous on the telephone.

'What a lovely idea. We could do with a game. Can you give me ten minutes and I'll be back to you with the answer?' The answer was positive: they would be pleased to play us the next day in Dublin. What I didn't know then but subsequently learned was that he had taken the opportunity to ring United's scout in Dublin and confirm that the pitch was as good as I had almost persuaded him it was.

So the following afternoon, there we were, third division Coventry lined up on a soft pitch facing Manchester United from the first division and a team of class. It included Harry Gregg, Noel Cantwell, Nobby Stiles, Bill Foulkes, Maurice Setters, John Giles, Albert Quixall, Denis Law and Bobby Charlton. At three o'clock, Manchester United v Coventry City kicked off in front of a crowd of 15,000.

If it seemed like a fairy story to start with, by half-time it certainly was: Coventry were leading by two goals to one. In our dressing-room there was great excitement and to add to the fun we could hear sounds of shouting coming from the adjoining dressing-room through the thin partition. There was very little I could say to improve on the performance so far, and instead of talking we pressed our ears to the flimsy wall and listened to Matt Busby handing out the mother and father of all blastings for allowing themselves to be a goal down to a side from the lowly third division. It served us right when not long before the end of the game, Bobby Charlton scored a brilliant goal to equalise and bring some contentment to both sides. After all, a draw was no mean feat. The icy conditions which were affecting England spread themselves to Dublin and Shamrock Rovers' pitch in the second half. We were all relieved when the ninety minutes were up.

As a result of this initiative, I was able to bring back a cheque for £200, not a fortune, but every penny counted in those days, and we had played a game of football at last. Personally, the thorn in the side was that it was Bobby Charlton who had scored the equaliser. It was not nearly as devastating as the semi-final of the Cup in 1958 between Fulham and United when, at Villa Park, his equaliser in another 2–2 draw sent the game to a replay, which Fulham lost, and I lost my chance to play at Wembley in a Cup final.

Back to real life, and the struggle continued to find the means to play a game at ice-bound Highfield Road. Someone thought of de-icing pellets; an experimental scattering over a small area of the pitch took place but the idea fell flat when we realised what it would cost to cover 8000 square yards. Someone else produced a de-icing machine resembling a massive hair dryer. The problem with that, as we soon discovered, was that once it had thawed a small area of turf, no sooner had we turned our backs on it than the ground had frozen again.

Bad luck seemed to breed bad luck, and on 18 February, with the team still hampered by the weather, our groundsman Ellick Smith slipped and fell while tending to a severe patch of ice and broke his leg in two places. It seemed as though we would never be able to play our away Cup-tie against Lincoln City. Nevertheless we were determined to play a league game of some kind. It looked as though we were about to succeed when on Friday, 22 February, the evening before our match with Barnsley, we appealed for our supporters to help us. We needed them at 9.30 a.m. on the Saturday morning to clear the pitch. We had resorted to the de-icing pellets and in addition had laid 500 bales of straw for insulation. On the following morning, over five hundred enthusiastic supporters turned up, armed with their shovels, and duly set about clearing the ground. Believe it or not, by three o'clock in the afternoon we had beaten the freeze at last and were able to play against Barnsley, winning 2–0, with goals from our cheapest and most expensive players, Jimmy Whitehouse, stolen from Reading, and Ken Hale whom we'd bought from Newcastle. Similar tactics enabled a 2–2 draw to be played against Colchester United. On Saturday, 2 March, we drew 0–0 at Northampton and prepared for the long-awaited Cup-tie at Lincoln City. It was due to be played on Monday, 4 March, but was postponed for the final time – sixteen times in all, which is still a record. It was eventually played three days later on 7 March.

Seventeen-year-old Ernie Machin made his debut as an inside-forward in that match and played a tangible part in a splendid 5–1 victory. We did not forget our supporters. To get to Lincoln City for a 7.30 kick-off, there would be no time for a meal first, so we organised a special catering coach to travel along with the supporters' coaches, which provided tea, coffee and hot dogs.

In the next round on Wednesday, 13 March, the team took the field at Fratton Park against Portsmouth. For a long time Pompey led 1–0 and it looked as if our run had come to an end, but with six minutes left Ken Hale managed to scramble an equaliser and force a replay. It took place on Saturday, 16 March; with home advantage we were leading by two goals from Jimmy White-house and it looked as though we were home and dry, but Portsmouth scored twice, Ron Saunders getting the equaliser. There being no such thing as a penalty shoot-out, the replay took place on neutral ground at White Hart Lane. Ron Saunders scored first for Pompey, but an equaliser by Terry Bly set the scene for a fine winning goal scored again by our free-transfer snip, Jimmy Whitehouse, who had scored in every round.

Laurie Pignon of the *Daily Sketch* wrote, 'The 16,750 crowd made enough noise for treble that number with the Coventry contingent continually filling the night air with their version of the Eton Boating Song.' Of course, we were all ecstatically happy, but even so I could see the danger of the Cup run to our other ambitions. That evening I said, 'A great win, but it complicates our promotion task. I'd rather get out of the third division than achieve anything else with Coventry City. We deserved to win and the lads are in a mood where they refuse to be beaten.'

So it was on to the fifth round and a home draw against Sunderland, managed by Alan Brown. The official attendance on the night was registered as 40,499 – the biggest crowd at Highfield Road for thirty years – and 4–5000 people were locked outside unable to see the match.

We had been kicked to pieces by Dick Graham's Crystal Palace team on the Saturday before, and four or five players were trying desperately hard to recover from knocks and bruises in time for the Monday evening. Fortunately, all came through and our young international, Ronnie Rees, who missed the Saturday match, was back in time for this splendid occasion.

Johnny Crossan scored for Sunderland after thirty-three minutes and quite honestly, despite the noisy enthusiasm of the vast army of home supporters, it looked as if Sunderland's classy superiority would see them through. At that time they were leading the second division and were a team unused to losing. Normality was cast aside. With only ten minutes left, Dietmar Bruck, our young midfielder, latched on to a loose ball outside the penalty area and cracked in a fierce shot which went into the net via the far post. The fans went wild. Thousands of delirious youngsters on the fringe of the pitch raced on like dervishes, clapping, back-slapping and congratulating anybody within reach. The FA Secretary, Dennis Follows, in the directors' box, graciously pronounced, 'Just a case of youthful exuberance, nothing to worry about!' for which kind thought we were most grateful. If those scenes were over-exuberant, imagine what happened two minutes later when skipper George Curtis, among a crowd of players surrounding the penalty spot, managed to get his head to a cross from a free-kick by John Sillett. Such a header should not have gone in from there, but unfortunately for Sunderland, Montgomery the goalkeeper had ventured just a fraction too far off his line and was helpless as the loping header dropped home under the bar. The ground exploded into frenzy once more. The problem from then on was to keep the crazy spectators away from the pitch and the players. Somehow, thankfully, common sense prevailed and the match was allowed to finish, the prize for the victors being a home draw in the sixth round against Manchester United, our old friends from Shamrock Rovers.

Sportingly, Alan Brown, the Sunderland manager, said, 'We have no complaints. Coventry deserved to win.' The Sky Blue song's co-composer, director John Camkin, decided to watch the game from the terraces. He reported afterwards that at one stage a woman had turned to him and said, 'Why aren't you singing?' and promptly hit him on the head with her handbag! We were understandably proud, too, of the quote from Mr McCabe, the referee, who had refereed two of our previous matches that season. He said afterwards, 'Coventry City are the best disciplined team I have handled.' That was quite a compliment.

Looking back, I have often wondered what it was that brought about such staggering success, in the hopes that I could pinpoint the source of it to pass on to ambitious young managers. I had made certain instinctive decisions, such as not wanting to be called 'Boss' or 'Gaffer'. The whole football world, and even my Mum and Dad, had caught up and were calling me 'JH'.

Secondly, I grasped quite quickly that to succeed, a football club must have a wide range of unselfish support from a variety of different directions, certainly from the board of directors, certainly from the manager, his staff and his players, and certainly from the rest of the staff. Our objective was to try to spread that loyal backing to wider spheres, for instance the local council, the local community and schools and local football leagues. We wanted them all to feel that Coventry City was their club and to support it actively, deriving pleasure from any success, as did those of us who were lucky enough to be closer to the heart of things. In order to do that, I learned to exert the maximum emphasis on the word 'we'. For a long time, I have cringed when I read or hear managers in football clubs talking about 'My players', or 'I did this', or 'I did that'. We became a 'we' club in a 'we' league in a 'we' city in a 'we' country.

In eliminating the word 'Boss' from the players' vocabulary, I reasoned that you can't expect a team to be treated as office boys from Monday to Friday and then play like senior executives when they're on their own on Saturday. I saw public relations as the most neglected part of football and my ambition was to encourage our followers, particularly those from our city, to feel part of our club and that our success was their success.

It was indeed a heady time for everyone but we were still

conscious of having to keep our feet firmly on the ground in a city that had its head in the sky – a blue sky!

We decided to take the players down to Fulham's old hunting ground before Cup-ties, the Warnes Hotel in Worthing. Although it took us away from the turmoil in the city of Coventry, we were overwhelmed, rather flattered if the truth was known, by the national press seeking to find out what the fuss was all about. One paper, the *Daily Mail*, interviewed George Curtis, our twenty-three-year-old captain giving his comments on the manager. 'I've never yet known him lose an argument. When you think you've got him cornered, he'll baffle you with science,' George was reported as saying. 'Since he came to Coventry, he has completely changed our training methods and our style of play. Our training is much more varied and enjoyable,' he went on, which was rather pleasing; but then George knew I was bound to read it and was thinking about his next contract.

Never mind the write-ups, Saturday was to bring us all down to earth, but not before we had sampled a glimpse of heaven. Over 44,000 people crowded into Highfield Road to witness the sad end to the gallant Cup run. Manchester United's stars deservedly won 3–1 on the day; the Coventry team, somewhat creaking in the joints as a result of the number of matches we had played in the preceding weeks and the emotional excitement of such games, was beaten but not disgraced. Matt Busby, as ever the gentleman, said some pleasant things about us, even admitting the extent of his relief. My own feeling was that had we not fixed the friendly match in Dublin during the freeze, giving Matt and his lads the chance to realise the strength of a so-called third division team, we might have caught them napping in the Cup-tie. As it was, they came to Highfield Road determined to produce their very best form on the day, which they now knew would be necessary to dispose of these upstarts. They did just that.

We took a deep breath and started back on the promotion trail, quite disastrously as it happened, with a game at Wrexham. For twenty minutes we played superb football, full of confidence as one would expect from a team having reached the sixth round of the Cup. Unfortunately, Wrexham scored a goal and it was as if every ounce of strength had gone from the players' legs: the previous energy, the style and the confidence just evaporated. We staggered on, relishing a summer's rest more than another game.

It's said that Alan Shearer is the richest footballer playing in domestic football. It's not coincidental, I think, that he is a striker, or an old-fashioned centre-forward if you prefer, a prolific goalscorer with the capacity also to link with other players and spread goals among his fellow attackers. You may think that's far removed from what happened at Coventry City during the latter part of that dramatic season. Having lived on the goalscoring strength of Terry Bly for eighteen months, it seemed to some supporters at least ungrateful and to others idiotic for me to purchase another centre-forward at the same time, this being before the time when strikers hunted in pairs; in those days you were either a centre-forward or you weren't. It's simple: goals win matches. Winning matches collects points and points win leagues. Though we all fall in love with a defender from time to time, Bobby Moore being the perfect example, most award winners play further upfield. Thus Terry Bly was a hero in the city of Coventry and not one person in ten could understand why a manager to whom they had freely given their trust should suddenly lose his marbles by purchasing another striker.

An uncomplicated reason for buying George Hudson (also from Peterborough) was that he had suddenly become available and there was no time like the present. There was the risk that I would lose him if I didn't move. The fundamental reason, though, was that I had seen signs here and there that, despite scintillating performances for us when he was hot, Terry was inclined to blow cold on other occasions. To be a successful manager it is essential to be ahead of the game. In making judgements it's not only necessary to be a step or two ahead of your supporters in exercising that judgement but also of managers of other clubs who are no slouches when it comes to finding the right answer themselves. It is vital to anticipate events, take a chance, if you like, by anticipating the direction in which a player's form might move. Sometimes form would improve rapidly and it would be necessary to move quickly in one direction. At other times, as was the case with Terry, I had detected signs that maybe he wouldn't continue to produce the sensational form for us much longer. The right time to sell, therefore, has to be before other managers recognise the weakening of a player's potency, enthusiasm or capability. In confusing or outwitting other managers, it's almost certain that you will confuse your own supporters. It's a game of bluff and counterbluff. The further ahead of the game you are, the less likely it is that your own supporters will understand. The best thing that one can hope is that sometime later, they may recognise the reasons which lay behind such seemingly abrasive decisions.

Later such lack of faith in my judgement was to occur again with George Hudson just as it had done with Terry Bly. History records that I sold both players for rather more than I bought them, particularly in George's case, making something in the region of £7500 profit. History also records that within a short space of time, less than two years, both players had fallen from the pinnacle which they had achieved in their careers in football into non-league football or into retirement altogether.

Forgive me for using these examples: I'm not reciting them merely for you to recognise what a clever old soul I was but to stress that some of the decisions which every manager will make, and which may appear to be ridiculous, are made with the understanding and intimate knowledge that only a manager can have of a player. It's his duty, aggravating as it may be, to remain silent, to accept the sometimes bitter criticism and to stand by an unpopular decision which he knows is for the long-term benefit of his club. In a nutshell, if you are going to outwit other managers, you certainly have to be prepared to fool your own supporters, without explanation. There was nothing more sinister in the events that led to the transfer of Terry Bly, and later of George Hudson, than that. It was pure, cold-blooded, unsentimental business for Coventry's balance sheet, but more importantly in the long-term, to win more matches.

The other indisputable point which had embedded itself in my mind after a year or two in the job was that players who are purchased will have been sold, in most cases, because their previous club and manager have found them wanting. It's not always the case; sometimes talent is unrecognised or players need time to mature and gain confidence in their ability. Certainly players past the halfway stage in their careers, who have moved around more than once, most probably have something about them which has given more than one manager cause to pass them on. With such players I learned that it is possible to motivate them for a season or two, but not to expect improvement or even consistency beyond that period. Perhaps it is a sad judgement on fellow footballers but, human nature being what it is, I learned that it is better to accept it than try to disprove it. When we reach the end of this Sky Blue story, you will see the composition of the team that eventually put Coventry City into the first division. There are eight or nine reasons why that theory proved itself. I found out later that sometimes it was necessary to splash out extravagantly on players to fill temporary holes which had appeared in a team structure through injury and who were never going to be sold at a profit; this was in times of genuine emergency, not panic.

I had rapidly formulated golden rules for myself in the years I spent in management. Once I realised how to use the transfer market, I disciplined myself accordingly, based on the fact that players on the move would give up to two seasons' reasonable service before falling back to the standard which accounted for their transfer from their previous club in the first place. I calculated that players over the age of twenty-seven or twenty-eight decreased in value to such an extent that, unless you were lucky, there would be little if any return on any transfer money paid for their services. So unless there was a compelling reason to purchase a player over the age of twenty-five, it could not be justified. Once a player had played out his two years, should he fall short of the standard expected of him after that time, there was still a reasonable chance of getting a fair return in the transfer market. In today's unbelievably extravagant times, despite superclubs becoming public companies with responsibilities to their shareholders, such prudence appears irrelevant. The income from Sky TV plus the floating of the superclubs on the Stock Exchange, as well as increasing pressure from supporters and the media, has made it extremely difficult to adopt and maintain a sane approach to the running of a major football club.

Back to the pitch, and for the record, George Hudson scored three goals in his first match, a win over Halifax Town, but it still didn't stop the fans asking questions. Coventry ended the season with a 3–1 win over Queens Park Rangers at the White City and four days later on tour beat Neumeinster by a similar score. On 24 May we announced that we had signed three apprentice professionals, among them a lad called Bobby Gould. Terry Bly left us in August. Two of our players, centre-half and captain George Curtis, and outside-right Willy Humphries, had been chosen by the magazine *Soccer Star* in their pick of the best division three team. Their manager was also chosen by the same journal as Manager of the Year. While the citizens of Coventry were spending their time arguing about the merits of transferring Terry Bly, necessary hard work was taking place in levelling the pitch so that for the first time in their existence the Coventry City team would be without the advantage or disadvantage of a fifteen-foot slope from one corner to t'other.

9

THE ONLY WAY IS UP

T HE summer came and went and we were seeking a way to open the season in flamboyant, typical Sky Blue manner for our home match against Crystal Palace. Late one night at a board meeting I had what I considered then, and still do for that matter, the most original idea I had while I was at the club. Each time Coventry scored at a home match, a massive firework would be released from the ground which would explode high in the sky and let the whole of the city know that Coventry had scored. Hopefully, a stock of ten such fireworks would cover any eventuality in that first game. Some members of the board liked the idea, others accorded it doubtful credibility and one charming director, Jack Smart, just couldn't bring himself to face up to the prospect of it, not the scoring of goals that is, but the suggested means of celebration. Nevertheless, I was given the licence to explore the idea. I telephoned Brocks, the fireworks manufacturers, and they offered to send a highly qualified explosives expert to discuss the possibilities. The real problem soon became evident: it seemed that a firework of sufficient calibre to be seen throughout the city in daylight was dangerous and would not be permitted. Such a device was contained in something which looked like half a coconut shell and a spent firework like that falling from the sky would clearly do some damage. As an experiment I dropped it on my head from six inches and I was not going to volunteer to test it from even six feet, let alone six hundred.

The explosives expert went back to the factory and later suggested a ground mortar, which would unleash a considerable bang. He came back with some colleagues to demonstrate the potency and suitability of the mortar on the edge of the pitch close to the halfway line. As they were about to light it, we were firmly advised to move back twenty yards or so. My eyes opened.

'Hold on a minute,' I said. 'What do you think is going to happen to the players and the supporters? Fifteen to twenty yards away? Do you mean to say we're in danger?'

'Well, yes,' came the reply. Nevertheless, we did explode it and with it out went my idea of promoting the club to the city during a match. We had to admit total defeat, much to the delight of our dissenting director.

What a disappointment it was on the following Saturday afternoon when we beat our long-term rivals, Crystal Palace, 5–1 in the opening match. Just imagine – in every national newspaper third division Coventry City would have made headlines by starting the season with a bang – five of them!

In spite of that win, the argument was still going on over the selling of Terry Bly. I had appealed to the supporters not to waste their energy on looking back. It was in the past now and to continue carping on about it wasn't going to help us to achieve our primary objective – promotion to the second division. Fortunately, the dynamic start in the first game was followed by an extraordinary few months. We followed the Crystal Palace triumph by winning 3–0 away at Notts County, who in the meantime had bought Terry Bly from us. It was a fairy story from Coventry's point of view. George Hudson, Terry's replacement, scored two of our goals. Point made!

Young Ernie Machin from Nelson had forced his way into the team and was developing a special on-the-field relationship with fellow Lancastrian, George Hudson. A 3–0 win in the third match at Walsall giving us a goal difference of 11–1 made sure that there weren't any spare tickets lying about. Such was the high that the following 0–0 draw at Reading was looked upon as total failure.

There were 27,796 people to see the return match against Notts County on Tuesday, 10 September. Coventry won 2–0, Hudson scoring one of the goals and burying the Terry Bly upheaval once and for all.

We lost our first match on 23 September, away to Hull City at Boothferry Park. I shan't forget it because the referee was Kevin Howley, who for a long time I thought of as an old adversary if referees can be described thus. In his wisdom Mr Howley judged that George Curtis controlled the ball with his arm in the penalty area. My eyes were pretty sharp and my mind as unbiased as it's possible for a manager to be and I reckon George was two yards from the touchline when he handled the ball. Whether it was intentional or not did not matter. Whether it was in the penalty area did. I could not believe that such injustice was possible. Nothing could bring back the point or eradicate the defeat. It became apparent to me, having to absorb that decision and others almost equally disconcerting, that it made no sense to complain about poor decisions publicly at the end of a game. I made my resolution never to dispute a referee's decision retrospectively. I used to voice this parrot-fashion to any reporters who questioned me. However, Kevin Howley's howler from long ago, for which I have now forgiven him (I'm not too sure about George Curtis), was infuriating. It's true, it did lead to my sensible resolution but at the time it created Coventry's first loss and bitter disappointment. I noticed following Arsenal's defeat by Chelsea in the semi-final of the 1998 Football League Cup, that Arsene Wenger has adopted the same 'parrot'.

Our season was progressing even better than the last. In a brief spell before Christmas, we scored eight goals at home against Swansea, and six away at Queens Park Rangers. I began to wonder whether I had truly stumbled on a soccer secret akin to splitting the atom. . .

During the summer, I had read a book written by Sir Adolphe Abrahams concerning body rhythms over a twenty-four-hour cycle. It sounded complicated and was new to me, but thinking of my own feelings of physical highs and lows, it made complete sense. Very simply it suggested that since the body had been prostrate for eight hours while asleep, no regular violent exercise should be undertaken until three or four hours after waking. The body would build up towards a fitness peak around midday which would then diminish to a low around 5 p.m. It would pick up again towards eight o'clock in the evening, sliding downwards towards the ultimate low point during the night. Quite clearly it revealed to me that from 3–4.45 p.m. the bodygraph was doing this ＿＿＿＿＿ whereas from 7.30–9.15 at night it was doing this ＿＿＿＿＿ . Give or take the odd exception, I had always felt much fitter during evening games than those in the afternoon.

I related those theories to our training routines. Our peak fitness sessions took place on Monday, Tuesday and Thursday mornings, from 10–12, after which the players would enjoy a formidable lunch, go home and relax, go racing, go shopping, but do nothing strenuous, savouring that comfortable 'after lunch' feeling. Yet on a Saturday the same body and mind which controlled it had to switch its regular habits, resting in the morning and being ready for a hard physical battle in the afternoon. It made such clear-cut sense to me that I changed the time of our main physical training sessions to take place at three o'clock in the afternoon, much to the annoyance of some players' wives, to whom, I'm afraid, I turned a deaf ear.

I think most clubs still schedule their tough physical sessions for the morning and I'm grateful. If I ever have to make a comeback as a manager, I'll need at least a yard's start at my age! I wonder, though, how many will read the above paragraphs and at least give them some thought?

Back to the promotion campaign which moved on steadily despite a blip here and there until a nasty accident to Ernie Machin, in a 2–2 draw at home to Watford towards the end of October, dented our prospects. It looked as though he would be out for at least two months and was to prove particularly damaging because of the understanding which he had built up with our newly acquired striker, George Hudson.

The FA Cup first round arrived and took our minds away from the league table, remembering our electrifying achievements during the previous season. We were drawn to face Trowbridge on their own ground in Wiltshire and I took the lads away to the old favourite training resort, the Warnes Hotel in Worthing, for a relaxing few days. They travelled down in their own cars and back via Trowbridge, stopping off to win 6–0 on the Saturday afternoon. We received a welcome from the Trowbridge hierarchy and supporters fit for a king; 6–0 wasn't the usual way to repay such generosity, but it saw us through to the second round of the Cup.

Bearing in mind what had happened last season, it wasn't surprising that the city of Coventry was beginning to suffer from Cup fever once more. We were drawn at home to Bristol Rovers, whom we had not long since beaten 4–2 in a league match – imagine the expectation! Yet to the astonishment and bitter disappointment of our supporters, we were knocked out of the Cup on our own ground. No manager likes to lose any game or be despatched from the FA Cup at any time, but that evening I can honestly report that I didn't suffer the depression which normally would have followed such a bitter defeat. I suppose it was because having seen the way we had collapsed in the League in the previous season due to our splendid Cup run, I had no wish to see the players run out of energy in the finishing straight once more. For such clubs as Coventry, the Cup's fun, the League's business.

We quickly forgot the Cup and returned to the problem of staying on top of the third division. We had made attempts to improve the atmosphere at the ground on a match day, launching Radio Sky Blue three-quarters of an hour before kick-off. With a disc jockey as host, the aim was to foster enthusiasm and eliminate boredom, creating a happy, positive atmosphere. In those days, spectators arrived an hour or so before a game and would stand, sometimes in the rain, often in the cold, waiting for

113

the whistle to blow. The least we could do was try to make that time pass quickly and enjoyably. At one point Godfrey Evans, England and Kent wicketkeeper, was our disc jockey. He had a waspish sense of humour and a good knowledge of sport and was a fan of the Sky Blues. The crowd loved him.

Insofar as away matches were concerned, we embarked on discussions with British Rail personnel, who were struggling with the problem of football supporters damaging coaches on their trains by unruly behaviour. The thought was that if the train appeared to belong to the club because the club had hired it for the afternoon, then supporters might take better care of it. We did a deal with BR to hire the trains and sold the seats to our supporters ourselves. Suddenly we were in the railway business with the Sky Blue Express and needed to find ways and means of filling the trains. We put our minds to work. The first thing we did was to wire each carriage for sound so that we could play music, which we followed with a news/interview/entertainment programme based on the activities of the club. We interviewed supporters about their attitude to the club, their favourite players or any topical subject. Sometimes injured players would join them and answer their questions personally. We were not only helping BR preserve their rolling stock but to start with we found such eagerness to travel to away matches that we could make a profit. When the team was doing particularly well, the trains would be full, but at other times business was not so good. Even Coventry fans, as is the case with every club, lose their enthusiasm for travelling to away matches when they expect to witness a defeat. It is easy enough to criticise this fragility but, if you think about it, there is an enormous difference between the pleasure of travelling home after an away success, and the same journey regurgitating the reasons which brought about a loss. It's all very well talking about loyalty but I see no reason why fans should not expect some pleasure in return for their expenditure. If they're disappointed week after week, it's understandable that their support should wane. Later, just when we were finding it difficult to fill the trains, BR decided to increase the hire charge. It became uneconomical to run such excursions and so everyone lost: a sad ending to a bright initiative.

As the season progressed, a vital league match was due to take place at Selhurst Park against Crystal Palace, who no doubt were determined to avenge the 5–1 drubbing in the season's opening game. I referred before to the aggressive nature of Dick Graham's team and the forthcoming match was not one for gentle souls. In the event, it was thrilling, it was rough, it was tough, it was dramatic and it ended all square. Although any professional footballer must have guts, physical courage and a healthy determination to win, there is a limit to this and I believe that Palace overstepped that mark. Bert Howe, their left-back, was not chosen for his ball-playing ability and had his name taken in the first half for a particularly nasty tackle on our diminutive, skilful outside-right, Willy Humphries.

Through no fault of any Palace player, George Curtis, our inspirational giant of a captain, gashed his knee and was carried off. I rushed to the dressing-room, where the Crystal Palace doctor was stitching it up. It wasn't a pretty sight: you could actually see the inside of the knee such was the severity of the injury, but George, unlike any other human being I have come across, did not seem to feel any pain as he was being treated. If he did, he didn't show it. There were no substitutes in those days and it seemed highly unlikely he would be able to play any further part in the game. We did not have our own doctor travelling with the party – a situation we later put right – and I had to count on the advice of the Crystal Palace medic. Without being discourteous, I felt I should not rely on the opinion of a doctor linked with our opponents with so much at stake. I left the doctor putting in the stitches and returned to my seat next to Derrick Robins to see how the game was going; we were a goal down. Our ten men were battling bravely on, when Derrick asked me whether George would take any further part. Deep down, having seen the injury, I did not think that even George could play on, at best he might hobble on a wing. As we were discussing it, the gentleman in question strode through the tunnel, straight out to the touchline, signalled to the ref and went back on, not to play on the wing, but to play centre-half and restore the numbers and balance to the team. George's bravery gave me the chance at half-time to stir the Coventry players to find a way to equalise at least. Willy was a talented player but a gentle person and not the kind of man whom we could expect to react to the mauling he had received from Bert Howe in the first half. I appealed to him, 'Willy, this is the greatest chance of your life to fight for right. Never mind Coventry City. Here is a big bully who is trying to kick you out of the game. We should have lost George and what has he done? He's come back with seven stitches. Willy, can you find the courage to go and use your skill to destroy this full-back? If he doesn't kick you to pieces, he can't stop you! So screw your courage to its sticking point and go out there and destroy him with skill!' Willy had a marvellous second half, scoring the equaliser which sustained Coventry's unbeaten sequence and meant so much psychologically at that time. When it came to handing out the medals, it was that two-point difference which enabled us to overtake Crystal Palace for the championship on the last day of the season. Willy and George had well earned theirs.

It was an extremely happy Christmas. We took part in as many joyful celebrations as we could muster, including the annual 'Pop and Crisp' party for the kids. In contrast, we were about to experience an appalling losing spell which went on for several weeks. After a 3–0 home win against Millwall early in January we were leading the division by nine points. Suddenly we lost the capacity to win at home and began to find opponents eager to beat the league leaders on their own ground. From a position of scoring 42 points from 27 games we found ourselves on 22 February still leading the division by two points from Crystal Palace, but with only 46 points from 33 games.

I thought a bit of drama and fun might well relax our players who were becoming increasingly tense approaching games, having appeared to have thrown away a certain chance of promotion into the second division, and so I agreed to take part in the students' rag week at Coventry Technical College. 'Jimmy Hill, the Coventry City manager, has been kidnapped,' announced the *Coventry Evening Telegraph*, 'and those responsible are demanding a ransom of £10,000.' Afterwards, when people questioned me about the suitability of entering into a student prank at a serious time in the football club's fortunes, I pointed out that surely a good cause should be supported in bad times as well as good – perhaps even more so.

Fundamentally, there were valid reasons for our loss of form, but it was hard to convince the players that it wasn't necessarily their fault. They knew only too well that it's possible to have a run where decisions go for you and the ball runs kindly. It's equally certain that sometimes the opposite will happen. Nearly always there is a catalyst and in this instance it was the absence of our most creative player, young Ernie Machin, and the in-and-out performances of George Hudson through injuries he incurred.

Looking back, it's extraordinary to register how quickly the fervour of some supporters dwindled. They continued to watch the team play, but they quickly lost faith in one or two players, and in the manager, because we had toppled from the standard we had set. It takes even less time for that to happen these days. Some did have faith though; Michael Grade, then a sportswriter with the *Daily Mirror*, said, 'Coventry are out of the wood. They may have gone nine games without a win but they'll be in the second division next season.' That was after a 1–1 draw at Watford when Bill McGarry, the Watford manager, showing far more confidence in the Coventry team than some of the supporters, said, 'Coventry gave nothing away and we played as well as we can to earn the draw. They are a fine side.'

It's one thing saying it and another proving it. Matters deteriorated further. Michael Grade watched us lose at home to Southend 5–2 on 13 March, the heaviest defeat of the season. He made no further predictions about promotion in his column. At that stage we'd amassed 49 points from 37 games and were still clinging to the top position having scored 85 goals for with 52 against. In second place, Crystal Palace, having played 36 games, were on level points. Ernie Machin still carried a troublesome injury, even when he was playing again, and George Hudson in Ernie's absence had been half the player he was when Ernie was alongside. As things stood, I feared disaster and knew that we needed an injection of something special in order to pep things up. After consultation with Derrick Robins, we agreed to spend some money before the closing date for transfers, Monday, 16 March. We needed an experienced striker who could score goals, was aggressive, and with as few nerves as possible, together with a confident midfield general who had sufficient skills to calm the nerves of those around him. I went south to Southampton for our dashing striker and signed George Kirby, thirty years old, at a cost of £12,500.

At the same time, I was able to persuade Tottenham to part with John Smith, the former England Under-23 wing-half, for £11,000. Thus for £23,500 I hoped I had bought what it took to keep us in the promotion battle and achieve our objective. I clawed £7000 back, selling Jimmy Whitehouse to Millwall for £4500 and Frank Kletzenbauer to Walsall for £2500. Kletz had been on the books since I had been at the club and Jimmy, as you will remember, had cost us nothing and had performed magnificently, the best free transfer ever. On 28 March with George Kirby's hat-trick we beat Oldham 4–1 and the rot had been stopped.

We began to pick up points again, yet a 0–0 draw at Millwall followed by a 2–0 defeat at Peterborough made it look as if, for all our efforts, the season might collapse on the last Saturday. Crystal Palace and Watford were still in strong contention. Crystal Palace had 60 points, two points ahead of ourselves and Watford, both with 58. We had a far superior goal average to Watford, which was a significant advantage, but things did not augur well for the Sky Blues. Despite George Kirby's impressive start, we hadn't been scoring goals and George Hudson, having played a game or two in the reserves, was making noises about feeling fit enough to come back into the team for the final game at home to Colchester. I was not prepared to discuss the team selection beforehand, although I knew exactly what I intended to do and that was to restore George Hudson to the centre-forward position, not only for that match, but if all went well for the whole of the next season in the second division.

The ending to this particular fairy story was that George Hudson scored the only goal to beat Colchester 1–0 and as a result of Crystal Palace losing on the day, Coventry City not only were promoted to the second division but went up as champions. There were 36,901 people in the stadium for that final match and nearly 16,000 on the following Wednesday for a celebration friendly against Spurs who won by the entertaining score of 6–5. George Curtis, our magnificent captain, who had not avoided criticism from some supporters during the unnerving slump, was deservedly voted Midlands Player of the Year. But we weren't finished. Within an hour of the end of the game, the builders began to pull down the stand opposite the directors' box on the far side of the ground ready for the construction of the new 5000 seater stand before the beginning of the next season.

Coventry's home league gates were 200,000 up on the previous season. Only ten Football League clubs averaged crowds of more than 25,000, gates having dropped by 350,000. Coventry's average gate had soared from 10,237 to 25,991 in three seasons.

10

CHASING PROMOTION

I T was a wonderful summer. I had been asked by ITV to take part in the Cup final broadcast as a summariser for Gerry Loftus, the main commentator. We broke new ground, too, by taking the players on a tour of Spain. There was nothing sensational about that but we did offer to take the players' wives which was an unusual step for a professional football club. So players, directors and wives, all one big happy family, flew off to the sunshine to take part in an unbeaten tour, albeit the matches were not against teams anywhere near the top echelon of Spanish football.

After that, I went off with my wife Heather and daughter Joanna to spend a holiday on the Spanish coast at Aigua Blava bay north of Palamos. It proved there is no such thing as a holiday for a football manager. New guests arrived generally on Saturday, but sometimes on a Sunday when I pestered unsuspecting arrivals for a Sunday paper, in order to catch up on the latest football news. On the first Sunday, I managed to procure a copy of the *People* and read that Watford were about to sign David Clements from Wolverhampton Wanderers. I had seen David play in the Irish youth team and he had made a strong impression on me. Wolves had purchased him for £7000, but it seemed were prepared to let him go. I managed to get a call through to Pat Saward, our youth coach, and asked him to alert Stan Cullis, the manager of Wolves, to our interest. I also asked Pat to get across to Ireland, find Dave Clements and begin discussions with him. The outcome of all this excitement was that within a few days we had signed David for £1500. A wonderful result for the club, but at the time not appreciated by Heather.

Later, watching the same Irish youth team at Wembley – a match which England won 5–0 – it was evident that had it not been for their goalkeeper, the Irish lads might have lost 20–0. The goalkeeper was Pat Jennings. I telephoned the chairman of Newry Town, for whom Pat played, and introduced myself to him. He was a touch offhand but we got round to discussing a possible fee for his very young player.

'Well, I don't know,' I said. 'I would think something like £2500 might be reasonable.'

'Don't be ridiculous!' he came back.

'Well, I'm sorry,' I said, 'but I think it's not an unreasonable offer for a young man of such limited experience.'

'Don't come your union arguments with me, Mr Hill!' was the unfriendly retort.

'Thank you very much,' I said and put down the phone. Soon afterwards, Watford signed Pat. They had a scout who was spending a lot of time close to Newry Town and its chairman and we could not compete. I found out from Pat several years later that he signed for Watford when he was asked because he thought they were the only club interested in him. The chairman of the club did not tell him that Coventry had been interested, otherwise he would have jumped at the chance to come to us. You win some and you lose some. We were still on the alert to find an outstanding keeper. After all, if a manager wanted to sleep at night, retain his sanity and his fingernails, it was imperative to have a safe pair of hands in his goalmouth.

During the summer we launched our Vice Presidents club for a maximum number of sixty-two local business executives who would have special privileges at Highfield Road including use of the Viking Room (the name still remains a mystery) with their own private bar and catering service. We also opened the Sky

Blue Club, alongside the dressing-room under the main stand. Members were welcome throughout the week, although the players weren't encouraged to use the facilities themselves as a watering hole. We discussed at a board meeting whom we might find to run such a club, someone who was experienced, with personality and who was scrupulously honest. After some reflection, I said, 'Well, I know someone who fills most of those requirements, but I'm not sure if he would be interested.'

'Who are you talking about?' the chairman asked.

'Well, my father as a matter of fact,' I replied. The outcome was that William Hill took over as proprietor and licensee of the Sky Blue Club at Coventry and moved into a local semi-detached house which we found for him and Mum. They spent what they considered to be the happiest three years of their lives with the Sky Blues. A major all-round victory for the family and the club, my best signing.

Season tickets were selling like hot cakes and, although it didn't make us the richest football club in England, we still felt confident enough to be able to spend if the chance came to improve our prospects of climbing higher up the ladder. Yet we weren't short of talent, especially up front, and when season 1964–65 started against Plymouth Argyle at home, I was faced with the problem of selecting from six forwards. That didn't include Ernie Machin, but the problem was Hudson or Kirby. I chose to leave George Kirby out of the side and was rewarded with a 2–0 win to start the season. We won the second match away to Ipswich by 3–1 and went on to win our first five games in the second division.

The game at Ipswich remains in my mind because my eldest son, Duncan, still on holiday from school, played a part in the win. I preferred to sit in the stands; at ground level in the dug-out I found it more difficult to see and analyse play. I took my seat in the Ipswich directors' box during the early stages of the game, with Ipswich pretty well all over us. I needed to make a switch in defence and the only way it could be done was to go out of the back of the Ipswich stand, run down its length, turn into the corner of the ground and then run down in front of the supporters to the trainers' bench. I didn't want to do that as inevitably it would start the usual nonsense of derisive remarks, cat calls and boos. So I gave Duncan the message for trainer Peter Hill to pass on to the team. Ten minutes later another change was needed and off went Duncan again. This time he was the target of some uncomplimentary comments from the spectators, and by the time he reached Peter Hill, under pressure, he promptly forgot the message. So back he came, was told again and then made his third trip to even noisier ribaldry from the locals. There was a happy ending though: a 3–1 win.

The return match against Ipswich we won 5–3 in front of 37,782 Coventry fanatics roaring the team home to victory and the top of the table. A local clairvoyant, Mrs Denise Chapman, had predicted that City would lose only nine games in the whole season and would be promoted. Most of those games she said would be lost against weaker teams. It didn't happen. She was much more accurate in her assessment of our family and my prospects: she said that I would suffer ear trouble, which I didn't have, and that my back would cause me problems, which it did. She also foretold that in 1965 Heather would give birth to a son, and that prediction was fulfilled when Jamie was born.

The first match we lost that season was away to Derby County 2–1, which we might just as easily have won but the law of averages dictated otherwise. Having won the first five matches, we proceeded to lose the next five, ending the run of defeats with a 1–1 draw with Swansea at the Vetch, and we all took a deep breath.

Meanwhile, we had appointed Charles Harrold, a leading Fleet Street journalist with a Midlands background, as our administrative manager. He was responsible for public relations, and also took on the task of raising money from all the commercial possibilities arising from our on-the-field progress. As an experienced broadcaster with the BBC, he took over Radio Sky Blue and set a most professional example. Not many clubs since have come anywhere near it.

Our offer of £30,000 for Crystal Palace's Under-23 goalkeeper Bill Glazier had been rejected, but there was one other goalkeeper in whom we had an interest. David Best had been playing exceedingly well for Bournemouth so John Camkin and I went down to watch him. Bournemouth drew 1–1 with Bristol Rovers at their Dean Court ground. We opened the negotiations with their directors immediately after the game but although we spent an hour or two in discussion, we could not bring any kind of a deal to a conclusion. A full board meeting would consider our £30,000 bid the following morning. We shacked up in a local hotel and next day sat patiently waiting outside the boardroom at the appointed time only to be told after an hour of twiddling our thumbs that our offer had been turned down.

'Right,' we agreed. 'Let's go and get Bill Glazier at Crystal Palace. He's the better goalkeeper of the two anyway and whatever extra we have to pay for him, it will be worth it.' Thus we broke the then record price for a goalkeeper, going back to Crystal Palace and raising our bid to £35,000. We came home with a most likeable young man with a very special talent.

But life was not all milk and honey. 'Coventry were as bereft of ideas on the field as they are full of them off the field and sank to their sixth defeat in seven games,' wrote the *Sunday Express*'s reporter after we lost 2–3 to Huddersfield in front of Harold Wilson, Huddersfield's locally born supporter. Entertaining the Prime Minister was a pleasure, losing to his team was not.

It turned out to be a strange transitory season. The biggest blessing I suppose was that Ernie Machin managed to overcome his injury and gain the experience essential for him to mature into the finished article. In November, we lost 5–0 at Bury and 3–0 at Charlton. We held our annual Soccer Ball a week after the thrashing at Bury and were comforted following that appalling defeat by the presence of celebrities like Fred Trueman, Colin Ingleby-McKenzie, Walter Winterbottom, Danny Blanchflower, Stan Cullis and, last but not least, Olympic medallist Mary Rand. At least some people still loved us; first division people supporting a second division club.

Conceding that number of goals called for action and in mid-November we sighed Alan Harris, brother of the legendary Ron, for £35,000, a sizeable sum for a full-back at the time, especially on top of the Glazier signing. It did show that having prospered through the loyal support of the citizens of Coventry we were prepared to invest substantially in the transfer market attempting to reward their faith.

However, one result which they, and certainly I, didn't enjoy was in the Football League Cup, losing at home 1–8 to Leicester City. We did have five first-teamers out of the side and were going through a very bad patch, but nevertheless eight goals against took some digesting.

Such was the injury problem at that time that we took on Ken Keyworth, an experienced and talented striker from Leicester City – on a free transfer it's true, but that was largely on account of the knee trouble he had suffered for some time hampering his career. However, his experience was going to be useful to us in the short and medium term. Since Ken was a striker, the usual questions were asked. Had George Hudson come to the end of his time with Coventry City? My answer was a firm 'No'.

While it was evident to the world that we were a long way from reaching the first division, the Minister of Sport Denis Howell, who sadly died in 1998, did agree to be our VIP guest for a friendly against Newcastle.

'All I have seen confirms my prejudices that this is the way football must go,' he said afterwards. 'The football follower of 1975 will demand comfort. He will want a ground where he can have a meal, have a drink, take his wife and family and feel part of the set-up. Coventry have succeeded in the participation aim in making the fan feel part of the club. Their interest is transmitted on to the field. The effect of warm and unflagging support from the crowd must have a beneficial effect on the team. I am very impressed by all I have seen. I am sure that if other clubs adopted similar progressive ideas they would benefit as much.'

One of the problems which emerged through that season was the form of Willy Humphries who had been a bargain buy, repaying his fee over and over. Yet in doing that, against the physical and aggressive attitude experienced at this level in the League, he had been kicked from pillar to post and inevitably it had taken its toll. He tended to edge more and more inside his opponent, instead of taking the challenging, more dangerous route on the outside, aiming to get in a potent cross. Occasionally I played David Clements, who had a strong left foot, at outside-left and switched Ronnie Rees to the other flank; I think that Ronnie was equally happy on either wing and it looked promising. I made up my mind and one morning had a long chat with Willy, putting it to him that maybe the time had come for us to part company. It was the most unenjoyable conversation I had as a manager. Willy had been a hero to the Sky Blue fans, not the least of them me. He had done so much for us during his time at Coventry, entertaining always, and he had never caused a moment's trouble. He deserved a medal for the Crystal Palace match alone. I felt an absolute heel. I explained that if I put him on the transfer list, it would immediately suggest to anyone who was interested that he was losing his value. It would be much better for him as well as for the club if he were to ask for a transfer. People would easily believe that he could have fallen out with a strong-minded manager such as myself and it would be more likely to entice interest. Willy saw the sense in what I was saying and agreed. The ploy worked and forty-five minutes before the transfer deadline on 16 March, he was transferred to Swansea Town for around £13,000. He was twenty-eight and had cost us £4500.

We suffered a major blow in April when Bill Glazier broke his leg in an unavoidable accident at Manchester City. He was unlikely to be fit for the start of the following season. You can imagine how demoralising that was after the euphoria of breaking the transfer record for a goalkeeper.

However, we still managed to have some fun and games off the field. As the season was drawing to a close, I was sent as the club's representative to the Football League's AGM. Up until then, and as far as I know up until now, clubs had only been represented at such meetings by a director. Once it became general knowledge that I, a mere manager, was attending there were all sorts of squawks and squeals from chairmen and directors of other clubs. The League was in an embarrassing position because legally there was nothing they could do to prevent Coventry from nominating me for that particular role. One reason I wanted to be there on behalf of the club was to propose a four up and four down promotion and relegation system throughout the League. When the time came round I did propose it and in fact persuaded the clubs to vote 25:24 in favour of it, but to bring about a change, Football League regulations needed a three-quarter majority so the proposition failed. Nevertheless, it was interesting to note that at that meeting, despite expressions of fear from the Football Association, the clubs voted to allow one substitute to replace an injured player at any time during the ninety minutes.

As the season ended, on Wednesday, 1 June to be precise, we appointed the Bishop of Coventry, Dr Cuthbert Bardsley, as the club's new President. With promotion in mind, we were anxious to get as much help as possible.

Later on in June, I went with the Internationals Club to Denmark to play against a Danish ex-international eleven, and managed to score a goal in a 3–3 draw. Nat Lofthouse and John Charles scored the other goals, so that wasn't bad company.

There was another extraordinary happening but nothing to do with football. On Friday, 13 August, the *Coventry Express* carried a picture of Miss Jean Harper of the Warwickshire Equestrian Sports Club, sitting on horseback alongside Alan Harris, Ernie Machin, Ronnie Rees and myself, described as the team that would play the National Hunt jockeys in a game of horse football for charity on 26 September. It was the beginning of my equestrian career.

Jean Harper had telephoned the ground explaining that she was organising this charity horse football tournament locally and would I and one or two of the Coventry players like to make up a team. I explained that I would love to but that I couldn't ride a horse to save my life.

'Don't worry about that,' she said. 'I'm prepared to teach you between now and then!' I had always wanted to ride; it was one of those things I'd always wanted to do but the opportunity had never arisen.

'Well, why not?' I replied. I didn't know if any of our other players rode but she knew that John Sillett did, and thought that one or two of the others would be interested in taking part. Hence the picture of the horse enthusiasts in the local paper and, soon to follow, the ridiculous sight of the manager and his team falling off ponies unused to conveying such idiots.

I had my suspicions about how all this had come about. One afternoon, after another practice for the big match against the jockeys, I noticed when John Sillett was leaving, Jean, our instructor, cast a very warm smile in his direction, to which John responded with an equally happy face. They were rumbled. Although John was married with three children it soon became evident that these two young people had fallen in love in a most positive fashion. They are still together to this day.

John was our star performer on horseback because he had ridden before as a youngster; it was through this he had met Jean at some horsey function in the area. For the rest of us, by the time the event came around, I suppose we could just about rise to the trot and stay on for reasonable lengths of time without provocation from outside. But we were to play against the National Hunt jockeys, not inexperienced as riders and as rough and tough as they come.

On the great day there were two sessions: one in the afternoon and one in the evening. In the afternoon, we managed just to trot into the arena before we were slaughtered by the jockeys six or seven nil, and retired gracefully, not enjoying our defeat. We licked our wounds and made our plans for the evening, when we dragged the National Hunt lads from their horses and rolled the pushball into the goal for a surprise win. A good time was had by all and off we went to celebrate.

Such an event would not normally change one's life, but it did mine. Standing at the bar I met a most sociable gentleman called Ted Edgar, of whom more later. In spite of our success, we didn't let these fascinating distractions take our minds away from our main target, and that was promotion to the first division.

11

SKY BLUE HEAVEN

As the 1965–66 season approached, there was still a managerial job to be done. Before we'd kicked a ball in anger, a local paper suggested that we had run out of ideas and would be unable to rekindle the excitement of previous years. Perhaps it was a kind of backlash because of the disappointment of not even being in contention for promotion the previous season. Anyway, last season's average attendance had risen to 26,620, and we started this one by announcing that we were intending to experiment with closed-circuit matches at Highfield Road and to be the first club so to do.

Whatever anyone thought, the publicity which we had experienced over past seasons had done us no harm, especially in attracting talented youngsters from near and far to the club, the most notable recent capture being young Willie Carr, whom we signed from Cambridge schoolboys. The Football League granted us permission to stage the first closed-circuit television league match at Highfield Road for the game at Ninian Park, Cardiff, on Wednesday, 6 October.

Our opening match was against Wolverhampton Wanderers, managed by Ronnie Allen. They had been relegated from the first division. They scored first and looked much the more sophisticated side, but our team wouldn't lie down. Finally, George

Hudson – who else? – snatched two half-chances in the seventy-ninth and eighty-fourth minutes and Coventry took maximum points. A significant selection a little later against Carlisle was a young man called Bobby Gould who managed to score a goal in a 3–2 win.

In October, the BBC's twice-weekly soccer serial, 'United!', was due to be launched. Brentwich United was to become the nation's favourite team and manager Gerry Barford, played by actor David Lodge, the well-known managerial face. I was employed as technical adviser in an endeavour to make sure that the football scenes were authentic, and the scripts, too, for that matter. I was always travelling around the country watching matches when 'United!' was transmitted, so it was some time before I realised that the alterations which I had made to some of the scripts were not actually being used. Such was the rush to get the programme in front of the public, there was supposedly no time for the actors to relearn their lines. I found out by accident one evening when someone said to me, 'I didn't like what such and such a character said to the manager that night.'

'No, he didn't say that at all,' I said. 'I changed it.'

'He did say something like that, I can assure you!'

The secret was out. My changes were not being made although they were hiding behind my name as adviser to the programme. I complained about it and in the end had my name taken off the credits.

The preparation for the first closed-circuit transmission of a league match at Cardiff on 6 October was fraught with tension and fear, due to seasonal fog. It was hoped that a dummy run would take place with the technicians and cameramen around midnight the night before, but the fog rendered it quite impossible. The finishing touches to the thousand fittings which each screen entailed were made only very late in the day and over 7500 tickets had already been sold to the expectant ones. Happily, on that turbulent evening the screens remained standing and the crowd was exhilarated by seeing Coventry win the match 2–1. Being present at Cardiff wasn't nearly as enjoyable as being back

at Highfield Road. At Ninian Park it was an uninspiring, unin-
teresting game with Cardiff showing little confidence in their own
ability. Of course, we were pleased to win even in a soulless
atmosphere; to earn two points making history and money from
the extra 10,295 highly satisfied customers who had shared a
thrilling evening at Highfield Road was doubly rewarding.

As for our chances of promotion, I predicted that Huddersfield,
who were then the league leaders, Manchester City, Wolves,
Southampton and possibly Portsmouth were the teams most to
be feared. The loyal and reliable Bob Wesson was understudying
Bill Glazier most successfully between the sticks, but in October
just when it looked as though Bill would be fit enough to return to
the side, he broke a cheek bone in training and had to be patient
for a while longer.

Whilst football in general was complaining about the lack of
healthy support for its clubs, so many of them experiencing
smaller gates, Coventry City's average for that season was
27,500. The supporters were expecting us to spend more money
in the transfer market. The success and excitement of the last two
or three years had created an appetite which, in some ways, was
working against the club. The fans tended to be quickly disappointed if in a run of matches players showed less than their best
form. As a manager, I reacted to this and remonstrated with them
to be patient because frustration could destroy the very target we
were seeking to achieve.

We were still in need of a goalscoring forward to play alongside
George Hudson, having sold George Kirby to Swansea, and at
Christmastime when Ray Pointer became available from Bury,
we splashed out £20,000 underlining our grit and determination
to gain promotion. Ray started the New Year with a hat-trick and,
as Kirby and Hudson had done before him, he made an immediate good impression on the supporters.

After an electric start to the season, George Hudson lost his
scoring touch as did Ken Hale, both showing signs of pressure at
this level. In the Cup we were drawn away to Crewe Alexandra.
Pre-match publicity concerned the Crewe manager Ernie Tagg,

131

who was described as a part-time milkman. A nervy 1–1 draw was followed by a 4–1 win in the replay at Highfield Road, with two goals from George Hudson. But the magic date of 16 March, the closing date for transfers, was round the corner. It was the time when transfer fees inflated to what might be their highest peak. If you wanted to sell, it was the perfect time.

Our old neighbours and rivals, Northampton Town, were seeking a striker and were well aware of the capability of George Hudson. Had we been leading the League with points in hand and favourites for the promotion race, it might have been a different matter. As it was, the performances which we were producing with George and Ken Hale in the side were not good enough, in my view, for us to achieve our first division dream. Thus, when an offer of £28,500 came in for George, I realised where my duty lay.

Once again, I made the unpopular decision, and stood back to wait for the inevitable bitter criticism. History was repeating itself; the lesson of Terry Bly had been forgotten and the supporters could not understand what made their manager take such an incomprehensible course of action. You, dear reader, know the answer because you have learned. If only it had been possible to reveal the truth at the time, life would have been pleasanter.

In the long term, I knew who was to replace Terry Bly, George Hudson and Ray Pointer as Coventry's number one striker. Bobby Gould was then just nineteen. Vying with him for a place in the side and scoring a goal or two was six foot three Dudley Roberts, son of Ted Roberts, a Coventry favourite of the past. Dudley was outstanding in the air, but maybe a fraction slow to be a top striker.

Whatever the rights and wrongs of the Hudson sale at that stage of the season, the team still managed to hang on to the chance of promotion by the skin of its teeth. When we beat Middlesbrough 2–1 on 2 May with goals from young Dudley Roberts and Ray Pointer, we were still in with a chance. I was, incidentally, extremely impressed by Ian Gibson, the Middlesbrough inside-forward, who scored their goal. Unhappily, only

132

19,704 came to this vital match which was something of a shock, bearing in mind the enormous support to which we had become accustomed. As is my nature, I retaliated with a moan in the local paper: 'The lads fought really hard and they have taken the promotion issue to the last match of the season. Yet they were deserted. It looks as though the city of Coventry does not deserve a first division football club.'

Since we had also sold Ken Hale, for £8000 to Oxford United, more than a few people felt that our chance had been thrown away, some even thought deliberately so. Nevertheless, we took the battle to the end of the season, playing away to Huddersfield who had been one of the promotion favourites, but who were now out of the race. Our immediate rivals were Southampton, who needed to win the last game of the season to stay ahead of us. Our lads could not have done any better; they went to Huddersfield and despite all of the tension surrounding the game won 2–0, both goals scored by Bobby Gould. Southampton did not slip up and were promoted along with Manchester City. Such was the expectation and disappointment that we had failed to get promoted, no one noticed, especially those who were missing from matches, that it was the highest the club had finished in the Football League – ever!

Alan Harris was itching to get back to London and Chelsea were equally anxious to sign him so that transfer went through for a £45,000 fee, again at a profit. John Sillett joined Plymouth Argyle for £5000 – a little more bunce for us – and Bob Wesson was transferred to Walsall for £10,000 having cost nothing. The bulk of that money went on buying just one player who was to turn out to be the missing link between narrow failure and elusive success. A richly talented Under-23 midfield player broke the Sky Blues' transfer record when we paid Middlesbrough £55,000 for Ian Gibson.

'I am certain I'll be happy here,' he said after the signing.

In keeping with our reputation for new ideas, we had agreed to play four matches in Europe in a unique venture to promote Rover cars. We were to make an eighteen-day, 2500 mile tour in eight most attractive Sky Blue Rover 2000s supplied by the company. We were to stop off for promotional conferences in Frankfurt, Vienna, Zurich and Brussels and at the same time play one of the local teams at football. This export drive had been given the blessing of Prime Minister Harold Wilson when he was our guest at the Huddersfield match earlier in the season.

We achieved a goalless draw in Germany against Offenbach Kickers, an interesting name for a team who, despite it, were very friendly. Unfortunately, in Vienna we did not hit the right note and lost 4–0 to the powerful FK Austria side. The tour was so successful, I'm afraid I have difficulty in remembering the scores of the last two matches. So what was the most important lesson I learned from that last season? It was not to drink more than half a dozen glasses of the fresh wine which is available in Vienna immediately after the grape harvest. It ended up with me singing an operatic aria to a hundred or so astonished Viennese patrons of a wine bar and Ray Pointer, less used to drink than his manager, losing consciousness completely. Nevertheless, the team came back to Coventry in good heart ready for a month or so's rest followed by a most exciting nine months' football.

During that summer I was selected for the BBC World Cup team for what proved to be the most exciting sporting event in the history of this country. Also in the eleven were Walter Winterbottom, Billy Wright, Joe Mercer, Don Revie, Ron Greenwood, a leading referee Arthur Ellis, Tommy Docherty, former World Cup referee Ken Aston, Johnny Haynes and Danny Blanchflower. I didn't have a major role to play: an interview here and there and an occasional comment about a match, but I was fascinated to see what went on behind a television operation of that magnitude. It was to stand me in good stead later.

I can still recall the emotion when the final whistle blew and the players turned to receive the acclaim of the crowd; standing alongside Joe Mercer, we had tears streaming down all four cheeks. It wasn't only that England won; I was thinking of all the faith and hard work that had gone into the development of coaching over the last few years. Walter Winterbottom was the original inspiration of this new era, although it was Alf Ramsey who was the hero of the multitude. Ron Greenwood, another fervent supporter of Winterbottom, produced three of the eleven heroes at West Ham. What a contribution that turned out to be towards England's success! The unforgettable evening was celebrated by Ron, Danish international Knud Lundberg and myself in a restaurant opposite the hotel where the England team and officials were celebrating.

While both England and Coventry City were on a high, there were still worries about the slump in gates generally and the difficulty many clubs were experiencing in staying alive. It was the same old story, just another era. We again recommended four up and four down to increase interest in the league structure. We also suggested splitting the season into two halves, with two competitions and two lots of promotion and relegation to sustain the excitement.

However, despite these collective problems, I was paid to enable Coventry City to win and we made a pretty reasonable start to the season. Before the start we were able to sign former Fulham winger Johnny Key. I could not believe he was on a free transfer. Having played alongside him at Fulham, I knew his real worth! We held our own near the top of the table until early in October when we lost two matches running, the first away at Preston 3–2, and the second 2–1 at Carlisle on the following Saturday. It wasn't so much losing two games in a row which was damaging to our chances, but it was the uninspiring performance of young Mr Gibson in those games. When the game was over in Carlisle, as fierce as the Coventry players had ever seen me, I chastised Ian, pointing out that his performance left a lot to be desired, or ungentlemanly words to that effect.

'It seems to me you are more interested in the result of the three o'clock race at Kempton Park than you are in ours at the same time on Saturday.' They were my final words.

It resulted in him showering, changing, going straight out to the waiting pressmen and putting himself on the transfer list, where he remained for some time to come. He was not in the team for the next four matches. Luckily, we earned seven points out of the next eight, before losing two games in a row to Crystal Palace and Huddersfield. The last thing a manager wants is to pay £55,000 for a player and have him play in the reserves, so I wasn't enjoying the situation much either. We had an injury or two, which gave me the opportunity to put Ian back in the side. I called him into the office and asked him if he wanted to play and that if he did, he must understand the reasons why he had been left out. Did he want that chance? He said he did and I asked him if he wanted to come off the transfer list. He replied that he wanted to stay on it. In the meantime, we had been knocked out of the League Cup by Brighton, struggling near the bottom of the third division, which wasn't all that enterprising.

During my time as manager, I used 'J.H.'s page' as a platform in the programme to be as honest as circumstances would allow with our supporters. I did my best to wrap the messages up attractively so that they would hit home. A burst of inspiration caused me to produce the following for the 15 October 1966 programme:

J.H.'s PAGE

Conversation between Father and Daughter

Joanna: 'Why are they booing the team as they come out, Daddy?'
J.H.:　　'Because they want them to do well.'
Joanna: 'Is that the way to help them do better?'
J.H.:　　'No, not really, but it is a bad match for Coventry, isn't it?'
Joanna: 'Yes it is, do they always play as badly?'
J.H.:　　'Lately they have not found their best form, but most of them have given great service to the Sky Blues.'
Joanna: 'What does Uncle George Curtis think about it?'
J.H.:　　'Fortunately he's so busy trying to stop Brighton he hasn't the opportunity to tell them.'
Joanna: 'Why are they singing dirty songs about you, Daddy?'
J.H.:　　'They like singing and dirt and they don't like me.'
Joanna: 'Why don't they like you then?'
J.H.:　　'What they really don't like is that the Sky Blues are not

scoring goals and beating everybody. The results are not good enough.'

Joanna: 'They've been pretty good up to now, haven't they?'

J.H.: 'It's now that counts!'

Joanna: 'What's that Gibson/Gibson business?'

J.H.: 'They want him in the team!'

Joanna: 'Do you want him in the team?'

J.H.: 'I want everyone who I think will help get the Sky Blues into Division 1.'

Joanna: 'Don't people trust you to do that?'

J.H.: 'Obviously not at the moment.'

Joanna: 'Have they ever trusted you before?'

J.H.: 'Yes, the week after we won the third division.'

Joanna: 'Will they trust you again?'

J.H.: 'Yes, the week after we win the second division.'

Joanna: 'Why won't they leave it to you?'

J.H.: 'Supporters always imagine they know better than managers – even Matt Busby – but that's what makes it so interesting.'

Joanna: 'It's a pity really because it seems such a nice club!'

J.H.: 'It's the most progressive in the country.'

Joanna: 'What are you going to do about it then?'

J.H.: 'Win.'

When I look back at my experiences as a manager and later as a director, they do illustrate what a monumental public relations problem a club has with its supporters. The game produces so many differing opinions about who should play and how they should play, which is, of course, part of the fascination. Yet it can lead to a constant stream of dissatisfaction which in the end is destructive. What is perceived as the truth about the game can shift from match to match, from person to person, from season to season. Everyone is free to have an opinion and to express it, even though it can be hurtful and even though it may have a negative effect on the very success which those involved hope to achieve.

Back to grim reality and the 3–1 defeat at Huddersfield which left us seventh in the table with Wolves on top. Ian returned against Cardiff City on 26 November and the team also included for the first time a young Leamington-born defender, Mick Coop. As a fifteen year old, Mick had been my first signing for Coventry City. (I called at his house in Leamington one evening to find that his mum and dad were out and this bright-eyed young man answered the door to us in his dressing-gown. I explained that I had come to talk to his parents about the possibility of his taking up a career as a professional footballer with Coventry City and would call again.) We beat Cardiff 3–2 and I was as pleased for Micky as I was for Ian Gibson. That was the start of a twenty-five game run until the end of the season without a single defeat. It was a sensational stampede for promotion. The only other personnel change I made was to buy Portsmouth midfield player Brian Lewis, with Ray Pointer, who had served us well for a brief period, going in part exchange. To my relief, we were knocked out of the FA Cup early.

My mother and father came to Highfield Road for the unforgettable match against Wolverhampton Wanderers on 29 April which virtually clinched promotion and eventually the championship. Wolves shocked but didn't silence the Coventry faithful by taking the lead as Peter Knowles scored, picking up a Derek Dougan pass, on the half-hour mark. In the second half, Ernie Machin equalised following a dose of Ronnie Rees wizardry, breaking Wolves' apparent grip on the game. Ian Gibson, Coventry's most expensive acquisition, scored a second, at which the pitch was invaded by hysterical Sky Blue supporters. Referee Norman Callender threatened to abandon the game if it happened again. Charles Harrold, over Radio Sky Blue, appreciating their excitement at history being made, appealed to the ecstatic Coventry fans to stay back. My proudest moment came when just before the final whistle Ronnie Rees made the game safe with our third goal. Of course I was jubilant – City were in the first division for the first time – but almost as satisfying was the fact that, responding to our appeal, not one person crossed the line to invade the pitch.

Mum and Dad helped cut the extra sandwiches needed in the Sky Blue Club for what was going to be the busiest day and night.

The excitement was unbelievable. It was frenzied, just sheer, unadulterated happiness shared by over 50,000 people. The historic party went on, as you may imagine, moving from the ground to the Leofric Hotel. I can just remember being taxied home with Mum and Dad around five o'clock in the morning. As I was about to climb into bed, my mother appeared at the bedroom door saying that Dad had a problem – he felt the room was going round. . ! He wasn't the only one. The whole world was spinning for me as a result of that extraordinary climax to my years at Coventry. It was a sensational day, and one which was personally deeply satisfying because of the joy it brought to the friendly people who had made me so very welcome, on the face of it reserved, but under the surface extremely warm-hearted. Somebody recalled that it was a night when everything but the air turned blue – bright sky blue!

12

THE END OF THAT PARTICULAR ROAD

T HE magnitude of our achievement becomes more apparent when contrasting the progress which Coventry made in playing terms during those five and a half years, with what we have seen happening since. Ridiculous sums of money are paid for players at home and abroad with clubs trying to buy immediate success. Easy come, easy go is an old expression but it is certainly exemplified by some of the wealthier clubs in the Premier League, and they're not alone. When I reflect on the make-up of our team in that final promotion season, I still find it staggering that so large a proportion was homegrown, although we did use the transfer market to our advantage, particularly with goalscoring strikers whose performances so often make the difference between success and failure.

We scored 74 goals of which 60 were scored by players who had cost less than £1550 in total. The bulk of the goals were scored by Bobby Gould, signed as a sixteen year old. Eighteen had been shared by David Clements (£1500), John Tudor and Johnny Key who had cost nothing.

Players who grow up with a club have something to offer in addition to natural ability. More often than not something is lost from a player who moves from club to club, perhaps even more so from country to country, as a result of massive money chasing

140

frenetic success. Opening up frontiers to so many players from overseas may have some beneficial effects theatrically and technically for a year or two. If it continues at the same rate it will certainly deny our own young men the essential exposure for them to reach the top echelons of the game. In addition, the result of the Bosman case has not helped to encourage clubs to develop their own players for the future. Manchester United have set a splendid example in acquiring a limited percentage of highly talented overseas players whose technical expertise rubs off on their glut of homemade youngsters to their mutual benefit. If England wants to progress internationally, our leading clubs will have to maintain that balance voluntarily, or the supply line will lack sufficient homegrown depth.

Looking back, I feel I belonged at Coventry City much more than I did at Fulham Football Club, although many rewarding personal friendships arose from my playing days there and some since. As for the spectators at Fulham, because of the barracking I experienced at times as both player and chairman, it's perhaps natural that I have never been overwhelmingly in love with all of them. It's fair to say that when Fulham reached their own particular league pinnacle in the first division, some of the cheers made amends for what had gone on before; but a player never forgets a crowd's ingratitude when he is doing his best for them and for his team.

As for the Sky Blues, I saw no reason why I should not continue managing them for many years to come. I was named as the Westclox Manager of Tomorrow, receiving a cheque for £500. Europe beckoned – a dream it's true, but in time with Coventry there would be fresh fields to conquer. The crowd of 51,500 watching our match against Wolves seemed to promise that if we gave them what they wanted there was no limit to their support. I was happy about the team, too, certainly in the striking department and in midfield. At last we were blossoming and with the Iron Man, George Curtis, masterminding the defensive set-up, things looked good.

Beneath the understandable hysteria there was a mass of

realism. I was only too well aware that we had climbed extremely quickly from the bottom of the third division. It was announced that first division football at Highfield Road would cost more. Terrace watchers would have to pay between sixpence and a shilling extra and the most expensive season ticket was to go up by £4 to £15. Seasons in the West Stand went up to £10. Our financial resources were not so vast that we could buy our way to the top of the first, even if I thought that was possible or desirable. Therefore, it would be necessary for the present players, young as many of them were, to be given time to adjust to the level of competition that they were about to experience. I had seen how fickle even the Coventry supporters' mood could be, changing from bliss to critical despair with the manager being the butt. I was prepared for that but had no long-term fears about turning Coventry into a team capable of competing for honours each season. There was always a chance, of course, that, should fortune forsake us as it does many teams which gain promotion in a hurry, we might struggle at the highest level.

All in all, the future seemed dangerous and exciting. I saw no reason for wanting to leave Coventry and had been discussing my contract with the board, Derrick Robins in particular. It wasn't greed on my part in relation to an annual salary or any kind of bonus that created the eventual breakdown. In the whole time I was there, I did not earn £35,000, and that was for five and three-quarter years' service. It also included a £10,000 bonus earned, as a result of a clause in my first contract, for reaching the first division. Neither was it a job offer from another direction; I had never encouraged anyone to think that my future lay elsewhere. What I did want was a contract for ten years.

I knew it would take some time to turn the Sky Blues into a team with sufficient support to compete for those top honours. Although one thrilling moment attracted over 51,000 people to the ground, reality spoke otherwise. I never even considered that the board would not understand my feelings and happily give me a ten-year contract. It was a shock when Derrick on their behalf came back and said that the offer stood but it was for five years.

He was very sorry, and of course he appreciated what I had done, but on the other hand because of views which he had previously held, he could not accede to my request. The views, of which I was well aware, arose over two failed ten-year contracts which had been granted to Ted Drake at Chelsea and Cliff Britton of Hull City, neither of whom had lasted eighteen months. I was deeply disappointed as I didn't wish to be compared with either Cliff Britton or Ted Drake. Neither Ted nor Cliff had anything like the relationship I had enjoyed with Coventry and with the club. To be honest, I was astonished. I was offering ten years of my life to the club and I could not understand why they weren't prepared to bite my hand off. Cynical ones have always believed, and probably wanted to believe, that I already had another offer up my sleeve. Nothing could be further from the truth. I left Coventry City FC not because I wanted to leave, but because I wanted to stay – for longer than they wanted me.

I really expected Derrick Robins to say, 'Okay, we'll do it,' or even come to a compromise and say eight years, or seven and a half and split the difference, but he did not and I did not budge either. But I couldn't leave Coventry City in the lurch. It is never easy to choose a manager and I knew it might take time, so I said I would carry on until such time as they had replaced me. Derrick said publicly from Venice that my resignation was a disappointment and a setback for the club, but not a disaster.

'We are grateful to Jimmy,' he said, 'for six wonderful seasons. We are now going to hold our heads up high and we're going to the top. The club is on too sound a foundation to falter.'

History has proved that to be true, to my joy, Coventry having survived thirty-two seasons in the top flight.

I said publicly that the directors had been trying for weeks to get me to change my mind and one of the reasons I was giving up was because of the strain a manager faces every day, football not improving one's life span, the worry that one is always living off someone else's performances. I said I saw the challenge, I had met it, but I felt that I had sampled enough. I also said, 'Managing a soccer club is the most difficult job in the world: five and a half

143

years ago I couldn't resist having a stab at it and now it's out of my system.' All of that wasn't true. I did it for Coventry City's sake.

The papers were tipping me to take a sports job with the BBC, bearing in mind that I had worked for them during the World Cup. At the time I was writing a weekly column for the *News of the World*, which would keep the wolf from the door for a while. I thought I might take a holiday; rest for a bit. Other than that, I hadn't the least idea what I was going to do.

You know you never win as a football manager, even when you win everything. A Mr Harold Atkins, a lifelong Coventry supporter, was quoted in the *People* as saying:

> We now need a football tactician, a man who can buy the right first division material and one who can make it click at top level. Although Jimmy Hill did a wonderful job as an image maker, with only five and a half years in the business, he is still in the novice class as a manager. He is not yet a Busby, Nicholson, Shankly or Revie and we shall never know now if he could have become one. There are managers in the first division who have proved themselves in the very top flight, so if we get one of these we could be better off.

Tony and Graham Pready said, 'We do not like Jimmy's apparent worship of money, but he has every right to better himself if he feels he can. The only thing we hold against him is the timing of his announcement and hundreds of people agree with us.' The reason I didn't stay, Tony and Graham, you now know – it had nothing whatsoever to do with money. The reason the announcement was left until just before the beginning of the season was that I was still hoping to stay. For the sake of the club I haven't spoken of this until now, but at this stage it won't be damaging. So many of those supporters from that era have long since passed on and an even wider number are not old enough to know what it was all about, but nonetheless I'm pleased to put the record straight. The last thing I wanted for the club was to bring an end to the progress we had made.

While all the contract negotiations were going on, Derrick was worried that my mind would be on other matters and that I might not give a hundred per cent to the job in hand. I assured him I would, but came up with an idea to put his mind at rest. If we stayed up at the end of the season, I volunteered, the club would make me a gift of my 3.4 litre sky blue Jaguar saloon; if not, I would pay list price. It was a deal.

Coventry's last match was away to Southampton, and City needed a draw to stay up. With Noel Cantwell in charge of the team by this time, I had taken my five-year-old daughter, Joanna, to the North Warwickshire point-to-point meeting. Before each race we walked to the paddock and I let her choose the horse that she liked the best. She said, 'That one, Daddy!' five times and unbelievably each came romping home. At 4.40 p.m. I said, 'Come with Daddy over to the car. I want to hear how Coventry have done.' The two of us listened to the results and among them we learned that Sheffield United had lost at home to Chelsea. Coventry drew 0–0 at Southampton, meaning that City were safe for another year among the élite, finishing third from the bottom. With immense relief I drove my daughter home in our own car, a lucky man if ever there was one.

On a lighter note, riding had become very much part of my life. After that honourable draw with the jockeys at Balsall Common and a drink or five with Ted Edgar, I learned that he was at a loose end. He was serving a six-month suspension from showjumping following a punch-up at Wembley, which didn't take place in the boxing ring under the Marquess of Queensberry's rules! That temporary loss of temper was responsible for providing me with a mass of horsey fun for twenty years. After the first couple of noggins, I began to explain just how much I had enjoyed my practice sessions and the event itself. Very generously, Ted responded.

'If you really want to ride, come over to my spot and I'll teach you properly: old-fashioned cowboy fashion!' He gave me his phone number and told me afterwards he thought that would be the end of it. Much to his amazement, I rang up and made an

145

appointment for Tuesday afternoon. When I arrived at their Warwickshire stables, it wasn't Ted the Master but Liz the Mistress who was to be my instructor. Ted's wife Liz popped me up on a friendly animal and I proceeded to jog round and round and round in circles, turning this way and that, rising to the trot, sitting back, putting my heels down, not gripping the reins too tightly, endeavouring to respond to all kinds of instructions. It transpired that she had been advised by her husband to 'Keep him going for an hour or two. Give him a sore arse and that's the last we'll see of him!' Well, Liz didn't quite do that. She was very courteous and helpful but still demanding. At the end of the session I eased slowly into my car and drove home. That night Ted asked Liz how I'd gone and she replied, 'Well, I think he's sore enough. I reckon that's the last we'll see of him!'

On the Wednesday evening I rang them again, asking to come over on the following afternoon. The answer came back 'Yes' and over I went. I explained to Liz that when I got home, I found I had taken the skin off the inside of both knees and thighs.

'Oh,' she said. 'Aren't they too sore to ride today?'

'No,' I said. 'I've plastered them up and I've put on a pair of paisley pyjamas underneath my trousers, so I've got three thicknesses which should help.'

'Fine,' she said. 'Up you get!'

I had another gruelling hour or so, jog jog jog, rising to the trot, sitting back, heels down. Liz was patience persaddlefied. It's all very confusing when you start riding a horse. Anyway, I survived it and that night Ted asked Liz again, 'How'd yer man go?'

'I think we're stuck with him for life!' Liz said.

And stuck with me they were.

Within a week or two I was riding out with them regularly every morning between seven and eight, finding it most exhilarating. Then it was back home for a quick breakfast and into the ground before nine o'clock, keeping me ahead of the game. The extra fitness that resulted from such strenuous exercise did me no harm either and I can thoroughly recommend it to anyone who has been thinking of getting saddled up.

The rides we took were mostly alongside or on roads, but other times we would cut across a field from one road to another and sometimes we'd ride on grass for a few minutes. Occasionally it would necessitate opening a gate and passing through and for a week or two that was the routine. Next, they began to select reasonable jumping places, a small hedge for example or a small post-and-rail fence where their pupil could be tutored. I would, in great excitement, follow them over the obstacles, sometimes astonished at just how easy it was to move with the rhythm of the horse and leave the difficult part to the animal. On the other hand, 'if you missed your jerk', as Ted put it, you were in trouble. For someone who had grown up in London, a city lad, it was a deeply satisfying thrill. It set me up for the long day's toil ahead which under normal circumstances would mean a training session in the morning, in the office in the afternoon, and going off most evenings to wherever football was being played to analyse teams or watch particular players in whom we might be interested. It was a full day but a healthy one and a delightful way of life, providing the team was winning.

Six weeks or so after I had started these enjoyable excursions, Ted casually said, 'You know, you should go hunting one day. You'd thoroughly enjoy it!' Quite honestly, I had no idea what that entailed; like most Londoners I had seen pictures of horses and hounds and foxes but otherwise it was a strange enigma. Nevertheless, my excitement at possibly taking part was intense. By then I had acquired a pair of jodhpurs and before I knew where I was, Ted had found me some riding boots kindly lent by a gentleman named Broughton-Lee who no longer hunted. He also produced a stock and pin and, of course, a bowler hat exactly my size, borrowed as well. He virtually dressed me himself, gave me a leg up on a horse at ten o'clock at his farm in Warwickshire and we hacked together to the meet.

By this time he had persuaded me to buy an elderly gelding, nicknamed Noddy, who became my tutor and preserved my life on numerous occasions. I had no idea where the name came from until John Sillett explained it to me some years later. The reason

147

my wonderful tutor nodded his head to the right when trotting was also the reason he was acquired at a knockdown price: the poor lad, similar to his owner, suffered from navicular syndrome, an equine equivalent of arthritis of his right knee. This affliction produced the nod and hence his nickname. However, Noddy looked after me and was my saviour and friend. He took me to my first hunt and he took me over my first jump, carrying me safely for the whole of the day. I can remember that first jump out hunting and I can still see Liz waiting to see whether or not I was going to make it. It was a small hedge and most of the field were safely over with a few others trying to pick a spot. Liz had also popped over and was in view a hundred yards or so across a field; she hesitated on the corner of a path turning along beside a copse approaching a gate. I saw her looking, thought, 'Come on, Noddy. Don't let Liz down!' and kicked on. Noddy jumped beautifully. Liz saw and with relief kicked on herself. I was away! If the truth were known I was more frightened of losing Liz than anything else. What do you do if you are on a horse in open country without the least idea of where you are? Liz therefore became my target and I had to stay with her.

I survived a few days out with the North Warwickshire Hunt, later progressing from Noddy to a younger horse, Snow White, and enjoying so much the thrill and danger of the chase. To be honest, the thought of the fox seldom came into my mind. All my concentration and every muscle were totally preoccupied with controlling the wonderfully athletic animal beneath me and making sure that we both arrived in one piece at our common destination, wherever it was. I came to understand that many people who hunt appreciate the work of the hounds more than they do the thrill of jumping the fences. I soon discerned the difference between the 'thrusters' as it were, continually prepared to put themselves and others in danger, and those who never seemed to be in a hurry but always managed to get where they needed to be.

Hunting in Ireland rings the same kind of bells as do tennis at Wimbledon, rugby at Twickenham or football at Wembley. It rings other bells, too, perhaps not so grand but nonetheless stimulating to the senses: pure pleasure with overtones of unadulterated fear. When Ted Edgar said to me one day, 'We'll go hunting in Ireland,' it wasn't a question, it was a statement of fact and in equestrian matters he was the guv'nor and I was the last person to disagree.

So one Sunday morning we set out from Jury's Hotel in Dublin, impeccably attired in hunting dress, in a rented car, aiming for Baltinglass for eleven o'clock. A waiter had informed Ted that it was about fifteen miles to the south and leaving well before 10 a.m. we seemed to have ample time to get there to meet the providers of our two hired mounts. As a driver, I'd back Ted with a fair start against Damon Hill. As a navigator, I wouldn't back him against Mark Thatcher. It turned out after fifty minutes hard driving that Baltinglass was nearer fifty miles away than fifteen and we still had a long way to go.

At around 11.30 we reached our first target, a picturesque village high street straight off a calendar, where we soon found our second target, a horse box in which stood our two new four-footed friends. Money changed hands as we inspected the horses. Ted chose his – I had the other one. We were in something of a panic because at home hounds would have been running minutes after eleven o'clock. We asked where everyone was gathering and a village store was pointed out across the road. Going inside, the place was deserted and we waited for someone to appear. Before long, the proprietor emerged from the woodwork and we ordered two large heart starters. After a sip or two we inquired about the day's hunt.

'Where has everyone gone?'

'They'll be along soon,' came the reply.

We glugged away at the port, as gradually our fellow hunters spilled out of church or bed, and within half an hour or so a voice was heard asking, 'Has anybody seen the Master?'

'Didn't he say he was going over to England for the weekend?'

'Be jabus, I think he did that. Perhaps we'd best get going!'

Meantime, we had become enmeshed in port and pastoral

149

conversation and a welcome to cherish. We staggered outside and mounted our patient animals. Dutifully taking our place in line, as we hacked our way from tarmac to fields I complained to Ted of a clicking noise coming from below. He dropped behind, reviewed the situation and confirmed that my mount had cast a shoe.

'What shall I do?' I asked.

'Kick on and keep on the grass!' was Ted's command.

We soon reached green pastures and soft, lush grass. I kept with the field as I had been taught, whereas Ted was exploring the territory, taking his own line. Suddenly a noise came from Ted's direction: cursing, sucking, grunting, squelching. Horrifically, Ted's horse was sinking into the mud. No matter what he did, however he puffed and panted, cajoled and shouted, the animal remained plugged. It became evident that he would have to dismount, which he did and went down in the quagmire almost as far as his horse. Another two or three minutes' muscular, mucky and masterful attempts to solve the problem eventually succeeded and a muddy, dripping Ted was back on board, this time upsides the acting Master. The latter spoke to the bedraggled Ted. 'And now you know,' he remarked profoundly, 'to be sure, what an Oirish bog is loik!'

It wasn't the greatest day's hunting, but one I shall never forget, particularly the sight of Ted, caked in dried mud from head to boot at 9.30 p.m., asking the Hall Porter back at the hotel for the key to his room.

13

LONDON WEEKEND TELEVISION

I N 1967, before August was out, I had a telephone call from Bagenal Harvey, the object of which was to arrange a lunch with a chap called Michael Peacock, who was 'something to do with television'. The venue was the Berkeley Hotel (the old site) and knowing that Bags was not a person to waste his time on worthless ventures, I was intrigued.

We met at the table and cheekily I ordered grouse for the first time in my life. I'd missed a few open goals, but not many culinary chances! Michael was businesslike and enthusiastic but did not seem to be deeply concerned with football or even sport. However, around pudding time he asked, 'If you owned a television channel and your rivals held exclusive contracts for the major sporting events, how would you compete?' Not an easy question to be landed with and the grouse fluttered uncomfortably back to life in my tum. Ignorance is bliss, for I had no knowledge of its purpose.

'I suppose,' I said, 'you'd be forced to devise your own competitions, which you would own. You'd need money to tempt the leading professionals to take part and presumably a sponsor might provide that if he could be guaranteed sufficient exposure. It's a three-legged stool.' Within moments it became apparent that I was being offered a job in television, but I did not know what. It wasn't until Bagenal and I were side by side in the gents' loo that I was able to ask, 'What job was he talking about?'

'Head of Sport, London Weekend Television,' was the reply.

'What's the salary?' I went on.

'Ten grand a year,' confirmed Bagenal. That seemed to me more than reasonable; I had already been offered £7500 a year by Coventry. In case it wasn't, Bagenal added, 'You can also buy 10,000 shares in LWT, which should become worth much more.'

'Great!' said I. I washed my hands, but not of such an exciting opportunity.

I came to learn later that while I was failing to come to terms with Coventry, my new employer had touted Bryan Cowgill, Paul Fox, David Coleman and Uncle Tom Cobley and all for the post and was reaching the end of his tether. Bagenal's knowledge of those goings-on enabled him to make his inspirational suggestion. It also enabled me to keep my word to Coventry folk that I would never manage another football club and I never have.

Since LWT was not due to broadcast until 1968 I did not have to put Coventry under any pressure to find a new manager. The chairman had flirted with the idea of Malcolm Allison, but didn't follow it through, and instead selected Noel Cantwell, then a Manchester United player. Sir Matt subtly was the guiding hand, killing two birds with one stone – recommending a prospective talented manager and at the same time getting a senior player, presently not always in the team, off the wage bill.

It was strange waiting for LWT's programmes to start. Ideas were flowing from all directions about what programmes might produce viewing figures to make an impression on the advertisers. Theories are one thing, to make them work in practice is quite another. The various department heads used a rectangular room at the GEC building as a communal office; GEC's chairman, Arnold Weinstock, was also a director of LWT. We were to sit at our desks, a mere hundred yards or so from Hyde Park, for many months before our programmes got on the air. Through listening to our neighbours' telephone calls, it wasn't long before we knew the names of wives, girlfriends, sons and daughters, bank managers, and occasionally those who were telephoning on business affairs. This closeness built up a kind of team spirit but it was soon to be shattered.

We were full of splendid programme ideas for LWT's baptism and couldn't wait for the time when the ensuing exposure would reveal the truth. John Bromley, our executive producer and previously mastermind for ABC Television's 'World of Sport', found himself approaching familiar territory. It was simply a question of continuing the programme under new management. Nevertheless, we were looking for innovative ideas to make an impact when the time came. I could not give him, nor did he need, much help in that area, though I did suggest that Richard Davies, the young presenter, might appear warmer if he substituted a more welcoming 'Dickie' for the Richard. So that's who he became.

Our football programme, 'The Big Match', was obviously going to be the second component in our winter weekend schedule. I was able to be more useful there with the choice of two star performers of whose talents I had become aware. John Camkin, the director friend of mine from Coventry City, used to provide commentaries for Anglia TV football games; the person responsible for the visual coverage of the matches was Bob Gardam. John was always eulogising about his qualities, not only in a professional, technical sense but for his improvisation and artistic feeling for the game of football itself. Thus, at LWT we wanted Gardam to direct the regular 'Big Match' programme.

Our choice as a commentator was someone I had met only once or twice in casual fashion, but to whose commentaries I had listened frequently when driving to and from scouting expeditions as Coventry City's manager. His name was Brian Moore. It is far from easy for someone who has not been a professional footballer to commentate for ninety minutes without offending the pernickety professionals who used to play the game, but I had never once been upset by any of the phrases or opinions that he offered.

So our choices were made – Dickie Davies was to host 'World

of Sport', following the legendary Eamonn Andrews; Bob Gardam and Brian Moore would produce and front 'The Big Match'. That was where the fun began. I telephoned the BBC sports department and asked if I could speak to Brian Moore. When I was told he wasn't in the office, the next question down the line was 'Who shall I say called?' Obviously I didn't want to give the game away that it was Jimmy Hill from LWT about to tap him, so I said briskly, 'The name is Hill,' and left it at that. I learned afterwards that when Brian got back to the office he was given the message that Lord Hill, who at that time was chairman of the BBC board of governors, wanted to speak to him. I was able to contact Brian later and over a long lunch offered him the chance to be our number one commentator. Much to my delight he agreed and his enormous popularity both in front of the camera and for commentaries over thirty years has thoroughly vindicated our choice.

Bob Gardam was not quite as easy. I had tried to track him down secretly in the Norwich area and had got as far as a caravan where he was supposedly staying at the time, only to be told by a young lady that he was no longer there. I had to go back to my old friend John Camkin in order to find out exactly where I could meet the elusive object of our quest and make him an offer to come to LWT. When I did eventually catch up with him, I soon realised that he had feelings of great loyalty to Anglia Television with whom he had started, as well as other strong local bonds. I emphasised the scope of the opportunity which we were offering, both artistically and nationally. He took some persuading but finally he agreed to come and we had captured the leading professional in his field.

John Bromley had already recruited Adrian Metcalfe, Olympic 400m medallist, from ABC Television, for his skills as an athletics commentator. He was also an experienced producer and executive. Also in that team was Ian Marshall, a racing nut, who coincidentally I had come across before when he was right-back in the Oxford University team I had coached.

With the signing of Brian Moore we had no need of any other front of camera personnel. Nevertheless, as a favour to Chris

Chataway, I agreed to meet a young fellow athlete from Oxford University, Jeffrey Archer, who apparently had ambitions to become a presenter. We chatted about sport and television for some time, but I had to tell him, sympathetically, that with Dickie Davies and Brian Moore already on board, we had no vacancies. In wanting to be helpful to my friend's friend, I pointed out that his manner with me had been determinedly serious, almost grave. As a presenter, he would need to show a more relaxed persona, perhaps a smile even?

'Oh no!' Jeffrey explained, his television face was nothing like the serious graduate visage I had witnessed during the interview.

Michael Murphy, however, was one of two successful applicants to join the sports unit. He was already with us in the accounts department and we had heard that he was a promising enough footballer to have played for Fulham reserves. Never one to beat about the bush, young Michael proceeded to tell John Bromley and myself along which lines the sports department should be run. John was somewhat taken aback by this arrogant performance and it was all I could do to persuade him to give Michael a chance, if only for Fulham's sake.

'After all,' I reasoned, 'we can always throw him out if it doesn't work!' We didn't, and some years afterwards Michael Murphy became Editor of 'Grandstand' and also of 'Match of the Day', presented by yours truly.

Another successful candidate was Andrew Franklin, just out of school but with an abundance of enthusiasm for the sport of kings; as it turned out, though, not much experience of the human world and particularly the City of London. Andrew was entrusted one morning with an important document to be taken from our HQ at Stonebridge Park to our London office in Old Burlington Street. Unfortunately, never having been a Boy Scout, he was unable to find the street, never mind the building, and travelled all the way back to Stonebridge Park still hugging the letter. Since those days he has progressed, hugging the rails I imagine, to a few winning posts including that of masterminding the highly popular Channel 4 racing output.

155

It was apparent at that time that more than one Football League club was complaining about the difficulty in making ends meet. The salaries which players had negotiated as a result of the end of the maximum wage were hurting. The obvious answer was for the clubs to pay players only as much as they could afford. I know from personal experience, that's easier said than done. Nevertheless, however difficult that task may have been, it was a more feasible course of action than to try to turn back history made seven years before. They had no chance. But it wasn't only clubs lower down in the League who were complaining about lack of income; Coventry City, still desperately trying to retain their first division place under Noel Cantwell, were also finding it difficult to balance their books. I couldn't help but notice, though, during his two years as manager Noel sold three players who had cost Coventry nothing yet had been much part of our journey to the top. John Tudor for £65,000, Ronnie Rees also for £65,000, and Bobby Gould for £90,000 all left Highfield Road.

Just before LWT launched itself and its programmes to the public, a party was held at the offices of Doyle, Dane, Berbach, its PR agency. At that time I was living in a small flat in Hampstead and on the Thursday before the weekend of the magic launch I took a taxi down to Baker Street. We hadn't been travelling long before the cabbie, inevitably, opened up a conversation:

'I saw you on the telly yesterday,' he said.

'Sorry, you didn't,' was my reply.

'Oh yes I did, mate!' he retorted confidently.

'I haven't done any television for over a year, I'm afraid,' said I. He was not impressed.

'I *know* you did!' he almost shouted at me and continued thus: 'My mates have often told me about certain lady passengers who have made suggestive remarks to them and in many cases have followed it up – one thing leading to another and another leading to one thing!' he chirped. 'Nothing like that has ever looked like happening to me until yesterday. I was in Fleet Street and this attractive bird waved me down. She had quite a few parcels and I helped her load up. She was chatty on the way to Hampstead, not far from where I picked you up, as it happens. When we arrived I offered to help her with her parcels and she accepted. At the door, she said, "Thank you," and on such a hot, steamy afternoon would I like to come and have a cold drink or a cup of tea. "Why not?" I thought. In a flash I found myself sitting in a luxury flat with a cup of tea in my hand, the television on. Next thing I know I'm on the floor on top of her, in front of the telly and that's when I saw your face! I *know* it was you!'

Confronted by that indisputable evidence my memory was triggered and I remembered I had filmed a promotion for the Gillette Cup final to be transmitted by LWT on its opening Saturday. Obviously the midweek company had given it a run and judging by yer man's description, one lady didn't see it. . . ain't life strange?

Having scooped the BBC over the contract to cover the Gillette Cup final from Lord's, it was a major part of an early Saturday night transmission, to precede David Frost's key spot in the schedule, an interview with the Editor of *Queen* magazine, at 6.45 p.m. In the history of the Gillette Cup the game had not once overrun 6.45, but it never pays to disregard sod's law. When the last over arrived it was exactly 6.45 p.m. and the result was still in doubt. The ignoramuses in Presentation, in fear of the powers that be, left Lord's with five balls to go and transmitted the live David Frost interview. What a start for a weekend television company for which, inherently, sport had to be an essential constituent ingredient. What a start, too, for the new, green as grass Head of Sport, having to take considerable flak from numerous directions for a decision made above his head by experienced senior executives, especially as they had all been alerted to the outside chance of an overrun beforehand.

Much more dramatically, as the result of the disastrous decision in taking the Gillette Cup final off the air with one over to be bowled, we lost the existing contract to cover the event for the next two years. It wasn't all misery, though. In jointly covering football's Home International tournament, we had lost to the BBC in the ratings battle by a ratio of only 30:25.

Whilst 'The Big Match' was to make LWT's reputation in the football world and among the general public, 'World of Sport' was a network programme; heads of sport and other series executives from the five major companies all wanted to have a say in its format. Regular network sports committee meetings took place to decide policy and discuss progress and ideas. John McMillan had been the managing director of Rediffusion Television, who had the midweek franchise before the reshuffle. Unfortunately, John had lost his niche there but in their wisdom his colleagues in other companies offered him the post of boss of ITV sport. It was a tricky and certainly unpopular job trying to create team spirit among the fiercely independent ITV companies. However, John was no fool. He soon realised that with the team we had put together at LWT at least there was a chance to ruffle the feathers of BBC's 'Grandstand', especially if the LWT crew were able to harness the support and strength of the network. It wasn't an easy task because BBC had most of the sporting contracts. To survive we had to find a means to get ratings, or otherwise submit to the inevitable and leave the field to the BBC.

One advantage was that wrestling achieved the biggest audience of all sports on a Saturday afternoon between four and five o'clock. Therefore, providing our results service was slick and professional, we would be able to hand over a majority share of the audience to the evening's family orientated schedule. Our sporting problem remained in creating an audience early in the afternoon and finding ways to hold on to most of it before wrestling came grunting to the rescue.

Early on, Brian Moore hosted a magazine football programme, 'On The Ball', for which we devised as many innovative ideas as possible to attract a young audience. One such idea was the 'Penalty Prize' competition where kids up to the age of twelve took penalties against professional goalkeepers. To initiate it, I was to demonstrate the format of the competition with Pat Jennings in goal, in front of the cameras. Stupidly I told our producer, Bob Gardam, my intention was to side foot the first one to the goalkeeper's right, having shaped up as if aiming to his left, into the bottom right-hand corner. Then I was going to hit the next five, all side foot, straight to the goalkeeper's left as near to the post as I could squeeze them. What I didn't know was that Bob had told Pat of the plot and he quickly moved over and made a simple save. In anger, I hammered the next five in, never giving him a chance! The miss was still transmitted.

Another strength was the contracts we had with many race-courses, and in that particular area we could provide healthy competition for 'Grandstand'. Because of this, an idea emerged to compress the racing action, using two courses to provide seven races. Thus the 'ITV Seven' was born. It reduced the lead-up to each race, but it did not seem to stop the punters from having a gamble. Betting or not, it was ninety minutes fun and most viewers loved it. So we had a popular football, racing, working man's start to the afternoon and a family finish, which the ladies enjoyed perhaps as much as the men, pulling in its loyal audience. The question remained of how to fill the 3–4 p.m. slot. For our own pride and prestige and to satisfy the ITA, we sought to transmit as many varied, attractive sports as possible. Our aim was to placate those who complained that they had never seen their favourite sport on television, let alone on ITV. So we resolved in that hour to satisfy them and the ITA, and at the same time preserve a sound ratings bridge from racing to wrestling.

One unexpected sport we succeeded in transmitting was polo. From a practical point, the ball is too small and the pitch far too large for viewers to savour the real essence of the game. Yet Tom Clegg, a young, enthusiastic and artistic director, captured perfectly the enchantment of polo on film. His cameras revealed the physical, competitive nature of the contest, the dexterity and courage involved, alongside the charm of children replacing and treading in the divots between chukkas.

Over the course of a year we were able to boast for our masters' benefit that we had covered almost thirty sports. It could be argued in our favour that those who were slow to change channels in mid-afternoon would have been introduced to sports they might previously never have chosen to watch.

We had devised a formula potent enough for survival and at the same time one that improved ITV's previous uninspiring reputation for transmitting sport seriously. From LWT's point of view, it was a financial blessing. Among the five major companies we were the controlling broadcaster, the others contributing to the programme budget, according to ITV practice.

Meanwhile, back in our communal room off Hyde Park it was still seeming somewhat strange to me, not having been in the entertainment business proper. For instance, an independent film producer, Frank Cvitanovitch, asked to meet me to discuss a proposition. When we sat down together I discovered he was interested in making a film about the Charlton brothers. He had been fascinated by the two lads, especially their journey from a mining community to World Cup winners. He would have been even more fascinated now, when you consider how much further they have both gone since then, in their different directions. It seemed to my naïve television mind a splendid idea, but I did wonder whether it was my dyed-in-the-wool enthusiasm for football which led me to be swept along by Frank's sugges- tion. Whatever it was, fortunately my fellow mortgagees in GEC's building seemed to like the idea, too. The outcome was that Frank produced a most moving film on a limited budget which was screened by LWT to critical acclaim.

Another gentleman came through the door with an idea for a mini golf series, 'Two Shot Golf'. It was based on marking out a golf green in circles of ten, twenty and thirty yards, each being the target for shots to the green from given distances. The distances were 200 yards, 150 yards, 100 yards and 50 yards. The idea was that each contestant would have a shot from each of those distances, aiming for the targets on the green. If the player got down in two shots by any means he would score 50 points. If he hit a target on the green of 10, 20 or 30 and missed the putt he would score accordingly. Thinking of my conversation with Michael Peacock about the three-legged stool before I was given the job, I liked the idea. It was innovative and I told the originator that I would think about it and let him know. In the meantime, having a connection with ESSO as a result of their successful World Cup coins promotion, I invited them to lunch at the Chinese restaurant opposite our Wembley studios and it soon became evident that they were prepared to sponsor such an event if we could set it up. Their exposure would come from the ESSO name on the competition. So I had the money, all I needed now were the players. ESSO were to put up a £5000 first prize plus reasonable subsidiary prizes. It wasn't easy to persuade the world's best players, even in those days, to operate for that kind of money. Holding the event in an attractive location would help, so we managed to get a course in Grand Bahamas to agree to host the tournament on beneficial terms. Don't ask me how, but we also succeeded in getting Gary Player, Jack Nicklaus, Dave Marr and our own champion, Tony Jacklin, to participate. We added a touch of glamour by enticing 007, Sean Connery, who for £1000 topped and tailed the series, demonstrating his enthusiasm and love of the game to viewers.

One incident with Jack Nicklaus frightened the life out of me; he was due at two o'clock for an afternoon session and we had the crew waiting and ready to go. At one o'clock there was no sign of the master. I had Jack's address in America and surprisingly, and with immense relief, I found that by telephoning inquiries I was able to obtain the great man's phone number. I called and explained to Mrs Nicklaus that there was no sign of her husband and he was due to be filming in less than an hour.

'Oh,' she said, 'he left in his jet not long ago. He should be there in about ten minutes!' Silly me! It was an introduction to the luxury world of sporting superstars, jetting themselves to work as it were – a hell of a long way from twenty quid a week.

I learned afterwards that Jack did not believe in anything other than 'tee to green' golf, as he put it. The only reason he had agreed to play in this event was that Mark McCormack had made a special plea on our behalf to help LWT, a new television company just going into business who were keen on sport. Jack played with reasonable enthusiasm but, uncharacteristically, was not too anxious about winning. Before he took to the skies again I sat down for a brief snack with him. I was eager to find out the likelihood of being able to sell the two-shot golf series to an American company. Jack proved to be a thorough gentleman but unshakeable from his own views, explaining his basic dislike of pseudo golf games. Nonetheless, he suggested that if I were to approach a man called Ed Dye at the American PGA perhaps they would help. Straight man that he was, he went on to explain that such a proposition would come up before the committee, of which he was a member, and he felt it right to tell me that his particular vote would be against it.

I couldn't have been more impressed with that conversation. It showed Jack to be a traditionalist with strong beliefs in the way in which golf should be played, but at the same time courteous enough to help me with the project. Most of all, though, he was honest enough to tell me (although he could easily have concealed it) exactly how he would vote when the time came.

At that time Tony Jacklin was probably the biggest name in sport in Great Britain and certainly in the golfing world. Everything he touched turned to gold. On the last day, the £5000 prize was obviously going to Dave Marr or Tony. In the final, Dave Marr was in the 30 scoring zone with a four-foot putt to hole for 50 points to win. Tony was in the 10 point scoring zone probably sixty feet from the hole. Tony unbelievably holed his putt for the £5000 and Dave Marr missed his four-footer. It was an extraordinary result and shows the way in which, when a sportsman is on a roll, luck stays with him. Sadly, it didn't remain with Tony *ad infinitum*!

I was not called upon to demonstrate my golfing prowess, but I did succumb to an invitation to put my foot into a game of rugby, and was delighted by the local response:

On a visit to Grand Bahamas to film 'Two Shot Golf', soccer personality Jimmy Hill, switching to the oval ball game this week, stepped in with an immaculate display as full-back in helping Freeport Rugby Club to a sizeable win over a team from HMS *Minerva*.

I wasn't only immersed in sport at LWT but learning fast about other departments. Johnny Haynes and I had become friendly with Willis Hall, the playwright and passionate Fulham supporter, and sometimes after a home game we would meet socially in the evening. An idea came to me for a play based around football; not so much the game itself, but around the passion it provokes. The FA Cup throws up exciting matches, especially in the later stages, and eventually the whole world wants a ticket for a special game, not least the final itself. I had seen and experienced personally the pressure put on professional players to find their relations and friends tickets for such matches. An idea had been mulling over in my mind for some time about a hypothetical situation where a handful of people found themselves desperately trying to get hold of a ticket for the FA Cup final – one maybe because he wanted to propose to his girlfriend and her father was a keen supporter of one of the teams; another as a sweetener in a business deal; another because he was just prepared to die for a ticket. At one of our gatherings I mentioned the idea to Willis to see how he would react. He liked it, so much as it turned out, that he wrote the play *The Ticket*, which was shown by LWT. From his fee, Willis most generously bought me a desk made from 'thank yew' wood at which I am now sitting.

Notwithstanding domestic confrontations at LWT, occasionally war broke out in full with the supposed real enemy, the BBC. I say supposed because at times, in endeavouring and often failing to reach an agreed competitive policy, we could be excused for believing we had more in common with the BBC than with other ITV companies. However, there was a distinct lack of any loving feeling at Wembley for the 1969 Cup final between Manchester City and Leicester City. The final was covered by both channels. The players behaved well but, claiming they had an exclusive contract for interviews, BBC staff attempted to break up an ITV interview with Mike Summerbee. An ITV outside broadcast manager, David Yallop, lost a tooth in the sudden switch from football to the noble art of lack of self-defence, and was obviously so disorientated by the whole experience he moved on to become a highly successful author.

Fortunately for us the war subsided, but not the competition and since that incident the Wembley authorities have made sure that agreed lines of rights and demarcations are upheld.

As a kind of peace offering, some time later, someone had the idea of challenging the BBC to a game of football for fun and a renewal of our friendship vows, perhaps even sharing a drink or two afterwards. The match was duly arranged and our selected World of Sport ITV XI turned up at the appointed venue, not all that far from Wembley. We waited in vain for our opponents. Apparently, BBC's sports boss, Bryan Cowgill, heard about the proposed match at the eleventh hour and forcibly withdrew his troops. Rumour had it that he objected on the grounds that having channelled his energies towards eliminating the ITV enemy, fraternisation would defeat the purpose.

A year after London Weekend Television had gone on the air, Michael Peacock, the managing director, came under attack from the ITA. In defending the range of LWT's programmes, he referred to such shows as 'On the Buses', 'Doctor in the House' and the 'Bruce Forsyth Show', all of which were doing reasonably well in the entertainment scene, and included a special word for sport. He explained that, when a separate ITV sports unit did not evolve as had been expected, it became necessary for LWT to fill the breach. Since then 'World of Sport' had been raised to a new qualitative and competitive level. It was not possible to create a department of forty people for sport and, considering the limited air time, not have something else give. Inevitably, the Public Affairs unit had to be reduced.

Little by little a feeling crept in that things were not right on the top floor. Rumours of arguments between the board of the company, the managing director Michael Peacock and pro-gramme controller Cyril Bennett, were rife in the canteen. As far as the sports department was concerned, we had received nothing but support from the MD in the enormous battle we were fighting against the strength of the BBC, even running to the purchase of a revolutionary HS100 machine. That mysterious formula meant nothing to me at the time, but it was the first of its kind to be used in television in this country to provide slow motion replays of sporting action. I joked that it was perfect for me, because when I played I was already in slow motion! That machine in itself was enough to demonstrate to the ITA, BBC sports department and others that we meant business.

It's easy enough to see what the problems were about in retrospect. Obviously, when a company is seeking to gain a franchise awarded by the ITA, it has to put up a potential programme schedule based on the loftiest possible ideals. When the time comes for those aspirations to be adopted in a death or glory match against a BBC schedule, the reality is somewhat different. Whatever London Weekend's long-term objectives, very quickly they had to adjust their sights and deliver a rating or go broke. It was said that Aidan Crawley and David Frost came together as principals of the company because they shared the philosophy of public service. There was speculation that Dr Tom Margerison, a qualified scientist, would become managing director of the company in place of Peacock. John Freeman, who was a director, had recently been made the British Ambassador to Washington and at that time played little part in it all, though a year or two later his influence, returning as chairman of the company, restored it to sanity and solvency.

The immediate outcome was that on Friday, 18 September 1969, Michael Peacock was sacked as managing director. In London the heads of departments met, including Frank Muir (Light Entertainment), Doreen Stevens (Children's and Family), Joy Whitby (executive producer of children's programmes), Derek Grainger (executive producer, drama), Terry Hughes (executive producer of general programmes) and myself. We were disappointed, to say the least, about the sacking of Michael Peacock. It has become even more evident as the years have passed that he was made a scapegoat for something which was inevitable. It was impossible for a new company to compete instantly and profitably against the established strength of the

BBC. Building a potent schedule which would attract sufficient viewers to survive commercially would take time and Michael wasn't given this because of LWT's anxiety to remain alive at whomsoever's personal cost. To be very honest, such executive squabbles were outside my remit and although I had the maximum sympathy for our departed MD, providing the company was prepared to back John Bromley and me in our struggle against the strength of the BBC's sports department, we were dedicated to continue with it. So we stayed for our own sound reasons while six of our fellow executives announced on 20 September that they were to leave LWT as a result of their dismay at Michael Peacock's dismissal.

Our problems were not only internal, but with other ITV companies less enthusiastic about sport with whom we shared seats on the network sports committee. Since most of them had seven-day franchises, that was understandable. To them a weekend was just two and a half days, to LWT it was the whole of our commercial life. They could perhaps stomach low ratings on Saturday afternoons. LWT couldn't. It was too big a slice of our bread and butter. Almost immediately, two points of frustration occurred. We had negotiated an option to cover that year's Ryder Cup for £5000 but, although LWT was prepared to give the air time to it, the other companies on the ITV sports committee turned it down.

Perhaps not surprisingly, the other ITV companies were not anxious to follow LWT's lead. ITV won the exclusive rights to the British hard court tennis championships at Bournemouth, but disappointingly the network bowed out and Southern Television couldn't get anyone else to share the costs. The venture collapsed.

Consequently, sport did not hold ITV in high regard. I did my level best to persuade the various associations to understand the advantage they would have if there were two bidders in the market place for their events and tournaments, so in the long run, helping us would be beneficial to them. If 'World of Sport' should die because of lack of sufficiently enticing events, the BBC would tell sports how much or how little they would pay them for transmission rights.

As if it wasn't difficult enough to launch a television franchise, ACTT union members had looked upon it as a heaven sent opportunity to unleash their grievances publicly and to turn the tables against their new bosses, before they'd had time to get their feet under them. The result was a strike for a week or two, which LWT defended resolutely with senior executives downing pens and manning the control room and the cameras to stay on the air. Fortunately for the company, they did not call on my technical knowledge or mechanical nous and were able to relay programmes until a welcome compromise was reached. As ex-chairman of the PFA, it was an opportunity to feel what it was like to defend the employers' goalmouth.

For the 1970 World Cup, LWT and the other ITV companies were determined to give the BBC a run for its licence money. An overall, across company team of directors, producers and performers was recruited. Although I had visited Mexico the previous summer, my own role in the competition proper was to be in the studio at Wembley alongside Brian Moore. John Bromley was the executive producer for the network and between us, with some help from the unforgettable Brazilian team, we achieved a TV sporting miracle – we surpassed the BBC for ratings for a football event for the first time ever. It wasn't accidental, it was calculated coldly and clinically and it worked. Perhaps they did have David Coleman, the best known and most experienced commentator, but he was only one man and ITV's commentary team was sound and professional. Yet the war wasn't won during the ninety or so minute games, but in the five minutes before, the ten minutes at half-time and the ultimate collective verdict at the end. We cunningly conceived the battle plan: a fully representative, qualified, opinionated panel. Representatives from England, Ireland and Scotland were needed who would not pull their punches, and would qualify their strong opinions but not without humour – Malcolm Allison, Derek Dougan and Paddy Crerand. As it turned out, the addition of Arsenal's Bob McNab occurred accidentally. Sir Alf Ramsey in his wisdom had not only left him out of the England squad but had sent him home into the bargain.

Bob's shy approach, contrasting with that of the other panellists, was immediately a hit, especially with the ladies who preferred a blush of modesty. He provided a perfect foil and we grabbed him for the whole competition.

It wasn't only the no-holds-barred, knowledgeable and passionate discussions which captured the public's imagination, but present company excepted, the participants were handsome, athletic young men. In addition, capturing the Mexican fiesta flavour, they dressed flamboyantly in carefree, colourful fashion. Whatever it was, it worked!

In a professional sense, without inhibiting our patriotic feelings, we began to appreciate and praise the artistry of the Brazilians. As game followed game, Pelé, Jairzinho, Gerson, Garrincha and Co. displayed their magical skills to the world and we gloried in their beauty. After England lost, unnecessarily in my view, to Germany we were theirs completely.

Before we dismiss England's performance and that fateful game, my opinion at the time, which hasn't changed incidentally, was that it was lost because of Sir Alf's mishandling of the substitutes. At home the tendency was still only to substitute for injured players. When leading 2–1 he left a weary Terry Cooper facing a fresh Jurgen Grabowski, with an equally fresh and highly athletic Colin Bell brought on to stand unhelpfully a yard from the touchline at outside-right. Peter Bonetti was blamed for not saving the shots, but with proper tactical substitution they could have been prevented at source.

England's loss was the world and ITV's gain. In contrast to our warm appreciation of Brazil, the BBC's army of panellists had appeared lukewarm. The public in large numbers switched loyalties and channels, reminding the BBC that at last they had an opponent to be reckoned with.

After Brazil's fine victory, the ITV panel received an invitation from the Brazilian Ambassador in London to attend the celebrations at the Embassy, at which we were thanked for our World Cup coverage, and particularly for our early and unqualified appreciation of the Brazilian players and their performances. On

Terry Bly – Sky Blue hero number one, bought and sold.

George Hudson – Sky Blue hero number two, bought and sold.

Second division champions, 1967 – the foundation stones underwriting over thirty years at the top.

Bobby Gould repaid a second chance by converting many more.

A tactful procession – manager on horseback, chairman on expensive wheels!

Behind
Dickie

Ernie Machin represented a £50 gamble
which paid off.

Spot the horse!

ITV 4
Derek

Good luck, Derrick and Noel (Robins and Cantwell) – I'm off because I wanted to stay.

Pri

Or
Ha
Fo

'Would you like to handle me in Europe. . . ?'
asked Raquel Welch.

Every boy's hero – Pelé.

Highbury 1972 – Tommy Smith (Liverpool), Pat Partridge (referee) and the emergency
linesman.

Ernie Machin represented a £50 gamble which paid off.

Spot the horse!

Good luck, Derrick and Noel (Robins and Cantwell) – I'm off because I wanted to stay.

Prince Philip was an enthusiastic supporter of our Goaldiggers' charity events.

Only the most enthusiastic made the Goaldiggers' team! Back row: *(left to right)* Dougie Hayward, Bill Taylor, Dave Underwood, Bill Dodgin, Frank Blunstone, Brian Mears, Theo Foley. Front row: *(left to right)* Michael Parkinson, Rod Stewart, Elton John, Jimmy Greaves, JH.

Behind the scenes at 'World of Sport', with two of my best signings, Brian Moore and Dickie Davies.

ITV 4 BBC 0 – on the World Cup panel in 1970 with *(left to right)* Paddy Crerand, Derek Dougan and Malcolm Allison.

'Would you like to handle me in Europe. . . ?' asked Raquel Welch.

Every boy's hero – Pelé.

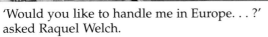

Highbury 1972 – Tommy Smith (Liverpool), Pat Partridge (referee) and the emergency linesman.

'Let's all sing together, Play up, Sky Blues! . . .' I couldn't say no when I was offered the chairmanship of Coventry City FC.

Two happy people – Saudi Arabian football takes off.

Sandwiched between twin pillars of BBC sporting strength, Bryan Cowgill *(left)* and Sir Paul Fox.

'BBC's not so poor players who strut and fret their many hours upon the sporting stage' (with apologies to Shakespeare). *Left to right:* Alan Weeks, Barry Davies, J H, John Motson, David Coleman, Frank Bough, Archie Macpherson and Tony Gubba.

leaving the Embassy a few hours later, I can remember the Ambassador saying, 'We have an old Brazilian proverb, "You have found the path to our house; you are welcome to tread it again." We are happy to extend this invitation to you.' Charming manners and breathtaking footballers – Big Mal noticed that the Ambassador's daughter was breathtakingly beautiful, too!

During the competition, Malcolm had caused a minor heart flutter among fellow panellists in revealing he was to lunch with Christine Keeler, notoriously linked with the political come-uppance of cabinet minister John Profumo. If we wished to tag along, we were welcome. Well, we would, wouldn't we? The subject occupied us for a day or two and having whipped ourselves into a frenzy of excitement and anticipation, Mal announced on the fateful morning – she couldn't come! Ah well, you win some, you lose some . . .

Adrian Metcalfe's baby, as a producer that is, was 'Sports Arena', these days a prehistoric forerunner of 'On the Line'. Our problem as always was to persuade viewers to sample the programme, and the route when you're in a hurry is to find a well-known popular face. One such, Michael Parkinson, had just taken a rest from fronting 'Cinema', a highly successful Granada programme. We knew he was a sports fanatic, a more than useful cricketer, and thought golf was a game only suitable for cranks. Consequently, I found myself swapping pints with him at a London hostelry at the end of which we reached some kind of agreement. The outcome was that Mike fronted and, with Adrian Metcalfe, edited this weekly sports magazine programme. It was extremely well received by an enthusiastic minority audience, but unlike 'World of Sport', to which the rest of the network had to subscribe, 'Sports Arena' did not enthral them sufficiently to throw yet more money in LWT's direction.

As if I hadn't enough to fill my days, I was invited to become a member of the Sports Council under Chairman Roger Bannister. Since Walter Winterbottom was its professional director, I wanted to accept. In addition, having a foot in that camp would not be a disadvantage professionally, and at the same time would enable me to play be it even a small part in improving the nation's sporting performances. One of the pleasures to follow was to present a talented seventeen-year-old golfer with an award for an outstanding performance in East Anglia. His name was Nick Faldo and six feet of me looked up at him then, and I still do. With me on the Council were Doug Insole, Norris McWhirter and Laddie Lucas, all with diverse sporting backgrounds, as well as a talented young Arsenal goalkeeper, Bob Wilson.

One day Lord Grade, then Lew and boss of ATV who held the Midlands ITV franchise, was put through on the phone by my secretary. He wasn't a regular caller.

'What can I do for you, Lew?' I asked.

'Jimmy, I need a couple of Cup final tickets. Can you help out?'

'Well, I could try,' I replied, 'but what about Billy Wright, your Head of Sport? Can't he help?'

'No, I don't like to worry Billy,' he answered.

'I'll do what I can,' I offered, 'but while you're on, could I ask why ATV is not taking "Sports Arena"? It's an excellent programme. In fact, when I was at the Orient, your brother Leslie came over specially to say what a fine programme it was and how much he enjoyed it!'

'That's why Leslie knows nothing about television.' End of conversation. He took his tickets but never took 'Sports Arena'.

Whatever the quality of that programme, it was doomed. When Stella Richman became controller of programmes it was inevitable that it would go. One evening, John Bromley and I took Stella to a Wembley international hoping to use our collective charm to persuade her in such a sporting environment. She enjoyed the football, the meal and all the wine with which we could jointly and severally fill her glass. At 2 a.m. she was still saying 'No!' and LWT kissed goodbye to 'Sports Arena', to Michael Parkinson, and not long afterwards to Stella herself.

In addition it had become apparent that Michael's financial horizons and LWT's were on different planes. Martin Sorrell, who now runs a huge American advertising agency and has become one of the world's richest men, then representing Mike, called in to see me to discuss if we still had a programme and what would be an appropriate figure for its presenter's fee. The figure he suggested meant that we could no longer afford Mike to front what at its best was a regional programme. Never mind the quality, I felt the reality of promoting sport on ITV.

Although the sports department was rapidly gaining in confidence, reputation and ratings, all was still not well at the top. In January 1971 Stella Richman left, apparently not having conjured up sufficient instant magic, although the national institution 'Upstairs Downstairs' was commissioned during her brief reign.

In February it was Tom Margerison's turn compulsorily to vacate his desk. We had always found him willing to help and appreciative of the sports unit's efforts. In the early days I had taken both Tom and Michael Peacock to watch England play at Wembley. Tom sat alongside me and in the first few minutes of the game popped the question, 'Jimmy, why do the players have eight shadows?' Twenty years in the game and I hadn't the least idea, or even noticed it before. I suppose that's the way a scientist's mind works, but it wasn't going to shape LWT's fortunes in the future. In those years of musical chairs we were hardly surprised when a month or two later Cyril Bennett returned as controller of programmes and I inherited yet another title, that of deputy controller of programmes.

'The Big Match', although only a regional programme, led the way in quality and innovation. We kept open minds, and were always ready to adopt fresh ideas. Thus when Arsenal reached the FA Cup final in 1971 and found themselves songless, facing Liverpool's emotional 'You'll never walk alone', LWT's sports unit came to their rescue by launching a 'Write a song for Arsenal' competition. We chose as the music Elgar's 'Land of Hope and Glory', and we were overwhelmed with stanza after stanza of words: moving, comic, historical, personal, the public's rhymes overflowed with passionate enthusiasm. Unfortunately, however, as they poured in, so did a breach of copyright protest from the Elgar Society. Our company secretary called an emergency meeting; 'Land of Hope and Glory' was out and 'Rule

171

Britannia!' was in. Luckily there were no restrictions on that one.

On the Wednesday evening I went to watch Coventry City play at Highbury. After the match I suggested to Bertie Mee that they might adopt the tune of 'Rule Britannia!' to which I would write some simple words and it would become their song. Showing enormous trust and, as it turned out, good sense, Bertie agreed; more than one newspaper had launched its own competition and too many songs would defeat the object. My next task was to write the words, which I did on my way home to my Hampstead flat. We launched the song in the *Daily Express*. *'Good old Arsenal! We're proud to say that name, While we sing this song you'll win the game!'* took off and three weeks later it was sung joyfully at the Cup final as Arsenal beat Liverpool 2–1. Arsenal got the Cup and I still get the royalties – it's peanuts, but satisfying.

For that highly competitive 1971 Cup final broadcast, our creative team again broke new ground by venturing into the mystical world of computer wizardry. We attempted to forecast the winners by engaging the metal brain cells of 'Cedric', as we christened our exciting piece of hardware. It didn't take me long to fathom, as I diligently awarded marks for each player's skills, athleticism, speed, aggression, goalscoring power etc., etc., that it wasn't Cedric who would make the forecast: he would only get the credit or the blame for it. It was I who was casting the die. Memory functioning selectively as it does, I'm sure Cedric predicted Arsenal's win, but all the computer science in the world could not have foreseen the Gunners' winning goal or foretold who scored it. George Graham took the credit for it and that would have been the end of the story had not a sharp-eyed videotape editor later that evening noticed that George's deceptive flick/dummy had not actually made contact with the ball. Eddie Kelly's unexceptional shot had avoided any further form of human contact before finding the net – Cedric knew!

About that time, Rupert Murdoch was taking a close interest in the company's instability, becoming chairman of the executive committee. As a result, the press increased its scrutiny of our affairs, particularly questioning the controlling involvement of an antipodean entrepreneur in domestic television. 'Panorama' sought to establish the facts and invited LWT to send a representative to defend its position. It was discussed at an executive meeting rather indecisively until, plucking up courage, I offered my services to represent LWT. I had seen it all from day one and understood the company's problems and I was relaxed in front of a camera; it was my job, after all. So my name was put forward, but the issue for the BBC then became rather different from the benefits or otherwise of a powerful Australian taking over LWT. The fear was that I might use the platform to draw attention to LWT (ITV)'s performance in sport, presently giving the BBC a run for its money.

Bagenal Harvey, whose clients had fingers in both pies, became a kind of pre-programme mediator. The BBC was quite happy for me to defend LWT, but didn't want me to use it as a means to promote ITV's successes in televised sport, particularly the recent World Cup. The BBC cautiously preferred to record the programme. If that was to be the formula, I contested that I should have similar transmission approval rights. In that stand-off atmosphere, we went ahead and the first take went out. On the subject of control of LWT, I wondered how owning 8.5 per cent of the voting shares could deliver to Rupert Murdoch the right to run the company. On the question of the quality of our sports output, I suggested that the BBC, with its history of leading the field in televised sport, was at last confronted with opposition of sufficient merit to compete healthily. It was a case of diplomacy and it enabled both sides to share a drink afterwards without hostility or loss of face. The next day I received a telegram from Rupert Murdoch which said: 'Understand you did great job on 24 hours last night. Many thanks and congratulations.'

In the area of light entertainment, one idea was for Frankie Howerd to tour the Far East giving concerts to our troops, which LWT would transmit. It was expensive and logistically difficult so the idea was quickly dropped. The story was to be part of LWT's press campaign at the Monte Carlo festival, a responsibility of the department I now headed. It was imperative, I judged, with the world only too aware of LWT's domestic shortcomings, to make an impact – a confident one if possible. As an ex-football manager, I considered the tactical scene and our potential strengths. John Alderton, whom I had met in Gerry's Bar on more than one occasion, and Nyree Dawn Porter whom I had never met, were, thanks to Frank Muir, due to appear in 'Please Sir!' and 'Never a Cross Word' respectively. It seemed to me that we should do our utmost to promote these two stars of our comedy output. All we had to do was to persuade them to go to Monte Carlo. John and his wife Pauline Collins, thank goodness, were receptive to the idea and Nyree accepted the invitation with professional courage; she had only recently lost her husband. The trio were old friends, which also helped considerably.

Professionally, I was looking for a return on our investment in time and money and the existing shows were old hat news-wise. John and Pauline enjoyed working together so when I was asked at the press conference whether LWT had any plans up its sleeve, I said casually that we were considering a series in which they might feature together. I admit I had little idea of the impact that announcement would make until Peter Hennessy, who was now the number two in the press and publicity department, telephoned with the news that it was headlined in one of the nationals. He was in a frenetic state.

'It says they're going to do it,' he challenged.

'Well, who knows, they might,' I squirmed. There was a certain lack of mutual understanding in the conversation but I comforted myself that at least LWT had some return on its outlay and perhaps Peter wasn't that comfortable with or confident in the judgement of an ex-football manager as his boss.

That evening, however, the ITV posse was to party together. We shared a splendid meal after which it was decided as a group to visit the Casino – a must in Monte Carlo. Someone suggested collecting a 'kitty' for a joint gamble. As a result of a contract with the Sportsman's Club in Tottenham Court Road, the original little chip from which London Clubs grew, I had learned something about roulette. If you want to sink or swim quickly you back single numbers; if you want a bit of lasting fun you back either red or black, odds or evens, numbers 1–18 or 19–36. Patrick Dromgoole of Westward TV was daring and wanted a quick flutter, so we decided to halve the funds and invest each according to his or her philosophy. Patrick's half disappeared predictably in record time. Our group battled on gamely, despite the taciturn disapproval of the croupiers, never having seen so much fuss being made over so little lolly. However, forty-five minutes later we emerged in triumph, having painstakingly won enough for the whole party to break even. It was almost better than winning the Cup! Also for a short time it diverted Nyree's mind away from her sadness and it was perhaps the very small beginning of the end of her personal grief. When the LWT hierarchy took her as our guest, limousine style, to the Derby in June she was most attractively back to life.

On reaching my room in the early hours, there was an urgent message for me to ring Roy Van Gelder, LWT's Head of Personnel, as soon as I could, whatever the time. All sorts of frightening thoughts entered my mind. Had the press conference rebounded? Had I overstepped the mark? I managed to get Roy at his home.

'When you come back first thing in the morning, don't go home, come straight to the office,' was the instruction barked over the crackling line, at which point it went dead. I tried without success to reach him again. There was nothing else to do but turn over and go to sleep.

Next morning I was away to the airport with John and Pauline. We had first-class tickets but were unable to claim our seats as all the first-class accommodation had been commandeered. However, we were not deprived of the essential, life-supporting alcohol during the flight. I was mostly preoccupied with trying to conjure up an instant series or play in which Pauline and John could co-star for LWT, and to persuade them to back up my bravado at the press conference.

When we arrived, there was a driver from a hire-car company waiting for me.

'I'm instructed to take you straight to the office,' he said.

175

'Okay,' I answered, 'but just let me phone first.' This time I succeeded in reaching Roy.

'There've been some changes,' he said. 'You're now part of a small executive team running the company. I'll see you shortly.' Never mind the sack! And I thought breaking even at roulette was lucky!

Not all that long afterwards, the uniquely talented John Hawkesworth produced a new series of 'Upstairs Downstairs' starring both Pauline and John. It became an overwhelming success for them and LWT.

Alongside the somewhat frantic executive role, I was still performing in front of camera, sometimes appreciated, sometimes not! Before one international at Wembley, I was to interview Sir Robert Kelly live for ITV. This was the dignified, dour and somewhat scary chairman of Celtic FC and of the Scottish FA. Commercials on the ITV network are spread among different companies and accordingly have to run to the second. Thus live interviews must also be timed to the second. What is termed a 'deaf aid' in the trade is concealed in one ear, through which the editor of the programme can communicate with the presenter. During an interview, it is normal for the editor to pass on a gentle reminder when the end is nigh, leading up to a final detailed countdown over the last ten seconds. On this occasion, Sir Robert had not been at all forthcoming, providing the flimsiest of replies to all my questions, which were on the verge of running out. However, in answer to my final inquiry Sir Robert took off. I thought he would never stop and he ploughed on through the increasingly violent guidance reverberating through my deaf aid.

'Get him off!' was the crystal clear instruction heard only by me. 'Wind him up, for heaven's sake!' Then 'SHUT HIM UP!!' which nearly blew my head off, as the ten second countdown began. I was coolness personified – or at least that's what I thought. Then I made a grave mistake: thinking we were only in vision from the waist up, I slipped my hand along the arm of Sir Robert's chair and gently squeezed his gloved hand hoping he would understand the signal to dry up. But we were not in close up and the whole world could see my action. Worse was to come. In pressing the glove, I realised that Sir Robert had an artificial hand and would not have felt anything anyway. So much for live television being fun!

My routine for a weekend during the winter months started on Saturday morning at the LWT studios for 'On the Ball' and continued at whichever London ground our chosen game was played. Accordingly, I arrived at Highbury looking forward immensely to a game between Arsenal and Liverpool. I took my place in the press box alongside one-time Arsenal hero, Bernard Joy. Early on the game was fascinating as the two giants strove for supremacy. After fifteen minutes the linesman on the far touchline, Denis Drewitt, slipped when changing direction and remained prostrate on the ground. It transpired that he had torn a thigh muscle and would have to be replaced, which proved not to be a simple matter. Obviously the match had been stopped and could not be restarted until a suitable substitute was found. After a while an announcement was made requesting any qualified official in the crowd to come forward and declare himself to the referee. Still nothing happened and the crowd was getting restless; fortunately not nearly as restless as a similar delay would provoke today – a sad reflection on current lack of patience and good manners and abundance of irritability. Nevertheless, it was becoming a major problem. I remarked to Bernard, 'If they're stuck, I know the laws and could fill in.'

'Why don't you go down and offer?' he said. I didn't go immediately, but since the delay was beginning to reach considerable proportions, I eventually went down and offered my services, saying to Pat Partridge, the referee, 'If you're stuck, I'm happy to do it.'

'You'll do me!' was the reply. 'Get changed quickly!' That wasn't as simple as it sounded: a light-blue tracksuit served the first half and black top and shorts the second, but unbelievably they could not find suitable footwear of any kind bigger than size eight – I take a ten! At half-time, thankfully, somehow they produced a pair of tens, but until then my toenails had been getting more and more bruised as I digested a painful lesson in how far a linesman has to run in a game.

The match was not the same afterwards and fizzled out to a 0–0 draw. Naturally, the crowd had their share of fun at my expense. Quite honestly, I was unaware of it as I came to realise the particular pressure under which I had put myself. Any mistake would undoubtedly make big black headlines. I kept my head down and concentrated like mad, particularly on vital offside decisions. I found that the well-timed runs of Arsenal's Kennedy and Radford created the most difficulty and called for precise judgement. Liverpool's attacking style with Keegan and Toshack did not. Both managers seemed to be happy to share the spoils and put the game behind them.

Before 'The Big Match' transmitted the programme on Sunday afternoon, I was able to check the accuracy or otherwise of my decisions on videotape, having read John Jenkins in the *Sunday Express*: 'Hill's first offside decision was greeted by friendly boos from the 47,000 crowd – the second a bad piece of misjudgement was angrily jeered. Poor Jimmy needed the slow motion cameras to help him out.' In the *Observer*, ex-soccer Blue, Tony Pawson, had written: 'Hill was immediately approved by both managers and referee Pat Partridge, a confidence he fully justified. There is no need for him to fear his own critical analyses of any playback decisions.' Hurrah for videotape and hurry on the day when it is used 'live' sparingly to reveal the truth. On that occasion it gave me a clean bill of judicial health for which I am enormously thankful, never having put myself under such scrutiny since and so preserving a clean sheet.

I learned afterwards that Pat had chosen me ahead of a twenty-seven-year-old Class 3 referee, Rodney Girvan, on the grounds of nervousness and fair play – he didn't want to pitch him in in front of over 40,000 spectators.

In November 1972, Raquel Welch was in London to promote her latest film. Someone somewhere had the idea of latching on to football's popularity and in particular to Peter Osgood, ringleader of Chelsea's on-the-field athleticism and off-the-field King's Road glamour. A passion for Peter's skills savoured by Raquel was the name of the PR game.

Three days' fun started in a studio within spitting distance of Tottenham Court Road and the Sportsman's Club. Dickie Davies was scheduled to interview Raquel, who was solely on the promotional path, but since we did not often entertain stars of such worldwide magnitude on 'World of Sport', we stifled any embarrassment. I still wore my various executive hats and judged that on such an occasion I should welcome our guest personally, which I did before leaving her in Dickie's more than capable hands. He was aided by John Bromley, who had managed to postpone his many arduous and widespread managerial tasks to be present at such an important function. The outcome was that my newly acquired film-star friend cancelled her Paris meeting on Friday; could I arrange a press conference here? We agreed for it to be held at the Sportsman's Club at 2.45 p.m.

We alerted the whole of Fleet Street to this enterprise, but it was evident by 2.30, when less than a handful of hacks had appeared, that this was not a conference fit for a superstar. In some panic we set to work. The staff at the Sportsman was not small: there were chefs, croupiers, waiters and office staff many of whom could pass themselves off as journalists. So by the time we sat down appearances were deceptive and numerically satisfactory and with straight faces our actors played their parts. The gag afterwards, which my journalist friends will forgive, was that one or two had nearly ruined the ruse by asking intelligent questions. . .

At five o'clock that same afternoon I was in for a bigger shock. Raquel rang again to say she had made arrangements to stay even longer and see her hero Peter Osgood play at Stamford Bridge the following afternoon. Could I organise it? Naturally I agreed and said I'd pick her up between eleven and twelve o'clock at the Savoy (where else?).

My problems were only just beginning. I had to find a film crew and a director to record the interview between Raquel and Peter. I tried Bob Gardam to be told by a friend that he was out for the evening at a gathering of the Old Elizabethans and would not be back until the early hours. I tried Mike Archer, who was also busy playing the violin in a performance of 'The Pirates of Penzance' at his son's school. The only contact I could make was with our not long since office boy, Michael Murphy.

'Can you get a crew for 12.30?' I implored.

'No problem,' said the confident young man, and came up trumps with a cameraman on time, on the day, at the right place.

In my chauffeur-driven limousine, I arrived to pick up my new-found friend on time and caught my breath at the most impressive combination of style and beauty. On a sunny November day the outfit was sensational, if not a touch daring weather-wise. A two-piece, light-blue trouser suit of the finest, softest suede embraced a fine white silk blouse. The trousers clung to the calves and terminated above the ankles, above a pair of flimsy stiletto sandals.

My companion requested some gum or sweeties, at which I signalled to our driver to stop, quickly alighted and came back with half the shop. The weather stayed calm until we reached the ground, where Brian Mears, the Chelsea chairman, greeted us. He had been warned.

'Wine or champagne?' he offered.

'Champagne,' was the reply.

Our highly professional film crew was at hand. I didn't introduce the young cameraman, but almost lived up to young Murph's expectations by describing him as one of the most promising young film directors in London. As far as I knew, he'd never directed a film in his life but, after all, it was hardly going to be 'Gone with the Wind'! After a glass or two, Ossie was duly produced, between them the stars sparkled for a minute or two and the morning's objective had been achieved. Life improved in relaxing fashion as we sampled the champagne until the time came for us to make our way to the only remaining stand at the Bridge at that time, in the far corner. Between it and us there were 150 yards, no shelter and the weather had deteriorated alarmingly. The cold wind and rain destroyed the effectiveness of our guest's umbrella as we half floated the distance to our target.

That stand is no longer there; when it was there were no lifts. Thus having reached our original objective, we now had a lengthy climb up unrelenting steep concrete steps. I sensed Raquel had had enough and was about to explode, but as we completed our stagger to the top an angel of mercy in the form of Mrs June Mears came to the rescue.

'Oh, you poor thing!' she sympathised, handing Raquel a huge brandy. 'Come with me and we'll make you comfortable.' They turned left and in cowardly fashion I turned right to join Len Shipman and his fellow directors from Leicester City.

For 'Big Match' television purposes, Raquel and I sat together during the match and to my mind she was a different lady from the public figure the world at large sees: 'Raquel' became 'Rocky', a very proud mother of her children. It was a scoop of its kind for 'The Big Match', to say nothing of the stories it provided for the relatives of her press interviewers. Before she left after half-time, blowing a kiss across the pitch to an astonished Ossie, she proceeded to ask me a question which would make most men think Paradise lay ahead.

'Jim,' she asked, 'how would you like to handle me in Europe?' After pausing to regain my composure and biting my tongue to stop myself from giving the obvious answer, regretfully I declined, explaining with as much charm as I could muster that sadly I was fully occupied in a variety of ways. I didn't let on that the past three days' drama was enough to last me for a lifetime.

The Internationals Club was founded in the early sixties over a glass of wine in El Vino's. Bagenal Harvey saw it as a way of establishing a link with the current top players as well as with the stars of the not-too-distant past. Apart from that, we thought it might create opportunities to raise the profile of football's élite in more sophisticated areas of society. One way would be to play matches for leading charities, both at home and abroad. It all came about because of a contract Bagenal had signed with ABC chewing gum to produce, for inclusion in their packaging, photographs and potted histories of current star players. On his behalf, I invited leading players to participate for an infinitesimal fee and membership of our club. A committee was formed which included Tom Finney, Billy Wright, Danny Blanchflower and Bobby Charlton. The idea was to select a superstar from each of the leading teams to be the club's representatives. Brian Clough, then scoring prolifically for Middlesbrough, was the sort of young, intelligent international we sought to recruit. Not having received a reply to my ABC chewing gum letter, I rang the club to make sure Brian had received it, to be told that he was on a cruise and would not be back for a week or two. That wouldn't be surprising these days, but thirty years ago a professional footballer on a cruise was different. Needless to add, Brian has proved unique since then in at least a hundred other different ways.

One unforgettable overseas' experience with the Internationals was a game against current players in Kuwait, with John Charles and Stanley Matthews in the star-studded party. The Kuwaitis were to a man clothed in pristine black and white, pretty well identically dressed. They are, or were, a far from tall race and the sight of the considerable frame of John Charles leaping to head a thumping thirty-yard clearance brought from ten thousand throats a sound of gasping astonishment like a massive rush of wind. They had never seen anything like it. On the other hand, they were totally aware of the legend of Stanley Matthews and their expectations were high. On the few occasions when Stan touched the ball, there were positive squeals of excitement. To be fair, Stan had continued to play professionally until past the age when most of us would have dandled a grandchild or two on our laps and he was then a year or two past that.

Unfortunately, we fell a goal behind and found ourselves in a difficult diplomatic position. The so much younger Welsh international and Spurs player, Cliff Jones, was becoming restless on the subs bench and was losing patience. Half-time came and we were still behind. I took the initiative and suggested to Stan that he might go all out for five or ten minutes before allowing Cliff to replace him. Big Dave Underwood, ex-goalkeeper for Fulham and Watford, our trainer, had his own phrase for it.

'Burn yourself out, Stan,' he ventured, 'and I'll give you the sign when to come off.' Five minutes or so into the half, Stan took a pass on the halfway line, shrugged off the years and in a trice dribbled his way past two Kuwaitis; the crowd was in a frenzy of noisy appreciation of the maestro's talent. Stan approached the penalty area and took on another opponent to even greater cheers, but the ball ran away from him and was stolen by a mean defender. The crowd took their first real opportunity to cheer their hero, glorying in the moment, at which Dave Underwood ran on to the field, captured Stan and at the same time encouraged the crowd to continue to show their appreciation of their man; a masterful diplomatic performance, which brought on Cliff whose comparatively youthful, scintillating runs enabled us to score and avoid defeat.

Most of our visits were to Holland. Every year by Dutch royal command a plane would land at Northolt airport and whisk us away to the land of windmills and wonderful welcomes. We played through the years in almost every major city in that hospitable country, always for the same charity: the Wounded Veteran Soldiers of our allies. Of course, as ex-professional players we couldn't be expected to offer our services for nothing. Neither did we, receiving an allowance of £2 a day which enabled us to buy our delightful hosts a drink.

In Holland the matches were between ex-pros of roughly the same age, but that wasn't the case when we agreed to play two games in the Sudan, again for local charities. I can tell you, Sudan is hot. Accordingly, we selected a much younger group of international players and ex-Chelsea, Fulham and England's Roy Bentley as coach. Our back four, including Arsenal's Bob McNab, had all represented their clubs in Europe and at least eight of the team were still playing professionally. Johnny Haynes was flying in from South Africa, but arrived after the game had already begun. The Sudanese were wonderful athletes and far from stupid as footballers. They scored twice in the first twenty minutes and ran us to death; it could easily have been six. Half-time was chaotic, we needed to sort matters out, but it had to be done on the pitch. Everybody was talking at once. It took some time to get anything like silence. I took control of the situation and at last the arguing stopped, giving me the chance to reorganise the team and include Johnny, who had hardly flown up from Durban merely to watch. As I spoke, the local brass band struck up and no one could hear a word. I had done my best I felt, as Roy Bentley and I sat down to enjoy the second half. The whistle blew.

'That looks better!' I said to Roy.

'It should do,' came the reply. 'We've got twelve men on!' After suitable further adjustment we still couldn't improve on the score, but at least the game was more balanced in the second half and some reputation was restored.

The weather was so hot that it was necessary to drink water constantly. Our hosts were kindly but by our standards rather taciturn. Footballers, too, are not always forthcoming socially. We were invited to lunch on the following day and filtered into a large, cooler tent. As we sat down for the meal it became apparent that the players were not sitting together but were intermingled with their hosts, clearly identifiable in national dress. There was a certain nervousness, really shyness, from both sides resulting in an abnormally long silence. It was broken by Barnsley's Steve Kindon observing loudly in a broad Lancashire accent, 'We've been lucky with the weather, haven't we?' We drew the second game in a much better performance and went home happy.

Around that time in the early seventies, I was approached by Doug Insole on behalf of the Isthmian League to recommend ways to encourage attacking football, sportsmanship and good behaviour, to attract better attendances and also to promote improved levels of refereeing – no mean task. A sponsor was sought to underwrite the project and before long Rothmans accepted the idea in principle awaiting my final recommendations.

It was a heaven-sent opportunity to try out some theories I had developed, but which could only be proved by putting them into practice. The first was the concept of three points for a win and one for a draw, the origination of the system that has now been adopted by almost every league in every country in the world as well as by UEFA and FIFA. I wanted an additional financial incentive for a clear win by three goals or more, the idea being to discourage a defensive mentality at all times even for a team leading by a goal or two. There were other extensions of this principle, which I put before the Football League clubs after they had adopted the basic idea years later, without success, but nothing has changed my belief in the logic behind them, and the ultimate beneficial effect for a spectator.

To improve discipline a financial carrot termed the 'Sportsmanship Pool' was created. In order to share in it, at a season's end a team must not have amassed eight disciplinary points (four for a sending-off and one for a caution). As it happened, that seemingly small incentive cut down offences radically and not one player was sent off in any game during the first season and the total number of cautions was reduced from sixty to thirty. Retrospectively, I'm not suggesting for one moment that £10,000 per week or more current players would change their way of life for a mess of pottage; I'm only pointing out that it worked then and professional players tend to respond to all challenges of any kind. So who knows? It was so successful in fact that not only did the Isthmian League go for it, but the Western League and the Northern League soon joined in under Rothmans' umbrella. The sponsors' message continued to inspire more goals, fewer fouls and higher standards of sportsmanship.

Although the promotion died in England after a few years, it survived for many years afterwards in the Channel Islands. Whatever tobacco has done to harm the world, it's strange that it was Rothmans' promotion that proved three points to be a winner. It might provoke some to ask why such an idea flourished outside the illustrious portals of the governing bodies for so long. I wonder how many other such embryonic ideas do not penetrate football's parliaments and consequently never see the light of day?

14

TRANSFERRING
TO THE BBC

Dᴜʀɪɴɢ late 1972 and early 1973, Bagenal Harvey was exploring possibilities at the BBC on my behalf. I had also set up my own sports consultancy, Jimmy Hill Limited, and was busy pursuing and investigating potential business opportunities for myself, including the link with Rothmans and the Isthmian League.

At ITV, the hugely popular 'Big Match' was still only a regional programme – the Midlands and North had scarcely heard of it – whereas 'Match of the Day' reached the whole nation.

In the New Year it became clear that the BBC was ready to double my salary at least, but in return for two or three times my current on-screen workload – £22,000 was a sum floated in the press, causing a certain Mr Arthur Lewis, the Labour MP for West Ham North, to urge the Government to impose a standstill order to prevent the BBC making such an offer. It seemed a funny old world at the time. I certainly wasn't born wealthy and had given pretty good value for money, I felt, as a stock exchange clerk, a player for Brentford and Fulham, a manager with Coventry and as a senior executive and on-screen performer for LWT. I hardly thought I was short-changing society. Restoring my faith in the credibility and sanity of politicians, the Minister of State for Employment dismissed the appeal.

As with Coventry City, my five-year journey with LWT had been a joyful ride: masses of teething troubles in house and with the ITV network, but they only magnified the satisfaction we gleaned from LWT's eventual salvation and achievements. In thanking me, bidding me farewell and wishing good luck for the future, John Freeman, LWT's chairman, was courtesy itself. We were all indebted to him for bringing stability and direction to the company in its hour of critical need.

I was to start with the BBC the next season, September 1973, leaving me with time to fill in other directions.

In April, following a meeting with Sir Andrew Stephen, the chairman, and Ted Croker, the new secretary, I was appointed commercial consultant to the Football Association, yet another first, I imagine. It marked the beginning of a change of attitude from the council, realising that the costs of administering such an enormously popular national game were not going to stand still. Such costs were largely underwritten by income from international competitions and friendly matches, so qualification for a share of the World Cup pool was essential, never mind the reflected glory. Someone must have had a premonition that Sir Alf Ramsey's team were not going to qualify for the finals of the World Cup in Germany in 1974 because the Association, urged on by Ted Croker, had woken up to the facts of future financial salvation.

One time-consuming ambition which I was asked to put my mind to was to find the means to fund a wholly owned national coaching centre. The FA then, as they do now, used both the National Recreation Centre at Lilleshall and Bisham Abbey for a wide variety of training courses and other activities, including get togethers for the England team. The ambition, still to be achieved, was to own one's own home.

We spent a fair amount of time considering Annersley Hall, near Mansfield, but the enthusiasm slowly petered out as the potential cost escalated and hopes that the Moores family of pools fame might underwrite such a venture never matured further than friendly overtures and responses. Because of the structure of the FA, the ultimate power lay in the hands of the ninety councillors, and it was not a simple matter to act on their behalf. In the autumn of 1974, following agreement reached at its summer meetings, the FA announced that it was to go commercial and offer the FA Cup and the Home International Championships to the world of potential sponsors. Before these matters could be brought to fruition, however, the summer arrived and with it the Saudi Arabian adventure (of which more later), as a result of which the FA agreed to terminate our relationship.

I also agreed to help my old club Fulham develop their off-the-field activities, largely because I'm very bad at saying 'no' when asked. Perhaps it is because I'm flattered and thus susceptible, and if that's a weakness, I own up to it. It has meant, though, that I've spent little of my life sitting on my backside. If that is a fault, it is to my family that I should go to ask forgiveness.

We set up a Supporters' Club for all those fans who wanted to play a more helpful role for the club than just attending matches. 'Fulham Fanatics' was to be their title, but Tommy Trinder thought that would suggest rowdyism and thus 'Friends of Fulham' was born. I tried very hard to avoid the recurring thought that it sounded like a Provident Society but as we all know 'a rose by any other name would smell as sweet'. What I was able to do was to persuade Don Durbridge, a smooth professional broadcaster, to be the host on match days and present a sophisticated image to our public.

We began negotiation with the local council to develop the Hammersmith end into a combination of seated stand, penthouses and flats, including a sports centre for club and public use. Don't ask me why we failed to get planning consent. Such decisions will always remain a mystery to me in a democratic society.

We arranged a friendly with the Brazilian team Santos and their world superstar, Pelé. As you can imagine, it was some occasion at the Cottage and a healthy crowd awaited the kick-off. Unfortunately there was a last-minute danger that the game would not take place because the Santos officials, having seen the size of the crowd, were seeking a revision of the contract. Eventually agreement was reached and the game took place. I wasn't there but learned afterwards that customs officers at London Airport caused the Brazilian party to miss their overnight plane by examining their baggage in minute detail. I never found out whether there was any connection between those events or whether it was purely coincidental.

The summer of 1973 flew by and although in some ways I felt on top of the world, I was not totally at ease with the prospect of fronting 'Match of the Day'. As a performer at LWT, I merely played the pundit to Brian Moore's programme host, in itself a much simpler task than the one for which the BBC was to pay me a not insubstantial sum. Such programme hosts, even in those days, were underpinned by a device called the 'autocue'. You would write out your opening lines beforehand, and these would be rolled at the appropriate speed before one's very eyes, large as life to the reader but invisible to the viewer – an essential piece of equipment for newsreaders as well as Her Majesty the Queen for her Christmas Day message, and even politicians use it for their party political broadcasts. I used to joke that in their case it was essential, otherwise they would not remember what it was they believed in! Joking's fine but the dreaded first programme approached as our summer holidays came to an end. I would need to master the art of reading autocue, with ten million pairs of eyes scrutinising my performance.

Before I appeared in a BBC programme, Sam Leitch, the Head of Sport who doubled up as a presenter of 'Football Preview', thought it would be a good idea for me to meet a certain Jonathan Martin, who was to be the editor of 'Match of the Day' for the coming season. An apparent favourite haunt, Arlecchino's in Notting Hill Gate, was chosen as the perfect place for a 'get to know each other' lunch. Sam was most anxious that we should hit it off for obvious reasons and accordingly was most liberal in his attitude to ordering, distributing and drinking wine. I'm not at all sure that I was in Sam's league, but I'm quite certain that Jonathan was not within a distance of either of us. In his defence, he competed nobly and the concluding picture that stays in my mind is of his holding on firmly to the lamp-post outside the restaurant whilst trying to bid his colleagues farewell. In practice he was not only a competitive and helpful editor, but moved on to be controller of sport, a fitting reward if ever there was one for surviving that original unforgettable liquid lunch.

On the first day of the season, I turned up at Lime Grove studios in the morning before travelling to the chosen match later. I brought with me my favourite suit, which was in reasonable condition but for my first BBC programme perhaps a last-minute press would achieve perfection. I asked Sam Leitch where I could get it ironed. In one sentence Sam brought home the bitter truth of the battle the BBC, with its carefully controlled licence fee, faced, and still does, in competing against the commercial companies.

'I'm afraid we've got nobody here who can do that,' Sam confessed. 'Why don't you take it to the cleaners?'

'Don't worry,' I said, 'I'll get it done when I pop home after the match.' Whatever the BBC's position in those days, it's become much, much worse now as the major sporting events are slowly ripped away from its repertoire by the greedy fingers of commercialism. I must confess, in my heady excitement I was oblivious to that underlying trend.

It was something of a shock for viewers outside the London franchise area to see my face regularly on Saturday night; even more so as the programme format called for me to spend a few minutes analysing the game the viewers had just seen. What has now become commonplace startled some, both within the game and outside it. I also did not realise until some years later, when it was pointed out by Jonathan Martin, that I had adopted a role in television sport which was unique and still remains unusual. Before I fronted 'Match of the Day', no performer had doubled up as both presenter and analyst. From 1973 until 1989, when the BBC lost the contract, that was how we operated. I would host the show as well as analyse single-handed, with forceful opinions, if they were called for, concerning the main match. Barry Davies or Bob Wilson read the news.

This turned out to be a double-edged sword. Not surprisingly, football writers did not necessarily welcome such a powerful voice, not always in agreement with their printed versions of events and who had the pictures to prove otherwise. The Sunday newspapers particularly did not enjoy their star sportswriters' views being dissected with surgical precision hours ahead of publication – who would? Therefore any fault which could be found with their aggravating rival would reinforce their campaign to prove that they were the voices that really mattered. I understood their antagonism only too well. They were joined, sometimes as allies, by directors and managers of clubs, to say nothing of wounded referees, who did not like the look of unflattering pictures, nor the sound of the bearded know-all who interpreted them.

I shared and sympathised with their problem. In those days I wrote a match report of the BBC's selected game for the *News of the World*. It was then thought essential for me to be at the match before scurrying back to Lime Grove to present the programme. This meant that before driving, catching a plane or taking a train, I needed to telephone my match copy through to the paper like any journalist, not having the luxury of checking the accuracy of any controversial happenings on videotape. The danger was, of course, that I might well be right on Saturday night and score an obvious own goal in Sunday's paper. Under such strain I confess there were times when in print I hedged my bets a touch. . .

Becoming acquainted with the laws of the game early, having coached as a relatively young professional player, proved a sound foundation. When controversial situations occur, if a person has a knowledge of the laws and lengthy experience of the nature and habits of professional players, nearly always his brain tells him on which side to come down. In addition, with the aid of slow-motion replay the truth almost inevitably emerges. Some do not appreciate it! The outcome is that an honest critic, searching for the truth and ready to proclaim it, is never likely to become universally popular, but I sleep reasonably well at night.

Stan Seymour of Newcastle United, Jimmy Adamson of Burnley and Malcolm Macdonald were early protesters about the new format which with words and pictures both condemned and praised the actions of players. Many supporters, too, did not like to hear their favourite players and chosen teams accused of unprofessional conduct or even of being dismal entertainers.

Envy in some cases played its part, too. Those less well-off souls who had read of my supposed salary ignored the fact that I was a one-off in my field at that time, leading the way in a style of broadcasting which was to become the norm, to an audience averaging over ten million people.

The BBC's contract entitled it to show only forty-five minutes of football action, the news and comments adding up to the hour. In amongst the protestations of horror at all that talk were comments from those who found an honest, professional approach to a game of football refreshing and enjoyable.

Whatever the reaction was without, within there was satisfaction. The BBC's programme review board reported, ' "Match of the Day" has gained immeasurably from the analytical ingredient so successfully introduced by Jimmy Hill during the last few weeks. People are obviously fascinated by it and there was no equivocation about the considerable extra value injected into the programme by Jimmy's linking and comment pieces.'

The above contrasted with Malcolm Macdonald's view that 'Match of the Day' could do with more action and less waffle. Since then I've noticed that Malcolm has done his share of waffling on television. Is the answer that waffling is fine, if one's doing it oneself? It's the others who overdo it. Whatever the arguments the ratings stayed high: towards twelve million at times.

It's perhaps interesting to reflect on the strong beliefs that I have consistently upheld from that day to this, underlying my editorial approach. Back in October 1973 I wrote, 'There are two things I hate in football: one is violent tackling over the top of the ball, and the other is players feigning injury and causing their professional colleagues and brother union members to be penalised by a referee. On television I can only point out the sickness, and if the guilty become ashamed then I might have done some good.' In essence, I have failed and so have others. In the case of 'diving', the recruitment of so many foreign players has turned a disease into an epidemic. All parties should take their share of the blame for failing to reduce both blemishes, which are still rampant, to acceptable proportions.

For matches in the north west, the BBC would charter a four-seater plane to ferry the producer Alec Weeks, John Motson or Barry Davies and myself to a game, a luxury which cost less than £300 in those days. I enjoy flying but when it is bumpy, as you will remember, my tummy does not and I get airsick. During the flight for an Everton game one Saturday, I felt terrible and didn't know where my stomach was. When we arrived at Goodison Park, I was the colour of Everton's shorts and staggered into the restaurant looking as if I was about to die. A most kind lady suggested I should drink a port and brandy. The words made me wince, but I took her advice – twice. By three o'clock I was almost well enough to play!

As the years wore on, with videotape machines galore at the Television Centre it became advantageous to remain at HQ and view not one, but sometimes three matches simultaneously – technology had replaced reality.

Despite my increasing confidence with autocue, other little gremlins somehow slithered their way into my somewhat nervous introductions. In linking to a rugby commentator, whom I had not met, I started smoothly, 'Now we go over to Paris to join Nigel Starmer Smith,' enunciating the three names correctly. Unfortunately, I went on to say, 'who has had seven craps as a scum-half for England!'

Another clear sign of the struggle that the BBC has to make ends meet was that make-up girls, while still functioning in the studio, were withdrawn from active service on outside broadcasts. Consequently, rather than inflict shiny noses on the nation we, the chaps, soon learned to travel with brush and comb and powder compact (a natty shade of American tan). In my bearded days larger and larger quantities of black mascara were employed as the grey hairs overtook their predecessors. Latterly, programme assistant producers, secretaries and other staff double up as make-up artists even for studio programmes. It does seem incongruous that the country's national television channel cannot afford to provide professional make-up for performances which are viewed by five million or more.

On the eve of the Grand National we used to bring 'Sportswide' live from Aintree at 6.45 p.m. In 1976 it had been arranged for some strange reason for me to jump the first fence on the Grand National course, not on foot but on horseback and not alone, but alongside Terry Biddlecombe, similarly mounted. Peter O'Sullevan was to commentate.

My knees were not exactly knocking at the prospect, after all I had jumped some fairly hefty obstacles in my time, but I was on a strange animal and we were jumping in cold blood. Nevertheless, I didn't panic until just before the cameras were ready to roll when Terry said, 'Follow me!' which I did, straight into the medical tent.

'Have you got a drop?' he inquired.

'Sure,' was the reply, and two large whiskies were produced. Until that moment I had not been really worried, but to think that one of my heroes and the nation's leading National Hunt jockey needed a heart starter changed my mind. It was too late to pull out – we were given a leg up and at Terry's suggestion made our way up the Mildmay course to stretch our horses' legs. The way back, after a healthy canter, necessitated a left turn to the start of the National course. Terry turned left, my horse turned right and headed straight down a path back towards his box, narrowly missing some trusting spectators. On reaching a grass clearing surrounded by trees, I rode my new partner directly towards the widest tree I could find and sat back. He was no fool, and he stopped. I thought I might save some face if I could get him back to the start and, surprisingly, he behaved perfectly. He knew who was master. . . We were soon back with Terry, who tactfully reacted as if nothing had happened.

'All ready, then?' was all he said.

'Yes, but supposing he jumps the first and I can't stop him?' was my fearful last cry for help.

'Jump the second, but for f . . .'s sake don't try to jump the third!' were Terry's pearls of wisdom.

We both jumped the first, Terry naturally without mishap. My fellow jumped well but pecked on landing and was nearly on his knees. I just managed to avoid going over his head, at the expense of pulling a thigh muscle. Once back in the saddle, and learning from experience, I lugged my steed to the right, sat tight and challenged him to jump the rails – he didn't. Afterwards Terry cheered me up by saying, 'If you had gone over his head he'd have kicked you all the way to the second fence!' Peter O'Sullevan described my 'staying on board' as a fine piece of horsemanship, but he's a good friend!

On the train up to Liverpool that day, I had happened accidentally to meet the daughter of the American Ambassador to London. Her father owned the horse L'Escargot and as a result of our conversation I became a firm supporter of the eventual winner to the extent of venturing a small wager on him. For dinner that evening, as a surprise, I scoured Liverpool for enough snails – it doesn't sound half as good in English – to feed our table. The next day, the day of the big race, I got up at the crack of dawn to see L'Escargot, a wonderfully fit and beautiful animal, seemingly announcing to the world his pedigree, his fitness and his confidence and that he was born to be the champion of that supreme race.

Unfortunately, I had to be at Aston Villa for the FA Cup semi-final between West Ham and Ipswich. I trust the teams will forgive me, but I let my eyes stray from the football action to Aintree for long enough to cheer L'Escargot home. Time spent on research is never wasted and I knew he was a certainty once he had jumped that first horrific fence!

It seems I'm never meant to see a Grand National. For many years the FA Cup semi-finals were always on that day and the BBC always covered one of them. In 1997, though, I was at

Aintree as a guest of the BBC, at sixty-eight ready to see my first live National and you know what happened – the course was cleared, the race postponed, as the result of a bomb scare.

Apart from L'Escargot, I've not been all that lucky in Liverpool. As a player, I can remember taking part in a 0–0 draw at Anfield, overshadowed by being carried off at Goodison with minutes to go. One off-the-field happening tested my affection for the city, although a scouser was not to blame. The villain of the piece was Michael Murphy, by that time editor of 'Match of the Day' and also responsible for 'Sportswide'. It was Michael's birthday on the Thursday before the Friday programme, and we had done justice to the occasion in the time-honoured way. We were about to go to bed when a group of young ladies, one of whom was also celebrating a birthday, arrived back at the hotel. The coincidence was too good to let slip and the champagne flowed afresh in mutual congratulation.

Editor Mike had to be at Aintree in the morning, whereas I needed to arrive only an hour or so before the early evening programme. The phone rang in my room in what seemed like the middle of the night. It was Mike: could he borrow my car? It was a Jaguar XJS V12. Murph said he would send a substitute car for me later in the day. I put the key outside the door of my room, turned over and went back to sleep; not for long as it turned out. A second call came from Mike producing the news that he had had a 'slight' accident – he had driven through the wall of a prefab frightening the life out of an unsuspecting couple who were peacefully enjoying their breakfast. The sight and colour of Murph's face was bad enough, but to absorb the nose of a yellow sportscar through their window took some digesting. It said a lot for my *sang froid* that my first reaction was to ask how I would get to the semi-final on Saturday.

'Don't worry,' he consoled me. 'We'll get you a car.'

'As long as you're not bloody driving it,' I said. Not too bad a loss of temper, when you think I never saw my lovely yellow Jaguar again.

It's not easy to front a live programme for fifteen years; it's inevitable that mistakes will occur – fortunately viewers love it when that happens. As a presenter it doesn't seem quite so funny, but time heals.

One Saturday night on 'Match of the Day' way back, we had reached my closing link without mishap. Barry Davies had read the news impeccably and handed back to me.

'Just to remind you,' I said, 'before you go to sleep, don't forget to put your cocks back!' I knew I had slipped up, but determinedly carried on informing viewers of the exciting sporting fixtures coming up in the forthcoming week on BBC. I was recovering quite well until I heard Barry make a strange snort unable to contain his laughter any longer. I battled on as best I could with the prepared words until through my deaf aid and Barry's came the editor, Jonathan Martin's, voice, 'Don't be a bloody fool, Barry, it could happen to you sometime!' As a result, an Eskimo would have had a better chance of understanding my last two sentences.

As if presenting wasn't dangerous enough, away from the camera I continued to hunt and even agreed to ride in a cross-country event. I had previously carefully followed Liz and Ted Edgar, with a lady partner, over a rather tame course in a pairs competition near Coventry. After my Grand National escapade, when it was suggested that a 'Nationwide' team should enter the full-blown Everdon cross-country event, I didn't agree without feelings of trepidation, maybe even of potential disaster. Suzanne Hall and myself were the novices in the quartet, Captain Alec Jackson from the Household Cavalry and David Turner, a champion point-to-point jockey, were to be our experienced companions. Jimmy, my reliable and trusty hunter, who was only just up to my weight, was available. I had tried to find, without success, an animal more like Desert Orchid to carry me. We searched far and wide but failed and the two Jimmys had to face the challenge together. I can see the first fence now: it was a post and rails, not all that high, but made tricky because it was at the bottom of a hill which then immediately climbed upwards.

197

We were quite late off and, because of this, saw the other teams performing. Most of them treated the first difficult obstacle as if it wasn't there, but there were still some who didn't and whose race ended almost before it started. Such happenings for me were the opposite of comforting. Unfortunately, having been on site for hours, at the moment I was needed I was, and not for the first time, ensconced in the Portaloo. I heard my name called out on the loudspeakers and as I emerged a breathless Suzanne panted, 'We're next! Good heavens, you look as white as a sheet!' Just before the start an urbane James Hogg stuck a microphone under my nose.

'Are you worried about fence number fourteen?' he asked.

'That's entirely academic,' I replied. 'I shan't get that far!' To be honest, I wouldn't have known fence fourteen if it came up and hit me in the face, but ignorance was bliss.

By that time I had magnified the degree of difficulty at the first jump tenfold. We scrambled over it in ungainly fashion, but were still together trundling up the hill. The Captain and David Turner soon forged ahead, but I had them in sight until neither Jimmy nor I could find a way over a sticky uphill jump which had to be done in two stages. At the point where I thought we would fail miserably I kicked on just once more and we made it – no points for style but we were back in the race. The next five minutes were as exhilarating as any on a football field. There was a line of fences – stout hedges – on flat ground and we flew over them like champions. In the thrill I had forgotten my team-mates – Captain Alec and David were far ahead and Sue a touch behind me. So pleased was I that I had also forgotten that the time that counted was the one scored by the third member of each team – me in other words. So a very tired person and an equally tired horse (think what he had endured!) gritted our teeth and staggered on up the hill again and over the last two fences, which by that time seemed larger than Becher's Brook, and on to the finish. I had never been as exhausted in my life and could hardly speak, but for 'Nationwide' cameras I described the experience – 'Just wonderful!'

Another challenge which I accepted during my 'Sportswide' days was to join in a different type of horsepower altogether, a kids' 'mini stox' race at Aldershot, the third annual BBC competition. I was to be 'miked' up, with a camera in the car. Unlike the other Hills, I was not born to drive fast, although I have covered thousands of miles in over fifty years on the roads. I borrowed a souped up Mini from Derek Warwick to race against youngsters round a mini racetrack, bumping and boring all part of the fun.

Unfortunately, it was a wet day and the practice runs I was supposed to have were limited to two. My newly introduced, unnamed mentor said, 'See how you go?' I roared off, foot down, frightening the life out of myself, completed the circuit and stopped.

'How's that?' I inquired. A shake of the head was not encouraging. I put my foot down harder and lapped again, even more determined, only to be confronted by a second helping of discouraging head shaking. That was my warm-up. Fifteen minutes later I was among a hefty field revving up for all I was worth and swish, the flag came down. Off we all roared and I was contentedly holding a place in the middle of the pack, when on a bend a mischievous and fearless young competitor knocked me, or rather the car, for six. By a miracle it wasn't six and out! I was furious, lost control completely, stuck my foot on the accelerator, swore into the mike and competed – aggression had replaced fear. Remarkably, I finished third – in a grand prix that's four points, and I felt like Damon. There was a small trophy for third place with which I was presented. As I was leaving a cheeky young lad said, 'It's not fair. I should have had that prize. You're too old!'

'Well, you're not getting it!' I said. 'You'll get the chance to win another, I won't!'

Despite the result, those who had seen me race would have known that I was not in any way related to Graham or Damon. I know from the number of letters I have received over the years that it has been the topic of debate in more than one pub, but in spite of a certain facial resemblance to Hill Senior, I am not part of the family. The similarity can lead to embarrassing confusion as it did once at a party hosted by Douglas Bunn after the Silk Cut Derby. A pretty lady approached me. . .

Chatting merrily she finished relating a story against herself when she had once mistaken Dickie Davies for Desmond Lynam. Pausing, she looked up at me and said, 'Tell me, just how fast have you driven?'

I looked down at the diminutive blonde actress who had posed the question. I admit that for once in my life I had no instant reply. I realised immediately and only too well whom she believed me to be, but it was finding the way to let her down gently that temporarily evaded me. 'Situational etiquette' Sir Bernard Audley called it. However, in order to find some thinking time, I did inform her that I once had to drive at a substantial speed in order to catch a ferry at Calais. She looked at me blankly. I remained speechless. I saw from her expression in the advancing evening gloom that the penny had dropped. The poor girl had done it again. Suffice it to say that on leaning back, embarrassed, her stiletto heels sank into the damp grass as she uttered a few choice Anglo-Saxon expletives. My responsibility as a gentleman prevents me from repeating them.

15

BACK TO COVENTRY

WHILE I was regaling 'Match of the Day' viewers with forthright opinions, Alec Stock, Fulham's talented and articulate manager, was making significant progress with the team to the extent that in 1975 they reached the Cup final. I was at Wembley with the BBC, remaining stoically neutral, but by that time I had parted company with Fulham to take up what I considered an irresistible offer to return to Coventry City as unpaid managing director. Saying yes again wasn't without its problems. Helping Fulham commercially was one thing, being proclaimed MD of a first division club was another. The world was entitled to question my neutrality as a broadcaster. I pointed out that I was earning a very comfortable living from the game of football. I could just take it and put nothing back, whereas helping Coventry was one way in which I could balance the account. Of course, there were those who were ready to pounce given the opportunity, and not giving anyone a chance to point an unfair finger at me during those seven years, or afterwards as a director of Charlton and chairman of Fulham, was professionally satisfying.

There was one extraordinary happening when Coventry were at home to Crystal Palace. I was at Highfield Road in the stand watching the game. A powerful header from a Palace striker hit the roof of the net and bounced down to be cleared hurriedly by Coventry's Mick Coop, seemingly off the line. The game proceeded and no goal was given. Fair play, I thought, that injustice is going to be seen by ten million people tonight, what can I do? Instinctively, I thought of rushing down and trying to restore justice. Calming down, I realised that, even if incorrect, the referee's decision had to be final. Supposing the position had been reversed, the referee would have rightly ignored my protest or anyone else's for that matter and stuck to his decision. On 'Match of the Day' later that night I had to reveal the truth to the world, though not to lucky Coventry – they knew!

In general the feeling had been that the Sky Blues were going nowhere, gates were down, results were unexciting and the diminishing crowd was losing confidence. Jack Scamp, the chairman, approached me in 1975 and asked me to join the board and once again the ingrained temptation to say yes took over. Anyway, I was never going to refuse a request to help the Sky Blues, with whom I had enjoyed over five such wonderful years, nor turn down my first chance to be a director of a Football League club. At the same time, I wanted to contribute positively in any way I could. Obviously I would not see the vast majority of matches, only the occasional midweek fixture, so there was no way I could be of real help teamwise, even if I had wished to be. My extensive commitments to the BBC as well as my growing consultancy work saw to that. Therefore the best contribution I could make was in advice and direction. As a result, the first unpaid managing director in Football League history was appointed. It was soon evident that news of the appointment had begun to rekindle the enthusiasm of those halcyon days in the sixties and in order to foster that attitude the club wanted to show that I was fully involved. Gordon Milne, the team manager, registered a certain perplexity and uneasiness at the change but before long he was able to reflect on a relationship based on understanding, support and positively no interference.

It wasn't easy being managing director of a club which was going to struggle to hold on to its place in the first division. Never mind the

51,500 who witnessed the match against Wolverhampton, the winning of which put them there, the average crowds since those years varied between thirteen and seventeen thousand. If there is a multi-millionaire prepared to underwrite a club's financial needs come what may, as Jack Walker does at Blackburn Rovers, a club can defy or make its own football gravity. There was no such person at Coventry and we had to cut our cloth according to our purse. At the same time, we had to hold on to that privileged, hard-won place in the future Premier League sun. Coventry supporters were the salt of the earth during those magical years in the sixties. We had our ups and downs but I came to know them well and they were part of my life. That did not mean, though, that their attitude was any better than any other club's supporters when their team was losing. They attacked the players, the manager and the board if it appeared to be doing nothing at all about the situation – such as spending money on other club's rejects. The fact remains that if every Premier League club spent its annual income equally wisely, Coventry would always be in the bottom six.

It may not be the case in the future, because of Bosman, but then the only workable policy was to recruit and train the best young players, knowing that some would have to be sold. The fees obtained for them would go towards paying wages healthy enough to keep the talented players needed to cling on to a place in the Premier League. You can create and invest in a youth policy overnight, but unfortunately the rewards do not arrive with the milkman the next morning. These days the milkman doesn't arrive at all, but then such a policy, if successful, could in time keep a club both solvent and competitive. Surely, you may well ask, if supporters are told those basic facts of their club's life they will understand, have patience and encourage the directors, manager and players even more, aware of the tightrope that is being walked. No, No, NO is the answer. The majority of people who follow football clubs do not want to be bothered with facts, excuses or explanations. Rumour and hearsay hold sway; they want a winning team and they don't care who pays for it or when his or her money runs out.

Initially, we splashed out £300,000 in the transfer market, backing Gordon Milne's judgement to bring in John Beck, Terry Yorath, Bobby McDonald and a little Scottish gem, Ian Wallace. We were able to spend that money as the result of a fanatical supporter who made the club an interest-free loan for such a purpose. The loan, together with the expected sale of Tommy Hutchison (which didn't happen), was meant to balance the books, as was the later transfer of David Cross to West Ham for £125,000, and Jimmy Holmes to Spurs for £120,000.

In 1977, in the same April week as Jim Blyth, our keeper, tore his knee ligaments we extended Gordon Milne's contract for a further two years. As usual, success-hungry supporters were baying for the manager's blood, without any regard for the bad luck which had made his job a nightmare. In the previous December, City was tenth in the table before a devastating crop of injuries rocked the boat, among them the young leading scorer Mick Ferguson, out for eight weeks with ankle ligament damage, and talented Ian Wallace, who was out for a similar period following a car crash. Can anyone explain why a board of directors takes account of such misfortune in making its judgements, to say nothing of fair play and decency, whereas on such issues, football supporters far and wide seem oblivious to reasoning and seem to regard a good, old-fashioned hatchet job as the answer to every problem? Chairman Jack Scamp pointed out that nine first division clubs had changed their managers in the last two years and were still in the bottom half of the table.

That season, 1976–77, the Sky Blues survived by a whisker following a 2–2 draw with fellow relegation candidates, Bristol City, as fate would have it, managed by Alan Dicks, my assistant manager at Coventry over a decade before. Stoke City and Tottenham were already relegated. Sunderland, who were away to Everton on the same evening, Bristol City and Coventry all had 34 points. One club had to go down. Any team which won would be safe. If points were level as a result of draws, Coventry had the worst goal average and Sunderland the best. Nearly 37,000 spectators turned up for the match and at kick-off time many

204

of them were still outside. In his wisdom, the referee delayed kick-off fractionally, not more than five minutes, so the game started late. This didn't seem to deter the home team as the Sky Blues led by 2–0 in the second half, and a loss would have relegated Bristol City on goal average. Bravely they fought back and as the game's end approached were drawing 2–2. A goal by either side would have relegated their opponents.

What happened next was that the players on both sides slowed down their pace; it was obvious that they knew that Sunderland had lost, having picked up the 2–0 result from supporters close to the action. There were quite a few following Sunderland's fate throughout on their transistor radios. Not surprisingly, and unfairly as it turned out, neither the Coventry nor Bristol City players tried to score during the last few minutes of the game. Whilst some of the crowd were aware of the good news, others were in ignorance and my action in pressing Radio Sky Blues' host to deliver the vital result to the whole stadium was misunderstood by those who didn't want to hear the truth. The inescapable fact was that the players had been going through the motions for a minute or two before the news was broadcast. Since it was such vital and welcome news for almost everyone at the ground, the sooner it was conveyed the sooner the relief and joy would be felt – what theatre, what drama, what entertainment! Radio Sky Blue had been broadcasting relevant football news during matches since 1961. Surely it would have been strange to change that policy at such a dramatic time, when only the players and some spectators knew the truth?

The events that followed were interesting to say the least. The referee confirmed that it was solely his decision to delay the kick-off and the club was not concerned in any way. Not surprisingly, Sunderland supporters were angry, feeling that they had been short-changed, not really wanting to accept that if their team had earned even a draw on that day, they would have stayed up and Coventry would have gone down

The matter would have ended there had not Alan Hardaker, the league secretary, written to the club reprimanding them on their part in the events of the evening. The Coventry board's response was to put the matter in legal hands, not feeling any guilt whatsoever either legal or moral. 'We want this decision rescinded and the stain removed from Coventry's name,' the board wrote. It wasn't long before we were invited to attend a formal meeting with the Football League and Chairman Jack Dunnett, a solicitor himself. We were simply asked to explain the happenings on that fateful night, which we did without any embarrassment. They thanked us for taking the trouble to attend and for providing the Football League with our account of what took place. It was accepted that we had acted with propriety and the matter was buried.

It was hardly surprising that Alan Hardaker and I should not appreciate each other's efforts to do what we believed was right for the game. We were different animals. It was perhaps more surprising that Derek Dougan, at that time chairman of the PFA, and fellow ITV panellist in 1970, should pour vitriol on me personally. The Football League and the PFA had been negotiating for some time over the procedure to take place at the end of a player's contract. The right of a player to leave a club at the end of a contract had been conceded by the Football League negotiators in 1961, yet afterwards not accepted by the clubs. As a result of the Eastham case, which came to court in 1964, that freedom was indelibly written into the laws of the land which have not changed. Now the argument was about how that freedom could be exercised within the regulations of the Football League whilst maintaining a club's right to contest what it believed its player to be worth. For some reason, the majority of clubs were in favour of conceding the current PFA claim, but Sir William Dugdale of Aston Villa and Sir Jack Scamp of Coventry, stood firmly by their convictions. They were not against the players' freedom to move, providing there was adequate and fair compensation. The proposition to impose artificial levels of compensation, which the clubs were supporting, would have meant that if the Sky Blues had sold Larry Lloyd at the end of his contract they would have received only £100,000 having paid a hefty £240,000 for him. I had the advantage, or disadvantage if you like, of looking at it through mercenary eyes. I knew what it was like to be on both sides of the fence and I was now on the paying side. For the first time for some years, Coventry City's balance sheet actually balanced.

As in 1961, there were forceful threats of a strike and a date fixed, 10 September 1977. However, the clubs met on 2 September at the Café Royal and accepted the amendment proposed by the Midlands clubs and the complicated compensation formula bit the dust. Alan Hardaker announced, 'At the end of his contract, a player can now say that no matter what he is offered, if he chooses, nothing can stop him joining another club. If there is a dispute about the fee, it will be resolved by an independent tribunal.'

That freedom was exactly what was negotiated by Cliff Lloyd and me on behalf of the players in 1961, and at last, sixteen years later, a system had arrived through which it could be exercised. Such a tribunal system has survived well, and despite criticism, still functions in part even after Bosman. It's still possible, and for heaven's sake essential if clubs are to be encouraged to develop young talent, for a player to be retained until the age of twenty-four. For them, in the pursuit of sanity, the tribunal system will still function. It's inevitable, though, that a young player some-where, sometime will be persuaded to take on the system legally, without a modicum of concern for the effect it will have. Clubs will offer any youngster looking like a potential superstar a long, long contract and save the money they now spend on nurturing the rest for transfer fees.

Meanwhile, back at Highfield Road, the next season, 1977–78, was far more restful and most enjoyable in a playing sense. Ray Graydon from Aston Villa was the only newcomer, but with last season's injury problems behind them the team and results were unrecognisable. The team finished seventh, scoring seventy-five goals, with Wallace and Ferguson scoring forty between them. In March, eighteen-year-old Gary Gillespie was signed from Falkirk for £75,000 and soon became the youngest captain in British football.

The 1978–79 season was far less exciting, not helped again by injuries. Through our American contacts we managed to get Steve Hunt cheaply from New York Cosmos, but Gary Thompson broke his leg in training and Mike Ferguson was again missing for a long period. It was then that we made the boldest of bids for Birmingham City's Trevor Francis, the first million pound player, but were defeated by the silky tongue of Brian Clough who was able to promise Trevor the chance to earn European glory.

Nevertheless, a respectable tenth, a point behind Manchester United, was far from a disgrace. Unfortunately, in the following season a miserable fifteenth place was bad enough, but losing to Blackburn Rovers in the FA Cup was not a high-flying performance. Despite those results and the grumbles about players who had left, there was a nucleus of considerable young talent emerging. Ferguson and Wallace were being supplanted by Gary Thompson and Mark Hateley, Danny Thomas, Les Sealey, Gary Bannister, Brian 'Harry' Roberts, Paul Dyson and others. It's true that certain star players were sold, just as others were bought. For Coventry and similar clubs to compete in the Premier League with a fraction of the income of wealthier rivals, they will always need to be successful traders. I had managed it, despite its unpopularity, years before with Bly and Hudson. Gordon Milne wasn't far off the mark in getting the best price for a player at the right time. Dennis Mortimer was the only one to spoil his record, being sold relatively cheaply as it turned out. He went on to become an Aston Villa hero, captaining them to the European Cup and playing for England. I don't begrudge Dennis his success for a moment, although it promoted a festering sore for us and eventually for Gordon. It's a tough fact of life that never mind how many successful deals a manager pulls off, it's the one that turns out disadvantageously that's remembered.

16

SAUDI ARABIAN KNIGHTS

M Y involvement with Coventry second time around coincided with the busiest and perhaps the most extraordinary part of my professional life, as Jimmy Hill Limited, my consultancy, took off. Three points for a win was flourishing with the Isthmian League, the Football Association had opened its doors to commercialism, Fulham had reached Wembley and, last but not least, I took a telephone call from a Mr Ian Fraser, asking for a meeting.

He had been commissioned to build a state of the art football stadium in Riyadh, the capital of Saudi Arabia. His contact was Prince Faisal bin Fahad bin Abdul Aziz, the son of the Crown Prince, with whom he had been meeting to discuss the project. The subject of the standard of Saudi football was broached and the Prince revealed his ambitions to accelerate his country's climb up the world football ladder. Initially that would mean becoming the leading team in the Gulf, above their historic rivals Kuwait and the intrinsically more powerful Iraqis. The thought was that an inspirational coach, manager or Messiah might be found to bring these ambitions to fruition but in double quick time. Prince Faisal asked Ian whether he could think of an Englishman who might measure up to the task.

When he arrived back in London, Ian, whom I didn't know

from Adam, contacted me. He suggested that, if I was interested, a meeting in Saudi Arabia could be arranged. It was an appealing idea. Just to be invited to that enigmatic country, the centre of the Islamic world, was exciting; to be given the chance to meet the Saudis and advise them on my subject even more so. It was too good a trip to turn down, despite my ever-increasing commitments. I booked and paid for my own ticket, assuming an independence (Dad's legacy again) which proved invaluable.

I really had no idea at all what I was going to find. Previous trips to Kuwait and the Sudan to play football were not quite the same as beginning a relationship, maybe a professional one, with a son of the next King.

On the fateful day, at the appointed time I was in position outside HRH's office in Riyadh, waiting a touch longer than was comfortable. After the usual introductions, I found the Prince to be a gentleman of considerable charm and passionate enthusiasm for the game of football, and even more enthusiasm for his country to improve its status in the Arab and world football scene. I had carried out some hasty research and established that there was very little organised coaching apart from the various national teams in their age groups. If a job was to be done, a major coaching programme would have to be structured, organised and fulfilled. I learned from the Prince of their intention to improve facilities at all levels, despite the climatic difficulties and immense cost. I was told of a master £25 million plan to create stadia, training camps and programmes comparable with any in the world. They would be in need of considerable expertise in staffing such enterprises. Ian Fraser was to supervise the building programme and the suggestion was that I might be able to mastermind the training sector.

Our conversation lasted for over two hours, which upset the Prince's schedule, but at its conclusion I promised to construct a blueprint and, if it was acceptable to the Prince and the Saudi Football Federation, to put it into practice. My ideas were accepted and at a rate of knots I formed World Sports Academy (WSA), persuading John Camkin, old friend and director of

Coventry City, to head up a team of talented young entrepreneurs with coaching, teaching and organising skills. We advertised and interviewed for the various posts, numbering over twenty, including the most vital task of all, finding a team manager who could inspire the Saudis to win the Gulf Cup, or at least beat their rivals Kuwait.

Finding a manager who was not only acceptable to us, but who would excite the Saudis, was not a simple task. History confirms that in that precarious occupation good men are scarce and most probably contracted, whereas those available have most probably recently fallen by the wayside; the Saudis would certainly not respect or pay handsomely for somebody else's cast off. The chosen person had to have what it takes to do a difficult job, not in Southampton or Sunderland but in Saudi Arabia. Of the limited possibilities, Bill McGarry was almost the only available candidate who measured up to the task. I'd known and respected him from his playing days. Apart from his skill as a player and record as a coach and manager, I was aware of his strict attitude to training, fitness and performance. If he overplayed that hand, I reckoned on John Camkin's diplomatic intervention to heal any wounds.

Getting results is never a simple matter; neither is getting the world to understand them. The least a coach can expect is that the critics wait to vent their spleen on their unfortunate targets until failure rears its ugly head. For some reason, perhaps the £25 million splashed in headlines, there wasn't the warmest of welcomes from some elements in Saudi for Bill McGarry. Mostly it appeared to emanate from the national press, perhaps trying to make him feel at home. . . In fact, one of the biggest immediate problems we encountered was the complete distrust and hostility of almost the entire Saudi national press. The £25 million contract reported in the British press – a wildly exaggerated figure – gave the Saudi press the expectation that our company, if paid such an enormous sum, would produce results. After our initial training camp for the national team in July 1976, we drew with Iraq at home in a World Cup qualifier. The impatient Saudi press were quick to declare, 'the British have completely failed to improve our football team's standard', and that 'the trip to London was in vain'. The SAFF (Saudi Arabian Football Federation), for whom WSA effectively worked, were very much like the board of directors of a Football League club, pressurised constantly by the press criticising their coaches' and teams' performances. It was difficult to understand the level of hostility to our attempts to help the Saudis climb to a higher rung of the world football ladder. Whether in victory or defeat, there was an unjustifiable xenophobic backlash. This criticism was instrumental in the early departure of Bill McGarry from the Saudi scene.

Anybody who knows Bill will tell you he would have done his best, but they would also know that he would not necessarily react by turning the other cheek to what he judged unfair and ignorant criticism of his stewardship. Whatever anyone said at the time or since, Bill McGarry was the first person to acquaint the Saudi players, and indeed the Princes, with the undeniable fact that, if success was to be achieved in competition with the rest of the world, strict discipline in preparation and performance was essential. They could not have made the considerable progress they have accomplished since in reaching the World Cup finals, without having taken that fundamental McGarry message to heart.

Unless he achieved results beyond the capability of his players, confrontation was inevitable and Bill had enough personal courage to argue his case with anyone. It was a situation that could not last for long and in the end in November 1977 Bill returned to England, a wiser, but slightly better off, victim of circumstance.

Life in Saudi Arabia then was a complete culture shock for all our British coaches and administrators. Arrival at Riyadh Airport in 1976 provided a taste of what was to become an everyday administrative reality for coaches and staff – the wait to get any task done. In those days, there was no air conditioning at Riyadh Airport, and two hours in immigration was normal. Any loss of temper would result in clampdown and utter non-cooperation.

The construction of a modern city was just getting under way; it is unrecognisable now, but in 1976 we were faced with an almost feudal bureaucracy. The Saudis were importing, and paying handsomely, sophisticated operators to build a state of the art country with spectacular hotels, airports, hospitals, houses and offices. Many parts of Riyadh resembled a huge building site and it was into this strange world that we ventured in August 1976, armed with interpreters and some paid local advisers.

Still, by Christmas 1976 our employees were comfortably housed, with cars and Saudi driving licences, and the company was established. Saudi officials had to approve minute items of expenditure and the process was not only tedious but time-consuming. We wanted to work at a western pace but by 1977 had realised the meaning of *bukar enshala* – tomorrow God willing. 'Will the Prince come in to work today to sign the papers?' was greeted with a polite smile, a shrug of the shoulders and an invitation to drink *tcha*, Arab tea. The pace of life could not be forced, one either adapted or took the plane home. Sometimes it was impossible to achieve an urgent administrative task without a payment of *bakshish*, and a local Mr Fixit, usually Lebanese, was a vital ingredient to the smooth running of any foreign company. Riyadh was full of Korean, American and European conglomerates all chasing the most profitable construction contracts of the century.

David Icke, ex-Coventry City goalkeeper, former BBC presenter and later self-proclaimed Son of God, was an early company casualty. Often tearful, he found it impossible to adjust to the Moslem environment without his family, and was soon on the Saudi Air flight back to London. Encouraged by healthy bank accounts, the rest of our employees successfully struggled to come to terms with life. Wives and girlfriends were not allowed and things were made just bearable by the construction of a squash court and by regular gatherings of expatriates, aided by the occasional sample of home-made beer and wine – all non-alcoholic, of course. Saudi Arabia was, and still is, a dry country.

During 1977 we established permanent coaching and admin-

213

istration bases in Jeddah and Dhahran on the east and west coasts of the Kingdom. The principal behind this action was to search for talent for the national team and to build for the future by establishing a structured coaching and training programme for the Saudi Under-19 and Under-16 players. Jack Burkett and John Manning were among the group of coaches we assembled to give Saudi youth players an opportunity that had hitherto been denied them – to receive first-class coaching and training. Our coaches selected the best players in both age groups to represent their country at international level. We had to build for the future whilst at the same time attempting a 'sticking plaster' job with the current national team.

The standard of the national league was not good enough to test the best Saudi players on a regular basis. The most talented of them could perform to seventy-five per cent of their ability in the majority of league matches and so developed, in Bill McGarry's words, 'lazy habits'. The paradoxical situation World Sports Academy were in was that our performance as a company was not to be judged on the basis of the results we achieved with our worthwhile youth programmes, but on current national team results against countries like Iraq, Iran and Morocco who were ten to fifteen years ahead of the Saudis in terms of coaching programmes. Their national leagues were much stronger. Whilst the Saudi Arabian Football Federation paid lip service to our youth programmes and encouraged them, they were under constant pressure from the press and their princely peers to achieve results after their disappointing performance in the last Gulf Games. In particular, they accepted that Iran and Iraq were ahead of them and defeat at national level was most likely and excusable. However, losing to Kuwait, as they had done in the last Gulf Games, was a national humiliation and disgrace. The success of WSA would be judged on our ability to confront successfully Kuwait, Qatar and the Emirates at the Gulf Games in April 1979.

Accordingly, during 1977 and 1978, the Saudis were not concerned with eighty per cent of WSA's work – organising the training and coaching of youth – but were obsessed with the performance of the national team. We strongly recommended creating grass pitches – there being only one in Riyadh. All international competitions were played on grass; the two stadia in Saudi Arabia were made of Astroturf. We tried to give them the best possible advice on how to build an enduring pyramid of soccer programmes. In practice, we could not organise a summer camp without written approval. We had no autonomy as a company. We were advisers to, not the replacements for, the Saudi Arabian Football Federation. We recommended action – then waited for the Saudis to implement it at their own pace, often slow or very slow. They were charming people in many ways, but not at that time proactive.

Unlike England, however, the Saudi national coaches had the advantage of being able to spend long periods in training camps with their players. In the summer of '77 we set up such camps in Coventry and Malmo and played a series of matches against English and Swedish sides over a six-week period. Our coaches attempted to reinforce sound habits and eradicate the damaging ones picked up through playing in the Saudi national league. We also wanted to develop team spirit and sought to create a bond between the players to enable them to function as a team and not as a collection of talented individuals. In January and February 1979, prior to the Gulf Games, we spent six weeks in Marbella and the South of France playing games against first-class opposition, including Real Madrid and Monaco. The SAFF had the authority to suspend the league for this period so that the national team could be properly prepared.

Touring abroad with the Saudis did provoke some interesting and difficult situations, seized on very quickly by both the Saudi and English press. At the time, remember, the world was in awe of the tremendous wealth the Saudis had been given by a geological lottery win. Princes patronised the Saudi league teams and readily rewarded their star players with expensive gifts ranging from Longines watches to Mercedes Benz cars and even houses. Yet the Saudi players were technically 'amateurs'. They

215

also lived in an environment where they had virtually no contact with the opposite sex outside their immediate family. Women wore unflattering flowing robes designed to cover the whole female form. They were not allowed to work, drive or reveal their faces to men outside their family. Imagine, then, the temptation to Saudi national footballers abroad when exposed to the fairer sex.

The Saudi Princes and Federation officials demanded the best when they toured and I remember introducing the Hotel Leofric in Coventry to the most helpful and enlightened member of the SAFF, Dr Fatah Nazer.

'Where is the air conditioning in this room, Jimmy?' asked Fatah. I showed him by opening the window. . .

When we played in the Asian Games in Bangkok in December 1978, we had two floors at the Oriental Hotel, arguably one of the best in the world. I also remember my eldest son Duncan, who was general manager of WSA, being given £80,000 in cash to pay for one of our summer training camps, an enormous sum of money to cater for twenty-five people for six weeks' training. Our partners could not be accused of failing to back their ambition with hard cash.

Outside Saudi Arabia, many other Middle Eastern countries in the late seventies were politically unstable and insecure. The Lebanon was embroiled in civil strife, the PLO were active throughout Syria, Arab argued with Arab, only united in their opposition to Israel. The Kingdom of Saudi Arabia, in contrast, was relatively calm, but trips to other Arab countries were accompanied by armed guards, suggesting that conflict was only one step away. The hotel in Damascus where we were guests for an international against Syria in 1977 had been closed two weeks previously after the police had fought a machine-gun battle with terrorists opposed to President Assad's regime. The lobby and stairway were riddled with machine-gun bullet holes; a number of people had been killed; hardly the ideal preparation for a football international, and we were more than grateful for the presence of the military on rooftops at every training session.

At the end of 1977, with the departure of Bill McGarry, we were required to appoint a new national team manager. The Princes,

Their Royal Highnesses Prince Fahad bin Sultan and Prince Faisal bin Fahad, were obsessed with appointing a Bob Paisley, a Bobby Robson or a Brian Clough. Saudi national pride demanded the best that money could buy. However, being manager of Liverpool and being the national team manager of Saudi Arabia were two completely different jobs requiring different skills. Working in the heat of Saudi Arabia, which could reach temperatures of 130 degrees Fahrenheit, in an alien culture, with Moslems who were sensitive and with a somewhat whimsical attitude to workrate, did not merit a conventional approach. It needed an agile mind from an energetic, youthful, intelligent and talented coach. It was not possible to appoint the kind of person who would have been most valuable, so we succumbed and appointed the biggest name we could find who was not under contract, Ronnie Allen, manager of West Bromwich Albion.

David Woodfield, Geoff Vowden and Malcolm Gregory (physiotherapist) had developed a mutually respectful relationship with our Saudi Arabian national squad. From the outset, Ronnie found it hard to adapt to the extreme cultural differences and did not impose himself sufficiently on the Saudi squad nor on our now tightly knit group of English coaches and administrative staff. He failed to devote time to learning his new players' Arabic names and called them by numbers which did nothing to endear their new coach to the players. Almost before a year was up, Ron was persuaded to return to England, not having made many friends, but that is not registered on a bank paying-in slip. With only six months left to prepare for the big test in Baghdad, our advice was to appoint David Woodfield. It was accepted with reluctance.

To maintain cordial relations with many unknown Saudi princes and with the local population through the press was an unimaginably difficult task. I can think of no better example of the problems we encountered than the 'Man Alive' documentary which was shown on Saudi and British television in the spring of 1977. In the opening minutes of my interview, I had been troubled by a fly and interrupted the commentator, who had just asked me about the progress of football in the last nine months, in order to despatch the insect. This was transmitted. The Saudi press were incensed by my lack of sensitivity, as was Prince Bandar bin Abdullah. Apparently there was a huge fly problem in Saudi Arabia, of which I was completely unaware. My crime was that I should indulge in such a trivial action whilst in the middle of a television discussion on such an important topic.

Later on in the programme, when asked to compare the relative merits of the Saudi and English football player, one of the WSA coaches suggested that the British players gave ninety per cent effort on average, whereas their Saudi counterparts gave only sixty per cent. The press inference was that the British had declared their players genetically superior. Afterwards I became friendly with Prince Bandar, following an exchange of correspondence concerning the innocence of my actions and the genuine intentions of WSA.

I had signed a three-year contract in 1976 to advise the Federation on all soccer matters with an optional two-year extension. The Saudis paid us a generous fee every month and we invoiced the SAFF separately for all our expenses: living, travel and coaching, plus salaries for company employees. Unfortunately, we did not ever commission or build any soccer pitches, the SAFF not having a large enough budget at that time. The majority of the profits we made from advising the Saudis and initiating their climb up world football disappeared into the financial bottomless pit of the North American Soccer League.

When we arrived in Saudi Arabia in 1976 there was a common belief that the Saudi player was past his best at twenty-five. Khalid Turkey, one of the most talented of the Saudi players, believed this. He was over twenty-five. The Saudis had a high degree of footballing skill, a natural talent, but they were generally on the small side and did not appear to be as strong as the Iraqis, Syrians or Iranians. When we played Iraq for the first time in 1976, physically it looked very much men against boys. The level of overall fitness was not high and they had an insufficient grasp of team play. Bill McGarry, Ronnie Allen and David

Woodfield did contribute to their overall tactical awareness, improved their level of physical fitness and imbued them with a feeling of collective responsibility. We also had noted success with some of the younger players who had developed better habits with their Saudi clubs. Inconsistency and an inability to perform under tournament conditions were problems which we never completely resolved. The Saudi players performed well in friendly matches, but found it difficult to reproduce the form demonstrated in drawing 1–1 with Liverpool, when taking the opportunity to compete in important international games and competitions. Yet, we only had a limited period of time to patch up this deficiency. In essence, the intense pressure of too much money chasing too little talent affected the players and perhaps even our own attitude on the big occasions.

Our national team preparations for the Gulf Games in 1979 continued with the Asian Games in Bangkok in December 1978, followed by training camps in Cannes and the south of Spain with games against Monaco, Real Madrid and Seville. It was now apparent to the whole company that our future jobs were dependent on a creditable performance in the Gulf Games, and defeating Kuwait was a priority. The SAFF would be judged on these results by their peers, the Saudi press and the Saudi people, and failure would mean WSA would be a convenient whipping boy irrespective of the innovative success we had with coaching and training Saudi youth. Failure would be ours and success would be the SAFF's.

We arrived in Baghdad for the Gulf Cup in spring 1979 with a fully fit national team. As now, almost every street was decorated with a portrait of Saddam Hussein and an army presence in the capital was an everyday occurrence. The Saudi team started poorly in the first two games and David Woodfield planned a shake-up for the match against Iraq, leaving out more established players and giving up-and-coming youth a chance. However, the suggested removal of Majid Abdullah from the starting line-up – at his best the outstanding Saudi player – was greeted by a personal summons to the Prince's hotel suite. He understood the need to reshuffle the pack, but disagreed with the decision to drop his favourite, the team's leading goalscorer and certainly most talented player. I discussed the issue with HRH but stated my unwillingness to impose our will on the national team coach. The Prince did not concede and suggested that if we acceded to his demands he would guarantee a new contract in September for three years. Principle triumphed over pecuniary interest and I declined to interfere with team selection. Although the Saudi team performed quite well against the favourites without Majid Abdullah, they lost 2–0 and the Saudi press went to town.

At that time, discussions were under way with the then United Arab Emirates' manager, a certain Don Revie, to take over as national team coach if our contract was extended. The Prince was happy with this choice but there was still fierce criticism of the Academy and our handling of the national team training and tactics. The tournament continued and climaxed with our fixture against Kuwait, which would effectively decide the fate of approximately twenty-five expat jobs, and the company contract – three years' work to be judged on ninety minutes' football. Win and the SAFF would be heroes, lose and we would be villains. We played well and dominated the match against Kuwait but could not score. Duncan and I were horrified when Majid Abdullah of all people failed to head a corner home from no more than three yards with the Kuwaiti goalkeeper frozen on his line. A draw meant third place between Iraq and Kuwait and was a considerable improvement on the previous Gulf Cup, but any hope of an extended contract went over the bar with Majid's header, the Federation vote being 4–3 against.

Despite that, I felt our coaches and administrators had performed well in an alien culture in difficult circumstances. They and the company had been well paid. Happily, we parted friends with the Saudis and took enormous pleasure from their qualification and far from disgraceful performances in the World Cup in America in 1994, just fifteen years later, and again in 1998.

17

THE AMERICAN
DIATER

Dᴜʀɪɴɢ 1977, I arranged for John Camkin to leave Riyadh and
travel to America to investigate the viability of making a
bid for a North American Soccer League (NASL) franchise with
the then commissioner, Phil Woosnam. The League was planning to expand from eighteen to twenty-four full-time professional teams. Detroit, Michigan, seemed to be an excellent
location because soccer, as a participant sport, was growing
phenomenally quickly in schools, colleges and Little Leagues.
The city of Detroit boasted the Detroit Lions (professional
American Football), the Detroit Tigers (professional baseball)
and the Detroit Pistons (professional basketball). Detroit was
seen as being a city with major potential for the establishment
of a fourth sport.

The reason WSA wanted to take on a franchise was to re-invest
the money we were earning from our Saudi Arabian contract.
Had we brought it back to Britain, ninety per cent would have
disappeared in tax. So John Camkin, encouraged by Phil Woosnam, teamed up with two local football entrepreneurs, Gordon
Preston and Roger Faulkner, and unfortunately as it turned out,
in the winter of 1977 we defeated five other American groups for
the exclusive rights to an NASL franchise. There were two
provisos – we could not sell the franchise for three years without

losing a pre-paid $250,000 bond; and Michigan Soccer Limited was set up to run the franchise with a group of American partners, who at this point had a minority shareholding.

In 1977 and 1978, World Sports Academy introduced approximately one million dollars of working capital into the US operation. The commissioner and the League had informed us, 'The game is commercially exploited to the highest degree and successful clubs are also making large profits, both from the gate money and also from the variety of commercial spin-offs related to the game.' As we later found out, this was completely untrue, 'bullshit' (I wish I could think of a better word) designed to sell a high-risk investment. Why then did I invest in American soccer? Apart from wanting an overseas investment for the Saudi money, football was my subject. If knowledge and experience are the twin pillars for success, I was superbly equipped. John Camkin and others – including my old friend Phil Woosnam – convinced me that professional soccer in the States would succeed and, in time, would prove a sound investment. We were delighted when our presentation was accepted, and our Anglo/American management team busied themselves with providing an administrative and playing structure for our entry into the League in the spring of 1978.

We estimated, based on figures provided by the NASL and soccer teams operating in the League, that $1.75 million was sufficient capital to operate a professional team for three years. In actual fact, this budget was completely inadequate. We spent our entire three-year budget in twelve months. During 1977, 1978 and 1979, on average gates of around 13,000, Detroit Express managed to lose around $1 million per annum and we were not alone. The situation could not last without increased capital; the possibility of Coventry City investing some resources, both financial and playing, could have been mutually beneficial.

Football, or 'soccer' as it is called in the States, was structured along similar lines to the American Football organisation with the top sixteen teams out of twenty-four, from four different conferences, making the play-offs which used a knock-out formula.

Play-off revenue was shared amongst all clubs. In 1978, for our inaugural season, we had recruited Ken Furphy to manage the team and signed a series of mature, seasoned British professionals: Steve Sergeant, Graham Oakes, Eddie Colquhoun and other loan players including some Americans. It was obligatory to play three American or Canadian citizens in the team. I was able to persuade Birmingham City to allow Trevor Francis to join Detroit Express for the summer. Trevor was an outstanding success on the field, scoring twenty-two goals in twenty games, turning a sound, spirited team into play-off contenders. We made the play-offs, had a 20–10 record of wins against losses, averaged 12,194 spectators for each home game and won the divisional title, but financially the cupboard was bare.

The philosophy of the NASL was founded on the principle of signing star names playing in luxury stadia, so attracting television coverage which would then bankroll the NASL as well as spreading the sport to the American public. American Football teams received a cheque for $5 million at the start of the season from television. The Express played in the Pontiac Silverdome, the home of the Detroit Lions, which had a capacity of over 80,000 people in an indoor, all-seater stadium. With our crowds and no large cheque it was uneconomic to use such an extravagant venue. The local college ground holding 20,000 would have been sufficient and much more cost effective. The NASL's grander plans wasted considerable capital. The New York Cosmos, funded by a multi-national corporation, had a team full of ethnic internationals and the major marketing *wunderkind*, Pelé, and did manage to average crowds of around 50,000. Fundamentally, this did not help other franchises to survive. Washington Diplomats, funded by Madison Square Garden Inc., signed Johan Cruyff, but still lost money. It turned out the greater the stars, the bigger the loss.

Apart from expensive stadia, it seemed that the league clubs were obsessed with the idea of giving away complimentary tickets to matches for a variety of promotions. Our average ticket price in the 1978 season was $3. We were persuaded to

223

surrender masses of free seats on the grounds of enticing new fans to watch the sport. The real cost of watching professional soccer in America was nearer $12 a ticket, and without a generous television subsidy, which was not forthcoming, WSA and our American partners continued to underwrite the ticket cost. This was a basic misconception which had to be changed throughout the League as a whole if the NASL was going to survive. You may imagine that our American partners did not take kindly to our protestations. After all, Uncle Sam surely knew all there was to know about running sport in the US of A.

Though there were large numbers of schoolchildren playing soccer throughout America, particularly on the East and West Coasts, their parents were largely indifferent to our national game, having been brought up on a diet of American Football and baseball throughout school and college. Children could not drive themselves and parents would take them to soccer games as a treat on an occasional rather than a regular basis. The overall standard of play amongst American schoolchildren was poor and the standard of coaching unimaginative, mostly undertaken by people with little knowledge or experience. I have seen it with my own eyes when visiting my three half-American grand-daughters in Texas, all of whom play soccer. Hence the standard of the compulsory American and Canadian participants in the professional teams was poor and the teams were largely filled with foreign players. The American audiences would have related more to an emerging American Pelé than a Brazilian one, although in New York, Pelé was king, a world superstar.

The American television stations had little interest in showing NASL matches. Audiences were small and advertisers were not keen to buy time. In the 1979 season we lost money in the televising of our away games, being forced to fill unsold advertising time with plugs for our forthcoming matches. Initially the press in Detroit, the *News* and the *Free Press*, gave the Express a reasonable amount of match coverage for both the outdoor and the indoor season. The indoor, small-sided league was based on ice hockey rather than the traditional English five-a-side game. In general, there was a lack of knowledge and understanding of the fundamentals of the game, by the press as well as the public. Writers became more comfortable predicting the demise of the NASL or recording the many partnership disputes than describing the game itself.

The 1979 outdoor season in Detroit was not as successful as the previous one. We averaged 14,058 fans per home game, but the team was not as consistent. Unfortunately, half the season had passed before our superstar, Trevor Francis, who was joining us for the summer again, was able to play his first game. We were rapidly running out of money and I was repeatedly involved in meetings and transatlantic telephone calls concerning the need for fresh investment. At this stage, WSA had paid almost $1 million into subsidising professional soccer in Michigan, aided and abetted by ten local business partners and two new general partners, paying $250,000 each for a say in the management and control of the team.

The board was unwieldy with too many individuals with differing views on how to make the franchise successful. In short, there was no consensus on how to make soccer work in Detroit, if such a way existed. The economy was totally dependent on the car industry which had slid into a vicious recession. Many jobs were lost and spending money was tight – not the ideal time to try and sell a new product. Yet the Express still averaged 14,000 fans in the 1979 season, qualifying for the play-offs but losing in the first round and emerging with an operating loss of around $1 million.

With at least two BBC programmes a week to contend with, I sent Duncan from WSA in Saudi Arabia (the Saudi contract came to an end in autumn 1979) and Graham Darby, WSA's director of business and administration, to investigate the situation in Detroit. In the first few weeks they discovered the debt was far worse than had been imagined, around $500,000 in unpaid bills. Roger Faulkner and Gordon Preston were removed from any further involvement in the day to day running of the club. We attempted to create some unity among the directors, and Ken

Furphy found a talented young South American, Pato Margetic, with dazzling dribbling skills, to replace Trevor Francis for the 1980 outdoor season. Two extremely promising Coventry youngsters, Mark Hateley and Gary Bannister, were added to the Express roster as well as a Yugoslav international, Peter Barolic. Despite that, five of our players were nineteen or younger and, youth being inconsistent, we failed to make the play-offs. Our average attendance dropped to 11,000 – hardly visible in a stadium built to hold 80,000. Cash flow drying up and our failure on the field resulted in increasingly vociferous disputes between larger than life partners.

The prime motivation Americans had for putting money into sports franchises was not necessarily love of the game but the tax savings they could make on their investment. A $100,000 investment into the NASL would save the investor an equal amount of tax. It was these tax write-offs which enabled the increasingly debt ridden and unstable NASL to survive as long as it did. However, even American millionaires will not continue to throw money away without signs that the team might at some point become financially viable. The problem was that, however well Detroit Express or New York Cosmos did, the League as a whole had to become financially viable.

Our American partners in Detroit Express were becoming increasingly disillusioned with the team, the media and public response to the franchise. Three years in Detroit, in a local economy riddled with recession, had taken its toll. Two of the directors, Gary Lemmen and Sonny Von Arnhem, were becoming more and more antagonistic towards each other and at one partnership meeting Duncan had to pull Gary off Sonny's throat. The volatile Sonny was soon removed from general partner status and Gary, who had a pragmatic business approach, Duncan and myself sought a solution to our problem. There were some pluses in 1980 on the playing side. Pato Margetic had electric pace and at nineteen was developing into a marketable asset. David Bradford toiled intelligently in midfield, Gary Bannister showed considerable flair and scored goals, playing as a central striker, but Mark Hateley found Astroturf difficult to adjust to and showed only glimpses of the player he was to become.

Off the field, our American partners would not invest further. The team was losing $1 million per annum – an amount that showed no signs of diminishing – and our hard core of ten thousand or so loyal fans in Detroit was not growing. The Detroit papers were predicting the demise of the Express.

Phil Woosnam and the rest of the directors of the NASL (each club had two representatives) must take full responsibility for the instability of the League itself. The whole structure was built on a false premise, that between 1977 and 1979 a number of teams in the NASL would be profitable. In reality the whole of the NASL was losing money hand over fist and teams like Tampa Bay Rowdies and the Vancouver Whitecaps, averaging over 15,000 per game, were losing similar if not larger amounts of money than ourselves. During the 1978 season only three NASL teams averaged over 20,000 per home game – the New York Cosmos (47,856), the Minnesota Kicks (30,926) and the Seattle Sounders (22,578). That seems healthy without knowing the average ticket price. The Washington Diplomats increased their average gates from 11,171 in 1978 to over 19,000 in 1979, but the cost of a ticket averaged $3. Giving tickets away was not the route to financial security.

Phil Woosnam, the commissioner, was too busy replacing ailing franchises to produce a comprehensive plan for the survival and success of the League as a whole. The NASL meetings were as discordant as our own Detroit Express partners' meetings. There was little honesty about the gravity of the situation in 1979; few club 'owners' were prepared to admit that their clubs were crippled with debt. There was no overall corrective plan for solving a crisis which nobody was prepared to acknowledge existed. It is hardly surprising that the NASL did not survive the early eighties and that professional soccer built on such fragile foundations collapsed. But for us, for the time being, it was not over.

18

TURBULENT TIMES AT COVENTRY

I N the summer of 1980, Phil Mead became president of Coventry and gave up the chairmanship role. I was invited by the board to take it on. I couldn't refuse; there was still so much to be done and the ideas were already forming in our minds. Phil was a remarkable man with the warmth to make good friends out of those who may have wanted to be his enemies. He saw only good in others, which I am sure was just a reflection of himself. If there's any influence from above keeping Coventry in the Premier League, I know from whence it comes.

With Phil as our president, our first project was to complete and launch our new modern sports centre, the Sky Blue Connexion. There were limits to any expansion at Highfield Road so it was built at our training ground at Ryton. We aimed to have the best training facility in Great Britain; to create closer links, away from matches, between the club, its supporters and others; and to add to the club's income from members' fees and regular sporting activities. The cost was £1.5 million and the hidden advantage was that as a wholly owned asset it provided collateral with our bank, so much more potent than the Highfield Road stadium.

I was able to persuade His Royal Highness Prince Philip to open the Connexion on a great day in November: a small bribe of one £10,000 cheque for the Duke of Edinburgh's Award Scheme and another for the footballing charity Goaldiggers clinched it. The £20,000 was subscribed by donations of £1000 per head from directors, vice presidents and others. Inscribed bricks recorded the names of donors. The top one says 'Alice and Bill' – my Mum and Dad – a thank you from me to them.

We had asked Alex Hay, from the BBC golf commentary team, to speak at the dinner. As is inevitable, time slips by quickly when one's having fun and I had been warned that the Prince's train was due to leave Coventry station sharp at 11.30 p.m. I promised to keep Alex informed about exactly how much time he had to speak. Before long the original allotted twenty minutes dwindled to fifteen, then ten, then eight at which Alex stood up.

'Forgive me hurrying,' he began, 'but I understand I only have a few minutes before His Royal Highness has to leave.'

'I beg your pardon?' exclaimed HRH.

'But I thought the train leaves at 11.30!' Alex stammered.

'It's *my* train!' was the royal answer. 'Please carry on!' So Alex did and the royal train didn't, not until Alex had finished his very funny speech, which was thoroughly enjoyed by everyone.

At the start of the 1980 season we formed a partnership, which lasted until 1996, with the Talbot Motor Company to exploit joint promotional links. I suppose I should not have been surprised that, in my recurring desire to lead the way, we were in trouble with the Football League yet again. Although shirt sponsorship was not allowed, in return for a healthy annual fee of £80,000, we sought to find ways and means of promoting our new sponsors and thus helping them emerge from their present slump and keep many local people in work, the same people we wanted to support the club. In order for our sponsors to get the maximum benefit from their investment, we had shirts designed for the coming season with a pattern based round a grand T – nothing more, nothing less. Viewers, if we were on television, would have to make their own link from the pattern to the sponsor. Imaginative of course; who would it harm? No one! However, it upset the FA and the Football League and both the BBC, by whom I was employed, and ITV. Everyone was consulting lawyers and in the meantime we were banned from the screens forthwith. We formed a company, the Big T Shirt Co., to make and market our own high-profile products.

Another promotional idea was to change the name of the club to Coventry Talbot, although this was suggested more from frustration than long-term practicality. By Christmas, four new shirt designs were submitted to the League and one of them was chosen, just in time for ATV (desperate because Villa v Southampton was frozen off) to jump in and transmit Coventry v West Bromwich Albion. Our game could be played because in 1980, also, we fulfilled a long-term ambition and installed at Highfield Road the first underground hot-water pipe method of undersoil heating. Other methods having been tried unsuccessfully, we took a chance that a device which enabled the Dutch to grow potatoes in icy conditions would bear fruit for us. The extensive network of pipes worked, and before long Liverpool and others followed suit.

Leading the way with Talbot was the beginning of a relationship which carried on for many years, with the name and ownership moving to Peugeot. Part of the original deal was that the chairman and players would drive Talbot Solaras. With some regret I sold my flash Lotus and switched to a Solara automatic, which was the first of a fleet of Peugeot/Talbot vehicles I have driven since. I can say that averaging 50,000 miles a year for twenty-eight years I have only once suffered a mechanical blip, when a throttle cable broke on a Tagora while on holiday in Spain, which was fixed in twenty minutes by a Catalan garage mechanic. It's a remarkable record, as was Peugeot's consistent support of Coventry City through so many years. I like to feel that the part the club played during so many campaigns returned the compliment. In 1996 Peugeot switched their alliance to the Coventry Rugby Club, who will need all the help they can get to regain the supremacy they enjoyed when I first came to the city.

At the end of the NASL 1980 outdoor season, Duncan received a phone call from one Terry Busby who implied that a number of rich Washington businessmen would welcome and support financially a new franchise in Washington. They did not understand the decision of the previous owners of the Washington Diplomats to pull out of the NASL in 1979, despite having averaged crowds of 19,000 per home game. It was suggested that the nation's capital was more likely to be a successful venue for a soccer team than our current impoverished Detroit. Why not move the franchise? We had a series of discussions with potential investors, obtained the approval of the majority of our Detroit partners, and on Friday, 27 February 1981 at precisely 2 p.m., the directors of the NASL unanimously approved the relocation of the franchise to Washington DC. We had pulled off a tremendous coup and were temporarily heralded by the Washington media as saviours for bringing soccer back to the capital. Perhaps, after all, with a fresh start on top of what we had learned from Detroit, we could make it work.

The venture was funded by the coffers of WSA, Gary Lemmen, and by an investment of $500,000 from Coventry City Football Club. The Coventry board and I envisaged the advantages of sharing in an enterprise that could give our younger players experience in the USA which would supplement their development and so benefit the club in England. If we could make it work it would close the financial gap between Coventry and its more prosperous first division rivals. On the field, as against the balance sheet, Steve Hunt, Alan Brazil, Gary Bannister and many other English players benefited greatly from this experience. We signed Malcolm Waldron and Trevor Hebberd from Southampton and kicked off on 11 April 1981 against Montreal at the RFK Stadium in Washington DC.

Immediately we had to face up to the old Diplomats' practice of giving away tickets. Their general manager would give 5000 tickets away for one match – no wonder the gates looked promising! We raised the cost to $15 for a family of four to see a Diplomats game. This was not well received but compared very favourably with $50 for a family to see a Bullets basketball game and over $100 to see a Redskins American Football game.

231

What transpired again was that the American public was not prepared in large overall numbers to pay to see a soccer game and enable the NASL to survive. The income shortfall could not be made up by sponsorship because the television stations were still not interested in showing soccer. Bert Abromovitz, a local PR man, summed it up to me when he said, 'You know what the problem is, Jimmy? If you gave 55,000 tickets away the stadium would still only be half full.' Our less expensive team struggled to live up to the impact the previous Diplomats had made, despite widespread media support. The fragility of the exercise was underlined when, following a 50,000 plus crowd for a great game and a narrow defeat by the Cosmos at the RFK Stadium, only 8000 turned up to watch the unheralded Tulsa Roughnecks the following week.

The search for investors to join the New Diplomats proved to be more difficult than anticipated, despite the encouragement of a persuasive local millionaire, Mel Estorin. Potential investors were wined and dined at home games and elsewhere with no tangible success. However, Duncan became involved in discussions with a wealthy supporter of the Diplomats who, at his country estate in Virginia, suggested that Paul Mellon of the Pittsburgh steel family and a great philanthropist was prepared to invest over three million dollars in guaranteeing soccer in Washington for the next three years. Typically thorough, his advisers investigated in depth the state of the NASL and many of their clubs. At 2 a.m. the phone rang beside my bed and a cultured American voice explained with much charm that his principal, Mr Mellon, had decided not to invest in Washington Diplomats. He went to great lengths to stress that this was in no way a reflection on my family or me personally, about whom his research had revealed only worthwhile and comforting information. He wished me luck. What a result: Ego 10, Finance 0. So it was back to the drawing-board and the pressing need to make something happen off the field and on it.

Previously Johan Cruyff had enchanted the Dips with his extraordinary football talent but had undergone a serious groin

Ninth World Cup and still a team man.
Back row: *(left to right)* JH, Barry Davies, John Motson.
Front row: *(left to right)* Alan Hansen, Des Lynam, Gary Lineker.

A man's best friend –
George.

A proud day when I received
the OBE. It rained, though,
and Bryony and I got wet!

Helping out without getting the needle! We knitted an enormous scarf for the
St Catherine's Hospice, Crawley.

Promotion and champagne for three Charlton supporters – Hill, Ufton and Grade.

A peak at heaven! A ten handicap alongside golfing gods – Trevino, Alliss and Ballesteros. Ronnie Corbett's pretty good, too!

The home team at play – sons, daughters, husbands, wives and ten grandchildren.

Thank heaven for Noddy! It helps when one of you knows what you're doing!

SPARKS tennis tournament, presided over by their Royal Highnesses Prince and Princess Michael of Kent.

Zidane and Co. fulfil France's World Cup dream.

Defender Lilian Thuram *(centre)* scored two goals in the semi-final. In seven matches only two slipped by France's goalkeeper, Fabien Barthez *(left)*.

Paraguay's mother hen and superstar – Jose Luis Chilavert.

England's young Lions, warts and all – Michael Owen (20) and David Beckham.

Did he fall or was he pushed? Mexico's Luis Hernandez keeps 'em guessing.

Hero and villain – Dennis Bergkamp dispatches Argentina's Roberto Ayala.

Neither Bryony and the family, nor anyone else for that matter, gave any hint, and so I fell for the 'This is Your Life' set-up hook, line and sinker. Terry Venables thought it was funny.

I was glad to be in Mexico for the 1986 World Cup, having been in the studios for LWT in 1970.

operation which was taking time to heal. The possibility of enticing him back entered our minds. First we had to establish his fitness. Leaving nothing to chance, I was able to persuade Coventry director, Tom Sergeant, a surgeon himself, to examine Johan in Holland and advise us whether he might be fit to play a useful part before the play-offs. Tom's report was encouraging; he should be fit within the month. Consequently we entered into a deal with Cruyff's agent, Dennis Roach, to play for the remainder of the season for a figure approaching $200,000. The reality when Johan arrived was that he was nowhere near ready to play, but anxious to undergo treatment from a clinic in Washington in whom he had total faith. He offered to manage the team in the interim but we explained we already had a manager, Ken Furphy.

However desperately we needed him, it would have been pointless and unforgivable to play him before he was fully fit. So we waited patiently for a return on our investment. It came in the form of three matches, the first of which I saw with 38,000 others against Cosmos in the RFK Stadium. Johan was in his own half immediately following a Cosmos goal, and almost straight from the kick-off, as the ball was laid back to him, he drove it directly over the opposing goalkeeper's head, perhaps sixty yards away, for a sensational goal. I shall never forget it, nor how much it cost. Our superstar played two more games but the hero had arrived too late to save the ailing Diplomats, who missed the play-offs by a point, and their season and life ended.

With no other investment forthcoming, and WSA, Coventry City and Gary Lemmen unwilling to provide further capital, the decision was taken to resign from the NASL. We all lost large amounts of money in a League which was run poorly, without a common purpose or objectives and which was doomed inevitably to fail. The NASL limped on for a few more years before collapsing and I listen most carefully now to any business proposition delivered in an American accent.

Back at Coventry we were preparing for a major breakthrough in presenting football to the public. We were going to insist that they all sat down, by providing only seats and eliminating terraces. For some years crowds had been dropping and it was to get worse. Everyone was searching for the answers and in that quest the increase of hooliganism emerged as a major factor in keeping people, perhaps frightening them, away from grounds. We had tried, as every club had, to find the solution to it. To deplore it was one thing, to eradicate it certainly another.

We had investigated every possible antidote for the disease; the most severe, as well as totally effective, remedy suggested to us was to take a thumb print of every supporter and have a checking device to gain final entry. Obviously the wider public would have to be persuaded that this unpleasant act was worth the ignominy. I coined the phrase, 'Thumbs down to beat the hooligans!' We would never have been able to put it to the test because there was not enough space at the entrances to accommodate the two essentials – paying and thumbing.

I accepted an invitation to attend a conference in London to discuss hooliganism and how to combat it. I shall never forget it because on that day, very early in the morning, I had a date with a horse. Having agreed to ride in the Mad Hatter's Charity Steeplechase at Plumpton, I had difficulty in finding a suitable mount. I pleaded with John Sillett, my ex-Coventry player and friend, to find me a trusty steed. At the eleventh hour he came good and if I could get to Cheltenham on the morning of the hooligan meeting, I could have a trial run on Wine Talk. You can imagine my excitement; I'd lost over a stone by refusing fattening (delicious) food and drink for four weeks, and my weight had dropped to 11st 9lbs.

I made the stables at the crack of dawn and was given a leg up on Wine Talk.

'What shall I do?'

'Just canter up to that slope and then give him a gallop to the top,' was the answer.

'Supposing I can't stop him?'

'He'll stop!' was the confident reply. 'If not just turn and steer him back here.' Wine Talk behaved like the perfect gentleman and I had a thrilling ride to the top and a gentle controlled journey back.

'Any advice for tomorrow?' I asked.

'Yes, he's gone pretty well for you, just sit tight and whatever you do, don't try to ride a finish!' I don't think that was a compliment.

However, I caught my train back to London and arrived in good time for the meeting. The speakers were informative and views from the police, psychiatrists, lawyers and politicians were voiced. Those there from the football world were looking for guidance and help but no one appeared to have the answer. At home that evening the excitement of the race obliterated the frustration of the day from my mind. I slept peacefully and awoke in the early morning gloom to be told that the Mad Hatter's race had been cancelled. Plumpton was waterlogged. The annoying fact remained that Wine Talk had already made the journey and the cost was down to me – without even getting to the start. I endeavoured to console myself with a massive fried breakfast of eggs, bacon, sausages, beans and mushrooms!

While we are on the topic of the sport of kings, there was an actual race in which I did eventually take part. Following my disappointment at the cancellation of the Mad Hatter's race at Plumpton, I could not resist an invitation some years later to ride in a similar charity scamper at Sandown. This time round it was Michael Ryan who drew the short straw, generously providing me with a horse, some necessary tuition at his stables at Newmarket and a plethora of prudent advice.

The day came and I arrived bright and early at the course, an absolute beginner if ever there was one which became increasingly evident in the changing room. My fellow jockeys seemed quite at home, accomplishing without a care all the routine preparations. I donned my jodhpurs and tied a stock with fumbling fingers, perhaps trembling more than would be thought acceptable for a grown man. I couldn't wait to get outside away from my experienced, totally relaxed rivals. Fortunately, no sooner was I outside the door when I bumped into my good friend Lord John Oaksey.

'My goodness, James! What a mess you are!' were his words. 'Come here!' At which command he more or less grabbed me by the throat and in a trice had retied the stock, virtually remoulded my headgear and stepped back admiring his handiwork. It was certainly the nearest I was going to get to looking like a jockey and I was as ready as I would ever be for the race.

I'm not making excuses, but some professional footballers have the reputation, deserved or not, for trying to defeat the enemy by unfair means. Mistakenly, I expected that, if not necessarily the jockeys, the Starter would represent the epitome of fair play, so that when the thrusters were twenty lengths or so in front of the fair and disciplined riders at the rear he would find a way to readjust matters. He did shout, 'Hold back there!' to which no one, except muggins, paid any attention. I wouldn't say I was left, because we were moving before the next race started, but a minority of other honest jockeys and I were badly behind. I persuaded myself not to panic and burn out my mount in an attempt to make up the lost ground too quickly. The next few minutes were heavenly. The speed was exhilarating and the fact that I overtook a rival or two even more so. I'm told we finished twelfth out of twenty or so runners, which I thought was at least satisfactory. My trainer's view, 'You never gave him a ride!' brought me down to earth. He was right, of course.

His comment wasn't going to stop me celebrating that I was still in one piece and on my curriculum vitae I could now put 'part-time jockey'. Whether it was nerves, bravado or just gratitude for having survived, I don't know, but I downed a glass or two of champagne. My driver interrupted the gathering.

'If we don't leave now we'll miss the plane,' he said. I woke up! If we missed the plane, there was no way I could make the 7.30 kick-off for Blackburn Rovers v Shrewsbury, a Cup-tie which the BBC was transmitting that evening. We made London Airport with minutes to spare; my driver was obviously a better pilot than his passenger.

236

No more talk of horses and back to the serious matter in hand. We discussed the hooligan problem at a board meeting. Nothing very positive having come out of the London meeting, we decided to explore the possibilities of an all-seater stadium. We didn't expect that it would eliminate hooliganism, nor that it would be universally popular, but it would make it harder to be a hooligan or certainly get away with hooliganism at football grounds.

The underlying reason why football has failed to rid itself of the hooligan element is that they get away with it. They are allowed to disgrace themselves and football again and again. There are degrees of hooliganism and I'm afraid the standard of behaviour, and in particular bad language, at grounds is still shocking. The guilty remain oblivious to the presence of women and children and graphically illustrate our society's fallen standards. The game of football is the victim, but it cannot provide the solution. That's the responsibility of everyone and particularly those who father us, teach us and represent us.

Recognising the above earlier than most, we announced to the world that we were going to create an all-seater stadium at Highfield Road holding just over 20,000 spectators. The news was warmly welcomed by the secretary of the Football Association, Ted Croker, but not by the 'I want to stand at all costs' brigade. It was an expensive exercise following the building of the Sky Blue Connexion and the loss in America, but both projects were conceived to increase revenue in future years. It took courage for the board to make such long-term commitments, which were later to rebound on me personally.

Life would have been so much simpler if we had thought just of the present, and if I had considered personal preservation, spending every available penny on ready made players. Buying popularity has never been at the top of my agenda, so we did what we thought was best for the club in the long run. Meantime, we had to survive on our wits and rely on our youth policy to fulfil our aims. In fact, the club did remain in the top division, sometimes admittedly by a hair's breadth, and won a major trophy, the FA Cup, in 1987 under the leadership of George Curtis and John Sillett, two of the original Sky Blues.

Whatever was happening off the field, however, in 1981 the team was hardly showing the same enterprise on it. Our numerous young players were unable to weave their considerable promise into a consistent winning pattern and the threat of relegation again reared its depressing head. As always, it was Gordon Milne who bore the brunt of the criticism, although it was inevitable that the board, too, came under fire locally for its policy of stringent financial management. Spectators were staying away, not only in Coventry, and the football world was still searching for the cause that lay behind the increasing lack of enthusiasm for the game.

I was in a strange position, sitting alongside Sir Matt Busby and Bobby Charlton on the Football League advisory committee formed to devise ways of reshaping football to counteract falling gates. At the same time, the Football League was taking high court action against me for remarks I had made about the way in which they had behaved during the negotiations with the BBC and ITV for the television contract. In the end we reached a settlement before the matter came to court, both sides agreeing to make no comment then or now. Peace, though, did enable me to continue with Sir Matt and Bobby in our task of coming up with recommendations to revitalise the ailing game.

Our three points for a win recommendation was already there to stay and eventually spread to the rest of the world. Only last year Franz Beckenbauer, in encouraging everyone to search for further means to increase the game's excitement, referred to its overwhelming success.

Other ideas suggested by our committee required changes to be made to the laws of the game which would have to be approved by FIFA's International Committee. Mr Havelange and Co. said no.

Some years later FIFA came up with a change of law to discourage the back pass and another to encourage goalkeepers not to fall asleep holding the ball. A foul throw is now awarded if a player throws in from the wrong place. A player cannot now be offside from a goalkeeper kicking or throwing in from his own penalty area. All those advisory committee changes were rejected by FIFA in 1982, yet have been adopted since. A key suggestion, which was rejected then and has been ever since, was for a referee to be given the power to award a penalty kick, at least an eighteen-yard penalty, for calculated 'last ditch' or cold-blooded violent offences outside the penalty area. That was one of the bees buzzing in my bonnet and the game would still be so much better and fairer with its adoption. The sometimes maligned Graham Kelly was an enthusiastic coordinator and disciple in canvassing these ideas well ahead of time and the rest of the football world.

At Coventry, we had given way at last to the mob feeling and bade farewell to coach Ron Wylie with a financial 'thank you' present in keeping with the board's evaluation of his work for Coventry City. We were to do likewise with Gordon Milne when he left, although for the time being he was kicked upstairs as we sought to find a candidate to satisfy our customers. The average gate had been just 13,099, but Coventry still had a side in the highest division. When I joined the club originally, they were fifth from the bottom of the third division. Manchester United, Arsenal and Liverpool would still visit next season, although we couldn't guarantee we would beat them.

Dave Sexton, who had a reputation within the game of being an outstanding coach, was our choice and we appointed him in the summer of 1981. The feeling was that with such a young, talented squad Dave would be the ideal person to guide them through those early tricky years both on and off the field and hopefully they would grow together into a formidable combination. Such progress would surely bring an end to the misery of our disillusioned supporters to say nothing of the peace of mind of the board of directors.

Whatever we hoped for, it didn't happen, and although there were times when the mainly young team promised much, on other occasions their inexperience cost points. In mid-season Steve Hunt, who had brought an indirect benefit from the

239

otherwise unsuccessful American investment, wanted to leave. Two points out of eleven games was enough to make anyone miserable, but Steve was told he had to fulfil his contract and battle his way out of trouble with the rest. Whoever was looking after City again in the months of March, April and May was working overtime because a mini revival resulted in yet another survival.

The following season, 1982–83, produced more doom and gloom. Although there were young players of great promise in the side, there just wasn't enough money around and neither was there really the appetite for trading which had been the case in the past few years. That part of Gordon Milne and Ronnie Wylie's reign had been essential to Coventry remaining in the Premier League and at the same time building for the future.

Dave Sexton was extremely popular with the players. He was capable, and still is for that matter, of delivering a fascinating two-hour coaching session which both players and spectators enjoy. I am sure retrospectively, and I think Dave would agree, that this is the role in which he is happiest, certainly the one at which he excels. Like myself, he might also argue that he was a better player than history records. However, the other aspects of a manager's job he did not appear to enjoy. It's true that in the transfer market he captured Gerry Francis, who was not only an international midfield player but was also an influential leader. More than anything else, it was probably that signing which kept Coventry in the top division.

However, football in general was still losing its appeal. Even the visits of glamour sides like Manchester United, Liverpool, Tottenham and Arsenal did not fill the ground and gates fell alarmingly, as low as 9000 at their worst. One might have thought that the people of Coventry would appreciate the quality of football they were seeing every other week, even though a fair percentage of it came from the visitors. Not on your life! More people came when the club was in the third division. Spectators like to see their team win more than they care about which division it is in. It wasn't just Coventry; there was a noticeable and damaging tendency for crowds to stay away.

240

Our supporters were particularly angered by the sale of Gary Thompson to West Bromwich Albion, and let us know about it. It was not a transfer carried out purely for financial reasons. Unlike today, the fashion was for one main striker, an old-fashioned centre-forward. We had two and although it was pleasant to have an embarrassment of riches in two such talented goalscoring youngsters, it wasn't easy to accommodate them both in the team's chosen tactical formation. More often than not Mark Hateley, being primarily left footed, was asked to play as one of the three front players, wide on the left. For a player of that height it is not easy to relax and acquire confidence playing so close to a touchline and Mark did not appear to enjoy it and his performance suffered. It's easy enough to say now that the two of them could have blended as joint strikers especially as that fashion has developed since, but it didn't happen then. So when the offer came and Gary was made aware of it, as against boxing and coxing with Mark Hateley for the main striking role, he took the chance to move to West Brom, a club with a more illustrious history. Again, the criticism could be made that the fee of £250,000 was nowhere near enough for a player with Gary's potential, but it was the market price at the time. It was the progress which Gary made afterwards that made it appear cheap.

Dave Sexton's personality being what it is, he didn't complain about the inevitable financial restraints and, although hardly a wheeler dealer, he was yet another manager who, for better or for worse, enabled Coventry, through a difficult season, to retain their treasured status at the top. Unlike many managers, he didn't spend a massive amount of time watching other clubs play during the week, keeping a weather eye out for any player who might be picked up cheaply, or player of promise who could be stolen before his real gift emerged. On the other hand, players were happy to play for him, but he was not a tough entrepreneur and until Coventry produces 40,000 supporters or more at every home match, the manager of their football club has to find the money to compete in other ways.

It was the chairman who began to take more than his share of

241

flak from the impatient public, desperate for the team to win something, or at least to win more often. Apart from other considerations, I didn't suffer with them at Saturday matches and perhaps it conveyed the impression that I wasn't sufficiently interested in the club, especially as my other activities made headlines for all sorts of reasons at that time. These activities did not stop me from giving enough time to the club to bring about the major changes and developments which occurred during my involvement. Most directors would have been happy to achieve that in a lifetime's stewardship.

19

THE SOUTH AFRICAN CONTROVERSY

THE summer of 1982 was not the happiest time in the world for me because of the problems at Coventry, and working for the BBC during the World Cup in Spain came as welcome relief. While there, Lawrie McMenemy phoned to ask whether I would like to manage an all-star team for a tour of South Africa. One or two well-known names had been offered the post and couldn't make it – could I? The word 'manager' was the bait I fell for. Deep down I have never really felt like a chairman. After all, chairmen are elderly chaps, successful businessmen, not ex-players. I would feel so much more comfortable, more relaxed in the manager's role, especially of a team including Ardiles and Kempes, two of Argentina's and my own special heroes from their World Cup-winning team. The lure to manage again made me open my mind to the challenge. Little did I know that it would nearly cost me my job.

It was only later after lengthy conversations with Lawrie that I began to understand the underlying implications. First such a tour would have to be sanctioned by the Football Association and as chairman of Coventry City I could not go without the blessing of the governing body. To get such approval was complicated. Sir Bert Millichip was with a twenty-strong FA delegation in a luxurious Madrid hotel and I took the opportunity to consult him.

'What was the FA's view?' was my question. I didn't get an answer then, but a friendly promise to let me know when the appropriate committee had ruled on the subject. By that time, the depth of feeling by those who really cared and the platitudinous preaching of those who thought they cared but were only in love with the good copy it would provide, was becoming obvious.

They had not, as I had, turned up years ago to an anti-apartheid press conference supposedly to support Bishop (then Father) Trevor Huddleston. Unfortunately, he didn't appear and neither did any of the other notable campaigners. I was left to field questions single-handed. I knew and believed in enough of the principles that lay behind Christianity to represent a firm view against apartheid's unacceptable face, but I resented the fact that I was left on my own to respond to these questions. I was there as an opponent in principle, but I had no detailed knowledge. I had never been to South Africa. Partly as a result of that previous experience, I wanted to see at first hand and inquire for myself and make my own judgement.

When I returned from the World Cup there was a press conference held to announce the prospective tour, which I attended still awaiting the FA's decision. In the absence of any news from Lancaster Gate, I caught the plane to Johannesburg, believing that before the FA made their ruling I would at least have the chance to visit the country and make my own assessment of the issues involved.

The first thing that astounded me was that at the initial press conference the representatives of the South African Football Federation were all black, very welcoming and obviously delighted by our presence. I asked a lot of questions of our hosts afterwards and found that the personnel of the average local football team was roughly made up of nine black and two white players, partially confirmed on the next day watching a local match.

Whatever the painful and aggravating results of that particular trip, they were almost balanced by one training session. At the conclusion of it, as is usual in the United Kingdom, we split up for

244

a six-a-side game. I made up the numbers on the opposing side to Ardiles and Kempes, champions of the world, and the memory I still treasure of that very brief visit was in scoring the winning goal.

On the following day, I played a game of golf as guest of a Swansea University friend of my daughter Joanna, at Kimberley Golf Club. I was one down at the eighteenth and holed an enormous putt from off the green to win the hole and halve the match! I thought the signs were good, until the news arrived that the Football Association would not sanction the tour. I made my peace with the black officials of the South African Association and came home.

On the following Saturday my other daughter, Alison, married an American – Chuck's a great guy. I just wish he'd been black.

Since that time I have rejoiced at the ending of apartheid in South Africa, just as I have been distressed by the horrific happenings sadly still occurring in other African countries. Here and there I have been able to offer infinitesimal practical help. I know where I stand on the issue, which is why I was furious at what was written about the non-tour and my theoretical role in it. It was more disturbing when it became apparent that the BBC hierarchy was being pressurised into taking disciplinary action of some kind against me. It was even promoted in some quarters that they should dispense with my services. Fortunately, a meeting at the highest level, arranged by my agent and long-time friend, Bagenal Harvey, enabled us to separate truth from fiction, spite and mischief and put it in perspective. At this distance, whatever else, I still treasure that winning goal in the six-a-side!

20

THE LEAVING OF COVENTRY

FOOTBALL had been a fulfilling friend in the past in numerous ways. Apart from the financial plus of Saudi Arabia, nullified by the dismal American venture, I had taken little out of the game and put an awful lot back. On the credit side I had been rewarded with the maximum amount of fun and more than my share of success, both as a player and manager and, up to that point, as a director. I suppose it was inevitable that fate would put a few low cards in my hand. One that caused me the utmost aggravation was the totally false impression that had been conveyed of my motives in the three-day South African fiasco. That was the most damaging emotionally, the American investment doing the financial damage. Being chairman of Coventry City Football Club was not my job; it was my passion, my hobby. Most people take up hobbies to relieve the pressure of the serious side of life, to provide relaxation and fun in their spare time. That's hardly the case when you're trying to defy all the odds in keeping Coventry's football team alive and healthy and in the top division, and as a bonus, scraping a minor honour once in a while.

When the Detroit Express franchise was on offer, there were four other interested parties prepared to take it on. Unfortunately, as it turned out, the case which I made on behalf of World Sports Academy was considered to be the best by the American League and we won. The champagne flowed and the dream which we had of having a team with connections on both sides of the pond was fulfilled. We hoped it would give us enormous advantages. We weren't the only ones, on both sides of the Atlantic, to assess that the future would be rosy. I had not taken the decision on behalf of World Sports Academy lightly. If I had brought any of the profit back from Saudi Arabia personally I would have incurred a gigantic tax bill. I was not in immediate need of cash so it made sense to invest it abroad. Accordingly WSA paid for John Camkin to spend three months in the States to establish the wisdom of such an investment and to find partners if we gave it the green light. Considering the competition in Detroit, it seemed we were on a sound footing.

There was and is a constant need to find ways to keep up with the Joneses. That was why the Sky Blues invested in America. I should make it clear that when the original proposition arose to invest in Washington Diplomats and for Coventry City Football Club to become part owners, I asked the board to make its decision to join the venture or not independently of me. They were examining the same set of conditions and opportunities which might be available to an organisation with a team on both sides of the Atlantic as I had done. As far as Coventry City were concerned, they were free to make the choice to join or otherwise. I did not vote on that particular item on the agenda.

When it went wrong, naturally it was the chairman who took the blame for its failure. Just as a manager would expect team spirit to be at its noblest in order to make its dreams come true, the same philosophy should apply to a board of directors. At Coventry it didn't. Again because of my job with the BBC, I was in no position to be at Saturday games, but I could easily imagine the miserable gossipy conversations which inevitably follow defeat, turning to the lack of influence of an absentee chairman. Never mind America, an excuse for a bad result and a convenient victim had to be found and the blame cast somewhere, or on someone. Quietly and surreptitiously the whispered and sometimes more loudly spoken words among the existing board must have turned towards the possibility of finding another chairman who would be there throughout the season, and with a hell of a lot more spare cash than the existing one.

I am not one, either then or now, to complain about looking for a multi-millionaire to underwrite the future of Coventry City; the cause was too important for that. However, perhaps one of our number was coveting the possibility of becoming chairman of the club, without the means, let alone the will, to underwrite its financial fragility. Perhaps such a profile was seen to be advantageous. Whatever lay behind it, I was not at ease with the situation. I became aggravated not so much by the rumblings from without, because through the years I had become used to the dissatisfaction of the crowd when things were not going our way, but more by the rumblings from within among my colleagues. On the one hand, one of the directors Peter Robins was writing me letters professing his loyal support of my position and at the same time must have been involved in discussions surrounding the possible end to my chairmanship.

All of a sudden the responsibility for the loss in America, which I had agreed to share if the board collectively thought that was fair, was referred to on more than one occasion. The fact that the original decision to invest in the American project was taken independently of me was conveniently ignored. That apart, during my eight years of rent-free managing directorship, the club had maintained its position in the Premier League, created its own £1.5 million training ground and sports club, built its own all-seater stadium, and installed innovative and successful under-soil heating, all of which seemed to count for nothing. The bone of contention was the failure of the club's American investment for which the board, as well as myself, were responsible.

We had accepted director Tom Sergeant's professional view as an orthopaedic surgeon that Johan Cruyff would be fit to play for Washington Diplomats in a month. In the event, it was nearer three and he had cost around $200,000 for only three games. Mind you, I don't think Tom or Micky French, another director, had anything to do with the deceitfulness which was occurring. I do believe that Peter Robins, despite smarmy notes of support, was like a spoilt child looking for a new toy, hoping that a change of any kind would ease the pressure, not discouraged in those thoughts by Ian Jamieson, who became chairman – but not for very long.

It was pretty obvious that I wasn't going to put up with the atmosphere surrounding my chairmanship. I could see that a problem was arising with our talented young players, notably Mark Hateley and Gary Gillespie, who were becoming disenchanted with the team lacking the capacity to hold its own in the first division. Perhaps they were looking for other fields to conquer.

Mark came to see me at the time for a chat, describing the difficulty of his home life, living in a small house without reasonable peace and quiet and with a young child and a wife who was feeling the pressure when he was away from home. Not unusual worries for a young footballer, but it was a warning light. It was imperative that we contracted our valuable young players and nearly always it was the relationship with the manager which counted. With Dave, money and contracts never seemed to be a priority – good football was. The club desperately needed to make over-generous contract offers to entice those special players to sign fresh, watertight contracts for our peace of mind. I had warned the board on more than one occasion of the danger. It would need boldness and perhaps to pay more than seemed prudent at the time in order to hold on to those precious registrations.

The relationship between my colleagues and myself was deteriorating rapidly and the mood was not a happy one. As a hobby I did not need it and I resigned. I offered to return my shares – well over 5000 – to the board on the basis that I would not be responsible for any of the club's loss in Washington. I had already lost every penny of WSA's investment, which I had to face up to. My Coventry shares – and you won't want me to tell you just how valuable they are now – were divided among the board of directors.

In the last year or so, the Sky Blue board had developed its own credit card for the use of directors and senior executives. I had one for a year or two and never used it for any expense, either personal or on behalf of the club. The evening following the board meeting at which I resigned, my good friend Tom Wilson and I decided to drown our sorrows and celebrate my new-found freedom in the Riffifi Club in Mayfair with a combination of champagne and orange juice. We were not going to drink common or garden bottled orange juice on such an occasion. We asked that fresh orange juice be provided, squeezed by some fair hand. When the bill came for our commiseration/celebration the orange juice cost rather more than the champagne. As a kind of sweet revenge, I took out my brand new, unused Coventry City credit card and apportioned the bill to the club. It was a sad end to an eventful chapter with many blessings, the biggest of all that Coventry City was solvent, still in the first division of the Football League and four years later went on to win the FA Cup.

Not long afterwards the board sold the Sky Blue Connexion for less than £500,000 and that £1.5 million asset was removed from the balance sheet. Even more damaging was that Mark Hateley was allowed to slip away to Portsmouth for an outrageously small tribunal fee. Portsmouth must have blushed for shame, or in self-congratulation, at being able to pass him on for a profit of a million pounds or more very soon afterwards.

The final straw came in April 1983 when the board submitted to pressure and allowed some supporters to stand, reconstructing the Spion Kop. It's revealing to record that the Department of Sociology at the University of Leicester in 1984, funded by the Football Trust, published a paper on the Coventry experience with its all-seater stadium. As you well know, selected statistics can be manipulated to inflate or reduce an argument. Statistics apart, the paper was not designed to promote me as a benefactor, nor all-seater stadia as the way forward for football. It used every feasible device to undermine the operation. I quote:

. . . The siting of away fans in the Sky Blue stand area and the changes in police after-match strategies introduced in tandem with the all-seater, made the post-match situation *more* unpleasant and potentially more dangerous . . .

I won't bore you with any more examples of the slanted nature of the report, but read retrospectively it's pretty obvious. Still, it's not the only time in my life I've been persecuted for being ahead of the game – but it did arise from an unexpected source. In 1986 the football world was devastated by the tragedy at Hillsborough and Justice Taylor insisted on all-seater stadia for clubs in the top divisions of the Football League.

21

CHARLTON ATHLETIC FC

O NE reason that I eventually gave way and agreed to become a director of Charlton Athletic FC was that, by doing so, I would also enter into a consultancy contract with Sunley Holdings, the club's benefactors. This involved opening and advertising housing complexes as they were developed, mostly in the south east of England. It was John Fryer, the chairman of the club and a director of the Sunley organisation, who was initially enthusiastic for the company to invest in Charlton. His senior partner, John Sunley, went along supporting the hobby of his fellow director as much through kindness to his business associate as for his considerable sporting and charity interest. I'm sure John Fryer enjoyed his involvement to begin with, because it provided some respite from the strenuous and unrelenting nature of his commitment to the business. However, after a year or two when he had begun to understand that being a director of a football club was a long way from being a relaxing pastime, he probably changed his mind on that score.

The second reason was that I would be rubbing shoulders with my old friend Derek Ufton. It would be a pleasure to spend more time together socially than had been possible in recent years. Finally, I suppose, it was that same old character trait – I never could resist a challenge. Charlton, with its ground threatened on

252

top of the general pessimism surrounding falling gates, was like a red rag to a bull if ever there was one.

I was hardly unfamiliar with the contemporary problems of football clubs. To start with in Charlton's case, their ground was in a mess and they desperately needed a training ground. Accordingly, building a relationship with Greenwich Council was vital. As always, some members were warmly supportive and others less so. It was essential to find a way through the political minefield to solve those basic problems, never mind winning a few matches.

The ground was owned indirectly by Michael Gliksten, previous chairman of the club, through a company called Adelong, to whom we paid rent. Without warning the massive terrace opposite the main stand was condemned, and its 3000 capacity reduced to nil. The cost of resurrection was huge and at that time out of the question. Idiotically, it seemed a terrace which had once held 30,000 was now not safe holding 3000. The club took the council to court but lost its appeal. Worse was to follow when the council condemned the terrace completely and made a move to Selhurst Park or somewhere else inevitable.

Of course, it was a devastating blow for everyone, but the board had to find an alternative to keep the club alive. What some supporters failed to understand at that point was that the board did not choose to move; there was no other option. It could be likened to the recent situation at Brighton; to survive they were forced to seek another ground. The damage had been done by a previous board. In Brighton's case, the crowds immediately dwindled to such an extent that it was impossible to make ends meet while still playing in the third division.

At Charlton, we entered into negotiations with Ron Noades of Crystal Palace to share Selhurst Park. Whatever the deal was, it wasn't one which was carved out gently or lightly because of the competitive nature of the two chairmen involved. Nevertheless, a deal was struck and it was a temporary lifeline for Charlton without which the club might have disintegrated completely. However clearly such facts have been represented to supporters, not only at Charlton but almost anywhere in football, there has always been a percentage of people who will not understand. From the outside it's all too simple to know better than those directly involved in making such decisions whilst remaining blind to reality.

I was asked to draft a statement containing the news. In it I explained as well as I could why the unpalatable decision had to be taken. The last sentence of that statement read: 'Nevertheless, if circumstances change at the Valley, the board will grasp any opportunity to return to their fundamental home.' They may not have been the exact words, but that was the sentiment I wanted to convey in order to ease the pain which the supporters were feeling. John Fryer, on reading the drafted statement, said that he would much rather eliminate that last sentence. He reasoned that if we wanted our supporters to adopt Selhurst Park as the place where the club had to be supported in the future, we should not plant ideas that we might one day go back to the Valley. It might encourage them not to support the club at its new rented home.

There was something to be said for that argument because there was then no certainty of returning to the Valley. John, as the ultimate authority, quite rightly had his way and the sentence was removed. I still maintain that it would have saved a lot of hardship and bad feeling to have left it in, by acquainting the supporters with the fact that they might not have been sacrificing their birthright for ever. Those who wished were able to believe that the board had walked away from the Valley heartlessly for a ground-sharing scheme which might suit their purposes better.

On the playing side, we were blessed with a bright manager with a stimulating personality. Unusually, Lennie Lawrence, who had taken over from Eddie May, had not had a majestic playing career as a professional before turning to coaching and then management. Unlike many of our high-profile managers in the Premier League today, he was fully qualified as a coach but a long way from being an international player. Yet he had a way of conveying to players with the utmost frankness and simplicity the route by which they could succeed as individuals and collectively on the field. I felt the tension arising from the playing side far less at Charlton than I had done at Coventry earlier or with Fulham later. What I liked about Lennie was that while not inviting interference from any direction, either the powerful Sunley organisation or the opinionated, ex-professional area of the board – Derek and myself – Lennie had no fear of opening up discussions on the delicate matter of players' form, worth, character and thus their fundamental use to the club. I think we were made to feel that whilst welcome to express an opinion, which no doubt he would digest, when the crunch came it was his own view he would back and nothing would turn him away from that. It was an adult approach to matters and one that was most beneficial to the club.

In the difficult circumstances, it wasn't surprising that the club did not run at a profit, either at the Valley or later at Selhurst Park. Even in times when the team was successful the balance sheet reflected a loss – not something which either John Sunley or John Fryer encouraged in the business which they ran successfully. I was only too accustomed to having a club's back up against a financial wall. However, it was a pleasure to be a spectator at midweek matches both home and away when the manager and his team did not disgrace themselves, eventually winning promotion to the coveted Premier League. It was a superb achievement and a great tribute to Lennie Lawrence and his boys. Sadly, the spectators were divided; some were happy to enjoy promotion to the top flight, regaining that long lost place; others, still feeling the disappointment of leaving the Valley, continued campaigning for a return to their home ground and perhaps saw less good in the playing success which the club was enjoying. Such stubbornness and inflexibility played a part in keeping the pressure on Greenwich Council and those who might have it within their power to bring about a return to the Valley. There is no doubt that persistent campaigning kept the memory of the club fresh in its home town, reminding the council of its historical obligations.

Ground-sharing was not without its problems. Directors of football clubs are used to getting their own way; having two such groups of people tied by an agreement, however carefully drawn up, to share facilities was never going to be an ideal situation. Apart from pressure within the stadium, there was other pressure from without as neighbours realised that having two senior clubs playing in the vicinity doubled the amount of inconvenience. Local groups put pressure on their council to remove these red-shirted interlopers. It was never going to be a peaceful, long-term solution.

Away from Selhurst Park and its problems, I can remember rejoicing particularly at one spectacular result – a 1–0 win against Manchester United at Old Trafford. A day like that certainly reduces the friction temporarily, but such joy was not signed up on a long-term contract and as the players struggled to get to grips with the higher standard, the urge and cry to get back to the Valley was as potent as ever. I was happy to play whatever small part I could in helping the club during those difficult years, but the two Johns, Fryer and Sunley, took the main strain when no one else was around. Since then, it's been a source of great pleasure to me to see Charlton back where they belong.

In 1987 Roger Alwen joined the board. Born in Sevenoaks, Kent, he and his family had been lifelong Charlton supporters, his mother having watched her first game in 1926, two years before I was born. Not long afterwards John Fryer fell ill and went to live in Florida, where the climate was kinder to his health. Roger bought the shares in 1989 accompanied by the immediate announcement that his aim was to take Charlton back to their home at the Valley. He devoted his time and boundless energies to helping convince Greenwich Council, encouraged by the support of so many loyal Charlton supporters. Finally, after all the years of heartbreak, toil and disappointments, the council agreed in May 1991 that the time was right for them to return to the Valley. On a memorable Saturday afternoon, 5 December 1992, Charlton beat Portsmouth 1–0 in front of an emotionally charged, capacity crowd of 8,337 people. Roger Alwen's dream, and that of the Charlton faithful, had come true.

Earlier, in 1991, two new faces joined Roger on the board: Richard Murray and Martin Simons. Both are staunch supporters and, together with their financial involvement, shrewd planning and good housekeeping, succeeded, following one of the finest matches ever seen at Wembley Stadium, in taking the club back to their cherished position in the Premier League. Each in turn took the chairmanship after Roger stepped down, Martin in 1995 and Richard in 1996.

The treasured ground of Charlton Athletic FC now has a stadium which can seat 16,000 people and before the year 2000 will have a capacity of over 20,000. From deep depression, the club has a healthy stock market listing, a much sought-after, young, loyal and successful manager, Alan Curbishley, himself an ex-Charlton player, and a flourishing youth policy which has produced, amongst others, Lee Bowyer who, at the heady price of £2.6 million, became a record signing for a teenager.

Roger Alwen has rightly joined Sam Bartram, Eddie Firmani and Keith Peacock in Charlton's illustrious Hall of Fame. I would confidently recommend my old chum Derek Ufton of Charlton, England and Kent County Cricket Club for inclusion.

22

THERE'S ONLY ONE 'F' IN FULHAM

THE most difficult part of this book which, unlike some highly successful sporting publications lately, has been written by its named author, is to reflect Fulham's recent history succinctly, accurately and fairly. To describe every nuance of my eventual ten-year chairmanship of Fulham would mean delving into details which the uncommitted might find tedious. It is at its best a romantic story, not of desert island proportions, but it does have charm and a heady finish.

Sadly, along the way, the sun seldom shone. When it did, the surrounding shadow of dissatisfaction, to say nothing of deception and greed, quickly dissuaded us from premature celebration. In truth, from the outset, to be chairman of the club was a burden. Until it became evident that nothing was going to prevent the gaining of the final, life-preserving planning consent, it was a miserable experience. It wasn't as if the different managers and players during that period were able to do anything to lift the gloom. In those circumstances, when a club is most in need of understanding and tender loving care from the terraces, it seldom gets it. In contrast, there are some kind, supporting souls whose enthusiasm doesn't wane as they steadfastly continue to encourage their team through the most wretched periods. Happiness was in short supply for them and us.

It all began towards the end of the 1986–87 season when it became obvious that Fulham FC were in difficulty. Ernie Clay, with Tom Wilson's help, acquired the freehold of Craven Cottage from the Church Commissioners, and then at a personal profit sold the club and all its assets, including that freehold, to Marler Estates, who already owned Stamford Bridge and Queens Park Rangers and their ground. Chelsea FC immediately bought their ground from Marler. The rules stated very clearly that no individual or family could be part of the board of directors of two clubs in the Football League, and the League made it clear to Marler in no uncertain terms that they would have to renounce one of them. At the time, Queens Park Rangers as a club had advantages over Fulham, but if ever planning consent could be obtained the site value of Craven Cottage would dwarf that of Loftus Road. There appeared to be a real danger that Marler would either wind Fulham up or merge the club with Queens Park Rangers (to become Fulham Park Rangers?) so as to release Craven Cottage for redevelopment.

It was a desperate time for Fulham and I was asked by a group of supporters to chair an emergency meeting at the Hammersmith Town Hall to which any interested party was invited. Whatever else I remember about that occasion, I certainly couldn't forget that I was on crutches. Playing tennis at the All England Club only a couple of weeks before, I had ruptured an Achilles tendon and had to have it repaired surgically, which meant that I couldn't put my foot to the ground having emerged from hospital only a day or two before with my leg in plaster.

The town hall was packed and those present listened carefully to the desperate account of the circumstances in which the club found itself. It would be necessary to appoint a completely new board of directors who had the wherewithal, or could find it, to finance the club in the future. The purpose of the gathering was to find a way to recruit and select such individuals and to create a new board as soon as was humanly possible. The resolution was that a small group of people, including myself, were entrusted with the task. We invited a chosen few who had expressed a wish to invest in the newly formed club, if the circumstances were to their liking, to a meeting to discuss the practicalities.

These wealthier Fulham supporters, among them David Dein and two interested friends, attended that historic meeting at the Wig and Pen club in Fleet Street and after some discussion were asked, 'How much might you be prepared to put into the club?' Eventually, when we added up, the total from every possible source came to £341,000. That was the figure with which the new Fulham began its life.

I had attended these meetings as a director of Charlton FC, but Bill Muddyman, one of the prospective investors, made a stipulation that he was only prepared to invest his money if I would become chairman. It would have made more sense for him to be chairman, but as he was a non-resident in the United Kingdom, he made it a condition of his involvement that I should fill the post for a period of two years. In the event, it stretched to ten. This put me in something of a dilemma. In many ways I felt I had done as much as I could for Charlton and their future was in good hands, so I resigned and accepted the challenge to become chairman of a club whose assets were a ground in urgent need of repair, then worth very little without planning consent, and with only £341,000 in the kitty.

It seemed logical to create a board from those who were the major contributors financially and so the Muddymans, father and son, Bill and Andy (£150,000), David Gardner (£50,000) and Cyril Swain (£50,000) became directors, alongside Tom Wilson and me who had virtually been conducting the club's affairs throughout this transitional phase. Thus the new Fulham was born. If I had expected that being chairman of a second division club would be a happy, rewarding experience, the supporters' magazine, *When Saturday Comes*, soon disabused me with the following sobering words, directly about me: 'No one person can be trusted to run a club no matter how altruistic they may be.' A refreshing welcome, reminding me that the next few years were going to be anything but a bowl of cherries.

Tom and I had meetings with Messrs David Bulstrode (then chairman of Marler Estates and also of Fulham FC) and Robert

Noonan, the chief executive of Marler Estates and the driving force behind the Marler plans. They were prepared to sell us the players at a price, but we could not afford to buy them, whoever made the valuation. A device had to be found for a feasible transaction to take place and for the new Fulham to have a ground as well as charge of itself. We negotiated a three-year lease for Craven Cottage and fortunately Queens Park Rangers coveted two of the team, Paul Parker and Dean Coney. The suggestion was made that Marler Estates should take the two players for QPR as payment for the rest of the playing staff, which would at least give us a clean start with some capital in hand. Naturally we didn't want to lose either player but survival was the only game we could play if there was to be a next stage. The deal was struck, I was appointed chairman of Fulham (1987) Limited and into battle we went.

During those last eventful two weeks, Bryony had not been at home; she had a nonagenarian grandmother in New Zealand whom she had been wanting to visit for some time and the opportunity had arisen so there she was, far away in the southern hemisphere. When she left, I was a normal human being walking around on two legs, and a director of Charlton. When she returned two weeks later, I was on crutches and chairman of Fulham! She has since declined to leave me for any length of time, thank goodness.

Over the next ten years there were three games to be played – on the field, of course; securing our home at Craven Cottage or elsewhere; and last but not least, financial survival.

We decided to give Ray Lewington, who was acting as caretaker manager, a run and our enthusiastic support. Ray was upset by a paragraph in a newspaper suggesting that Dave Bassett might be taking the job. It was true that a friend at the BBC, Chris Lewis, who was a particular pal of Dave's, had suggested to me that he would be interested in Fulham and we had met. I explained our financial position and whether that was an unwelcome revelation or, as I suspected, I was being used as a bargaining tool, it didn't matter because Dave joined Watford soon after.

Minus Parker and Coney we managed to win enough games to hold our place in the second division and give ourselves breathing space. Ray and I had a good relationship but not all that long after it came to an end. With most managerial sackings, the sequence is something like this: the team hits a bad spell and the crowd begins to lose confidence in various players and their manager; that puts more pressure on the players, who are less likely to recover their form; the results do not improve; the pressure is turned on the board, who nearly always do their best to be loyal and pass a vote of confidence in their manager. History tells us that such confidence will not last for ever. In that atmosphere, it's extremely unusual for a manager to find a way to save his neck. Buying a couple of talented, fresh faces, especially belonging to goalscorers, can sometimes save the day. Such a last-resort cavalry charge into the transfer market can only be achieved when it can be funded. At most clubs it can't and certainly not at Fulham at that time.

Our policy, supported by the Muddymans and our bank, had to be to trade, hopefully successfully. That's the way in which three-quarters of league clubs survive, exemplified by John Rudge of Port Vale, a brilliant manager supported by a wise chairman guiding a club which has consistently defied the odds of financial snakes and ladders. To survive, a manager's judgement of a prospect has to be sound, and he must have the ability to create a successful playing method and atmosphere, so that all his existing players appear to be valuable prospects to others. It would be delightful if that was all there was to it, but there is a snag, I'm afraid. It is that young players who might become worth a bob or two, excepting one in a hundred, are not the most likely lads to gain a club promotion or even save it from relegation. So while supporters are screaming for his head, the poor man under such scrutiny fights to survive by balancing those difficult and delicate conflicting managerial responsibilities.

The truth is that directors appoint managers; supporters sack them in most cases. It also follows that if directors appoint managers, it is they who are held to blame for their chosen one's failings. It's certainly their responsibility, but my experience has taught me that it's easier to back a winner at Cheltenham. If you had seen, as I have, the names and managerial experience of those who applied for jobs over the years, you would realise they are divided into two camps: (1) those who have no managerial experience, many with no coaching qualifications either, and (2) those who have been managers, but have been sacked once, twice, three times or more. That's the result of our pretty sadistic system and after all these years I still don't know the answer to it. I know it's no use asking the supporters to understand or to be patient. I've tried over the years in a thousand programme articles without any success. They bay for blood and usually get it – after all, the customer is always right.

During the last few months of Ray's reign, Alan Dicks joined us on his return from coaching in the States. Alan was my assistant manager at Coventry during the successful sixties. He had gone on to more success with Bristol City but spoiled matters by staying too long. That's another 'survival' maxim I learned as a manager. It's not easy to keep stimulating the same players, particularly passing strangers – either keep a healthy turnover going or they'll see you to the door first.

I did not want the absolute responsibility of appointing an old friend, so I suggested to the board that we should bring Alan in alongside Ray to freshen things up with a new face. It was up to them to say yes or no. Alan's experience, the novelty of new ideas and his friendly personality seemed to be popular so the appointment was made in July 1990. Unfortunately, Alan did not stay the course. In January we received a warning from the FA, for with 165 disciplinary points we were among the League's worst offenders. What was even more depressing was that normally it's teams whose players are second to the ball who collect most disciplinary points, and consequently far fewer league points. That message was clear!

So it was back to an advert in a national newspaper, not *The Times* or the *Telegraph*, for another dip, dip, dip selection. However, this time round it seemed that we were on to a winner. Don Mackay, not long having left Blackburn Rovers, was among those who applied for the job. Don had experience and some success at Bristol City and appeared to have been squeezed out at Blackburn to accommodate a high-profile figure, who turned out to be Kenny Dalglish. No one could complain that it was the wrong decision for Rovers as they went on to win the league championship. Perhaps, though, that was our luck. Don's personality, warm manner and Scottish brogue put him ahead of the other candidates, but he had been sacked more than once before. . .

The players seemed to take to him and all that directors can really do once they have made the appointment is to sit back and pray. Because of continual financial restraints we didn't expect miracles. We enjoyed a more than acceptable relationship with Don despite that and I don't remember a cross word or difference of opinion spoiling it.

I have been accused of being many things in my life, some true, some unfair, but I must confess that although I am not a New Man, I do consider myself to be reasonably romantic. However, there was one occasion which severely risked damaging my reputation. During this period of intense flux at the club, on a cold January morning in 1991 Bryony and I were married. We were three days into our honeymoon and were heading for a confrontation between Cambridge United and Fulham on the Saturday, the sole reason for choosing East Anglia in preference to the Caribbean. . .

Having celebrated the event at home on the Wednesday, we drove to Suffolk to stay in a small guesthouse where we had been once before, and where they served an evening meal if required. It was quieter and more private than a hotel, and just what we needed. We were the only guests that night, and after a delicious meal we climbed the stairs armed with a bottle of champagne given to us by our hosts. I made the mistake of turning on the television. Bryony came out of the bathroom to see me lying fully dressed on the bed, the clicker in my hand. Up on the screen popped a familiar face: Mr Lynam.

'Ah! "Sportsnight"!' I said with glee. Bryony's face was a picture of horror.

'It may be your third wedding night, but this is my first!' she cried. Not wanting to appear too churlish, but ever the professional, I closed the subject by saying, 'It is my job, you know!' I won, but I've been paying for it ever since. . .

Saturday arrived and the weather was foul. It was a bitterly cold afternoon and in spite of the inclement weather the roads around the outskirts of Cambridge were congested with cars, coaches and too much traffic in general. We arrived in plenty of time before the kick-off and spotting the floodlights in the distance we made our way to the ground. Pulling up outside double iron gates we asked two police officers the way to the directors' car park. The younger of the two told us to head back from whence we came, follow the one-way system and then ask again when we saw the next policeman. We did as we were bid, renegotiating the horrendous Saturday afternoon traffic. It was now drizzling and becoming foggy and thoroughly unpleasant. We drove the two miles or so around on the ring road only to be told once we got there that the directors' car park was back the other way. Once more we found ourselves outside the original gate and patiently asked our boys in blue the same question. They gave us further instructions and off we set once more, only this time when we did find the other policeman, he directed us miles away into a field where, with much relief, we could see the familiar Fulham Supporters' coach amongst others in the distance. We drove across the grass but could see no cars parked nearby. Now desperate and with time rapidly running out we turned round and drove the now familiar path back to square one.

We did not have to put it to our new friends that we had a problem. It was already twenty minutes after kick-off and we had seen nothing of the game. The younger of the two policemen shuffled in his shoes, went pink in the face and muttered apologetically that the directors' car park was just behind him – the very same gates we had stopped in front of forty minutes before.

A year or so later Bryony's brother, Neil, was listening with half an ear to a programme called 'Confessions' on Radio 1. One of the tales of woe began to strike a chord as it unravelled. A young chap was on the line relating that some time ago he had been a special constable on duty at a football match, Cambridge United v Fulham. He had been asked to direct Jimmy Hill no less, who happened to be on his honeymoon at the time, to the directors' car park. He had given the wrong instructions three times which meant that his interrogator missed the kick-off and twenty minutes of the game. His conscience had been troubling him ever since and he ended his story by saying that after that experience he resigned immediately from the force and was no longer a special constable. . . Fulham lost 1–0, the only goal being scored late in the game by a promising, athletic youngster, Dion Dublin. I've forgiven him since, his heroic efforts on Coventry's behalf having preserved their Premier League status.

But let's get back to the real problems. We were encouraged at first by a much more successful second half of the season and a respectable ninth place. Approaching the 1992–93 season with optimism but without the wherewithal to be extravagant, we became desperately disappointed with our results as we realised the end-of-term report would inevitably read, 'must try harder'. Our fears were confirmed. As our off-the-field struggle for survival continued, the playing side offered little or no comfort. Never without hope, we gathered our strength and stoked up our enthusiasm for the 1993–94 season. What a sad one that turned out to be. In the relegation zone with three-quarters of the season gone, we were in dire straits.

We appreciated that Don was working under financial restrictions and pressure to reduce costs. Excessive injuries do not encourage staff reductions and we were experiencing more than our fair share. I perhaps should have been awakened to the fact that all was not quite well when we entertained the team to an early evening supper at home in Sussex. The idea was for a game of golf first for those who played and a bowl in Brighton for those who didn't. Unfortunately, it was a cold, rainy day. The golfers survived it and so did the rest, although apparently they hadn't done anything except hang around the shops in Brighton and get soaked. Since I was the overall host of the day I began to feel guilty about what was meant to be an enjoyable day off.

The team had been home before, one summer for a barbecue. They'd never forgotten it because the coach driver, uninvited, beat everyone else to the front of the queue, shovelling four large chops and several sausages on to his plate. That captured the spirit at the time. However, on this occasion, although it seemed most had enjoyed it, we felt a flicker of unease.

More points were lost and slipped away as one disappointment followed another. Still in the relegation zone, we were far from confident facing the Orient at Brisbane Road. Picking the right team was difficult because of injuries and there were few alternatives for selection, position and tactics. As normal I popped my head in the dressing-room to say, 'Good luck,' noticed that Simon Morgan, our captain, was fuming, and came out. I found out later that the mood had arisen because Don had changed the team and the formation three times in the previous hour. It wasn't a very happy prelude to a vital match, but I consoled myself that growling players sometimes vent their anger on their opponents.

I could not believe the way we played in the first half. I had never seen such a dispirited group of footballers anywhere at any time. They looked to each other for help and none came. Orient scored once and it could have been five, although their performance was hardly sparkling.

After all we had suffered to keep the club alive, I could not sit and see it thrown away. I consulted the Muddymans and Tom Wilson.

'I think I must try and sort it out,' I said. 'We cannot just sit back and watch another half like that.' Fortunately they felt the same way. It's not very pleasant watching one's team play with neither method nor spirit.

So I went into the dressing-room, asked Don to take a back seat and then extracted honest answers from miserable players playing in unfamiliar roles. We changed the team around: John Marshall was happily restored to his favourite right-wing spot and Ara Bedrossian to midfield, among other adjustments. We equalised and were unrecognisable from the eleven who produced that relegation-loaded performance before half-time. As

267

luck would have it, Orient scored a second time, an unstoppable piledriver from way out, but spiritedly we fought back for a draw. It had become clear that Don could not continue to be our manager.

Once again the loyal and dependable Ray Lewington took over as temporary manager. I promised him personal backing in the dressing-room and on the training ground. It was to no avail. Despite putting up a brave fight, we finally succumbed, losing to Swansea at the Vetch on the last day of the season.

Judging by the number of points we needed to stay up, it wasn't going to be our season anyway. I didn't think, though, that I was going to be driving to Swansea on the last Saturday with the team needing to win to stay up. I took Bryony for comfort and a supply of handkerchiefs and watched us lose 2–0. I had not been involved in a relegation since joining Fulham as a player in March 1952 when they were already in the danger zone. That relegation was out of the top division, not into the bottom. It wasn't the end of the world, but it didn't half feel like it. But we were still alive and we were still battling to regain Craven Cottage, so the chairman of all people should not weaken. Instead of driving home, more than three hours away, I suggested we should stay overnight at The Bear in Hungerford to drown our sorrows in good food and wine, and then drive to the Berkshire for a game of golf after breakfast to avoid the misery of the telephone on Sunday morning. It was blissfully therapeutic and just what the doctor ordered. If only the lads had controlled a football in the way I guided the golf ball we would have been saved! On Monday morning I woke up and realised how truly horrible it was.

It was back to the drawing board and the desperate plea in the 'Situations Vacant' column for potential managers to apply to the club. The letters came in and the interviews took place. Our record was not good, never mind the financial problems; they made life difficult, but it's results by which clubs and their directors are judged.

In many people's eyes, especially those within sight of the Isle of Wight, we were off our heads to choose Ian Branfoot, who had been Southampton's manager during depressing times. Despite his local unpopularity, he had still kept his team in the Premier League. Ian also had a splendid reputation for signing and schooling young players, including Alan Shearer, and was well-respected by his colleagues in the game. He explained that his plan would be to bring with him Micky Adams, as player-coach, whom he would groom for managership, taking over as and when seemed prudent. There was no argument among the board, the package seemed sound.

Ian began to reshape the playing staff, nursing the young and leaning on the oldies. Micky mixed coaching with playing, troubled by a slowly deteriorating knee. After an uncertain start, when Micky played he oozed class and confidence and became a warm favourite. Nevertheless, it wasn't the most successful season and as the club's financial position and un-relenting planning problems and delays became more debilitat-ing, the team slipped down the table. It's easy to say those frustrating events should have no effect on the playing side, unless you've been involved in the game for as long as I have. I'm superstitious, too, and the effect of that shortcoming was that I had a deep underlying belief that matters would not improve on the pitch until we had solved our seemingly never-ending ground problem.

I would like to report that the next season, 1995–96, brought some joy and some reward for our efforts, but it wasn't to be and our patience and stamina were stretched to the limit. We were not all that far from falling into the Conference and it wasn't easy for anyone to keep faith. Perhaps the continuing drama surrounding the future of Craven Cottage gave our supporters something to occupy their minds or at least a straw of some kind at which to clutch. For our part there was no way out, other than to continue to fight on all fronts. I clung to my superstition that one good happening would lead to another. . .

Ian Branfoot had never been a popular manager and for a number of reasons for the 1996–97 season we decided to make the planned promotion and appoint his *protégé*, Micky Adams, in his place with Alan Cork as his assistant. A change of any kind always buys a board time and in addition, Micky had clearly proved in limited appearances that he was at least a class or two above his new charges. After our long struggle it was time for a change of luck, thanks to our persistence and the justice of our cause.

We were blessed with a fantastic season, thank goodness, taking some pressure away from the board, who were occupied to the full with the culmination of the long campaign to repossess the club's home. The game that clinched our promotion was at Mansfield and those of us who were there will not forget the emotional response from our own supporters nor the compassionate understanding of those from Mansfield who generously shared in the celebration. The team had regained its pride, the perfect prelude to the club regaining its home by the river.

That had not been an easy task either, with the added disadvantage of there being no referee to see fair play among the parties involved, from Ernie Clay, David Bulstrode and John Duggan to Mohammed Al Fayed and Uncle Tom Cobley and all between 1985 and 1997. But that's another story. . .

From the outset we went overboard in our determination to create a democratic club, conscious of how the new Fulham had arisen and had been funded. It became evident before very long that, however strong those intentions, when it became a matter of life or death, the decisions of those who had largely taken on the responsibility for the club's survival had to hold sway. We formed a board of management which included representatives of all sections of the club: the vice presidents, the Riversiders and not least the supporters' club. We also invited the council to nominate a representative and they chose Gordon Prentice, now a Member of Parliament. Despite some harrowing moments when we appeared to be pulling in different directions, that committee proved a valuable tool for the task of regaining Craven Cottage, although its members didn't always see it that way.

What was happening off the field dominated our days, not surprising considering the nature of events. The ownership of Craven Cottage had changed hands from Marler Estates to Cabra Estates for a staggering £83 million. Originally we had negotiated a three-year lease with David Bulstrode of Marler, terminating in 1990. It was about to end with John Duggan and Cabra Estates in control. A variety of schemes were contemplated for when the lease ended. Hammersmith and Fulham Council rejected two Cabra plans – a Quinlan Terry concept for 224 Georgian-style flats, with the Cottage as a pub, and an alternative scheme for a three-sided residential development surrounding the pitch and stands. The council drew up its own plans, which the club supported, inviting Cabra to adopt the scheme or otherwise a compulsory purchase order would go ahead. If that plan had succeeded, the council would have owned the ground outright with the club renting it. It would have been some time before the victorious clash of cymbals had subsided and in the cold light of day it became apparent that at that time there was no one in the world with sufficient funds ready, willing and waiting to under-write the expensive consequences of its success. Never mind any rent, the premises were desperately in need of repair and the club was losing around £500,000 per annum.

There was also a limit to the Muddymans' resources as far as Fulham was concerned. During those difficult times, Bill sup-ported the club financially by means of loans, interest calculated and rolled up. There came a moment when Bill's finances were stretched and I introduced him to a Saudi Arabian friend of mine in an attempt to provide immediate capital to ride the crisis. It didn't work out because Bill would not give up control of the company involved and found other means to weather that particular storm. The directors, too, jointly and severally guar-anteed the club's sizeable overdraft. The undesirable fact of financial life for Fulham and so many similar clubs is that they lose money every season, because competitively they pay the players more than their balance sheets can sustain.

It was, and is, all very well for people who didn't have the responsibility of keeping the club alive and solvent to criticise the board's actions *ad nauseam*. I can tell you, it is totally different when it is personal. At that time of crisis, and since, there have been plenty of pretentious critics pouring scorn on the knife-edge decisions we took. I can understand some of our most passionate supporters, fearful of the future or lack of it, becoming angry in their frustration. What I abhor above all else is someone like Simon Inglis who, in writing about the history of Craven Cottage, retrospectively coloured my actions, and those who had joined me to save Fulham, as if some of the unpopular decisions we took, or might have taken, were from choice. It is a simple matter to be spiteful about the behaviour of fellow human beings when the bank statements are not falling on one's own doormat. It would be arrogant and untrue to boast that the Fulham board had seen the whole plot, including the astonishing increase in land value from 1990 until now. What we did have in our different ways was a feeling for the club, a sense of duty and a determination to battle on and, with luck, provide a foundation for a future at Craven Cottage and also, one day, in the Premier League. Why not? We'd been there before, and I'd played a small part in that journey on the field.

To compete for and maintain a place in the Premier League sun now requires a ground holding 20,000 or more; to challenge for honours, 35,000 to 50,000; if the name of the game is to compete unconditionally, even bigger. Manchester United, for example, extended its current site to hold 56,000. In contrast, Huddersfield Town, Stoke City and Derby County found their ambitions restricted by the impossibility of extending their traditional homes and have made tactical, sensible moves to fresh sites capable of accommodating any increased demand, should they go bananas on the field. I don't ever see 50,000 people getting in and out of Craven Cottage on a Saturday, let alone an evening, sandwiched as it is between Hammersmith and Putney. If Mohammed Al Fayed's ambitions are unlimited, the club will have to move.

A public inquiry into the whole business was scheduled by the

Department of the Environment for 30 January 1990. This put enormous pressure on Cabra Estates who made an approach to Fulham almost hours before the inquiry was due to begin. The approach came on a Saturday whilst I was on duty with 'Match of the Day', but I was only too well aware of the nature of it and what it might mean in terms of public response. When the conditions of Cabra's offer were described to me by my fellow directors, I realised that there was no practical alternative to accepting it. It was very easy for those who were not funding the club, or responsible for its debts and salvation, to say we should have turned down the offer. It would provide money to pay off the overdraft, fund the purchase of a player or two and under-write a future for a couple of years at least. Whatever anyone thought, we were not in a position to support the consequences of refusal. For all the criticism we faced at that time, I took the trouble to share a pot of coffee with long-term supporter and historian of the club Denis Turner, a fervent supporter of Gordon Prentice and the Hammersmith Council, no one more enthusiastic. When I explained the exact terms of the deal alongside our limited capacity financially to cope without it, he agreed that there was no option. On the other hand, I understood Gordon Prentice's disappointment and frustration, but long term his involvement did no harm to his political future.

The Cabra deal meant £2 million up front, £4 million on vacating Craven Cottage and a further £5 million if and when Cabra acquired the planning consent they wanted for the site. There was a bonus if the site's value increased to over £50 million. The club had a new three-year lease, but would leave if and when planning permission was obtained. There is no reason to suppose we could have survived those early years, if we had not accepted this deal.

The public inquiry eventually took place and I was subpoenaed to appear when my carefully worded statement, crafted because I had by then agreed not to support the compulsory purchase order, left the door open for anything to happen.

When November 1990 came, and with it the end of the first

273

lease, the order was not granted, neither were Cabra's new plans passed, and even more surprisingly the council's own scheme was also rejected. A funny old hat-trick! Sooner or later, we had to find a new home before Cabra produced a plan which was approved. We could not stand still and consequently investigated every avenue that was open to us. It didn't stop us praying for a miracle reprieve, but neither did it reduce the misery for our long-suffering supporters, still lacking any compensation from the field of play.

Sharing Stamford Bridge was an obvious choice for some sound reasons – it was in the borough; it had been reconstructed to include two home dressing-rooms; it was to be equipped for the Premier League; and it made economic sense. None of the other avenues we explored was proving feasible, popular or better.

We spent some time endeavouring to establish with Chelsea a formula for ground-sharing. We suggested £5 million for a long-term lease which effectively would give us a share of the equity in the stadium, but we never entered into any detailed discussions. More time was spent on the essential practical details of co-habiting.

We didn't forget our supporters. It's impossible with the noisy ones anyway, they always let you know what they think. At this stage we invited them to join us so that we could tell them the whys and wherefores and gather their current views. It was a sensible meeting and every possibility was explored. On a show of hands on the wisdom, never mind inevitability, of moving to Stamford Bridge, it came out fifty fifty as near as dammit. Life's never simple, is it? Whether we were forced to go by circumstances or chose to go, we knew our audience was split right down the middle. A bonus was that there was some sadness, little bitterness and much sympathy. Initially there appeared to be similar understanding between those who were negotiating the financial details of the ground-share operation.

On the June day when I was due to go on holiday, I was enjoying a family birthday lunch in an Italian restaurant in

Tolworth when the news came through of a prospective deal with the Royal Bank of Scotland, who were lending money to Cabra Estates. Whichever way you looked at it, it was a much healthier situation than had existed at any time during my stewardship. I went on holiday confidently expecting the ground-sharing discussions to proceed smoothly, knowing there was a possibility we could stay at Craven Cottage if they didn't.

We were committed to securing for Fulham FC at least a share in another ground long term. We were prepared to invest the capital which at that time appeared to be available to us – from Cabra and the Football Trust – to achieve that end. Chelsea's preference was to grant Fulham a shorter lease than we wanted, and they proposed a rental which Fulham would have found impossible to pay. Our club would have been a poor relation in a stadium in which it would never have had the sovereignty which it now enjoys at Craven Cottage. That episode, it seems to me, was a classic example of an ill wind blowing somebody some good. I had gone on holiday in optimistic mood and was surprised to find on my return that the deal had turned sour.

Ken Bates blamed me publicly, but we would never have been forgiven, quite rightly, for leaving Craven Cottage without securing irrevocable rights to play at Stamford Bridge. I wrote to the Royal Bank explaining the situation, with the result that we remained at Craven Cottage under the terms and temporary comfort of a deal with them.

The Royal Bank of Scotland were first mortgagees in respect of Craven Cottage and their initial intention was to wind Fulham up and realise as much money as they could from a sale of Craven Cottage. It is understood that they had advanced in excess of £10 million to Cabra Estates against the security of the freehold in the light of valuations of the order of £30 million for residential development, which of course assumed that planning consent existed, but it did not.

Public opinion and the risk of receiving critical press coverage caused the Royal Bank to have a change of heart. Consequently, in 1993 they agreed to grant a new lease of Craven Cottage to

Fulham for ten years on the basis that in the early part of the lease term, little or no rent was to be paid, but Fulham had an obligation to obtain planning permission for partial development of the ground, so adding to the value. Associated with the new lease was an option for Fulham to acquire the freehold from the Royal Bank for the sum of £7.5 million.

Soon after, Cabra experienced a fatal blow in again failing to get planning consent, this time for a less pretentious, more sophisticated scheme. In November, liquidators were appointed and Cabra's reign was over.

Tom Wilson continued lengthy negotiations on the club's behalf with the Hammersmith and Fulham Borough Council Planning Department, the Port of London Authority and the National Rivers Authority. Other bodies had to be consulted and although the council were very supportive, planning application was not made until the spring of 1994. Due to the sensitivity of the application and the numerous issues which had to be addressed, it was mid-1995 before the council approved Fulham's application. The matter had to be referred to the Government Office for London because it would be a Thames-side redevelopment. Matthew Carrington MP, the Conservative member for Hammersmith and Fulham, began to take a close interest in the situation. Tom Wilson and I went to the House of Commons to see Mr Carrington, at which stage he was marginally encouraging and at no time implied that he might be responsible for causing Fulham's application to be put before a public inquiry. In the event, this is exactly what he accomplished and early in August 1995, John Gummer, the Secretary of State for the Environment, informed the interested parties that an inquiry was to be held. It may be that decision would have been made without Mr Carrington's intervention because Mr Gummer was reputedly always highly concerned about riverside schemes, but I was not impressed with the performance of our local MP.

The public inquiry was held in February 1996. The inspector gave his decision surprisingly quickly and granted consent for 142 flats and three new all-seater stands which would enclose the ground at the Bishop's Park, riverside and Hammersmith boundaries. The Stevenage Road stand is, of course, a listed building, as are the Cottage and the Stevenage Road turnstiles. This was the first really encouraging sign either on or off the field that we had experienced – there was a possibility that the club might have a future and a value. Strangely enough, the board showed splendid team spirit up to that point.

Ever since the prospective partial redevelopment of Craven Cottage was first publicised, numerous developers had approached us through Tom Wilson with a view to negotiating terms under which they would be able to construct and sell the residential units. The Royal Bank of Scotland remained close to and interested in this situation and, indeed, because the planning negotiations were taking so long, generously extended the time during which the club was to remain rent free and paid our legal costs for the inquiry.

A further setback occurred in early 1997 when Lady Berkeley, a local resident, brought an action in the High Court against the Secretary of State for the Environment on the grounds that his inspector at the public inquiry had paid insufficient heed to environmental matters – particularly relating to the River Thames – in reaching his decision. Judgement was fairly quickly given against Lady Berkeley, who was ordered to pay costs. There was the threat of an appeal against this judgement but as far as I know, no further litigation has, as yet, taken place. I made it my business to seek out Lady Berkeley and to try to understand her case, as well as for her to appreciate ours. I admired her tenacity and courage; I had also fought a few unpopular battles in my time. However, I did not feel that our development plans were fundamentally damaging to the river's ecology, but I was sympathetic to her concern.

Contrasting with other frustrations, these delays were to prove beneficial in one delightful way. The property market was rising rapidly and our financial situation was looking rosier by the day. We were within spitting distance of being able to repay the club's debt to Bill Muddyman, buy back the freehold from the Royal

277

Bank and have enough left over to redevelop the ground. Hour by hour conditions looked more favourable. Tom Wilson, who had spearheaded our campaign culminating in its ultimate success, had been handling negotiations with interested development partners. In addition, three groups had approached me with a wish to underwrite the club's future, as well as the property deal. It didn't take an Einstein to realise that this impoverished club, abandoned by Ernie Clay to the developers, was at last in a position to deal from strength.

The simple truth is that Tom and I revealed the approaches that had been made to us to Bill and to the rest of the board. In contrast, the first time I saw or heard Mohammed Al Fayed's name mentioned in connection with Fulham was in what may well have been a flyer in the *Independent on Sunday*. It was never communicated to Tom or myself as directors of the club until we had resigned. We decided for Fulham's sake not to attempt to establish whatever rights we may have had. After ten years of struggle neither of us could bear the thought of a bitter legal battle spoiling the double blessing of home ownership at last and promotion for the club for whom we had both competed as young men.

We had negotiated a reduction on the price of Craven Cottage with our landlords to £6.75 million. The Muddymans, referring frequently to the Royal Bank hierarchy as 'hard-nosed Jocks', had also put as much pressure as they were able on the Royal Bank. In the later stages, they even threatened to mount a legal action arising from the contents of a letter to John Duggan which had perhaps inadvisedly been written by the manager of their Pall Mall branch. This letter intimated that the Royal Bank of Scotland would support his company, Cabra, in its contracted financial obligations to Fulham. The Muddymans' legal advisers would seek to prove that, at the demise of Cabra, the Bank became responsible for that undertaking. Subsequent events swept away the urge to acquire this particular golden goose, as the possibility of another, more precious golden egg emerged, without any further financial obligation or risk. But at the time this issue divided the board and made Tom's position impossible, because of many years of mutual business activities in terms of property advice with the Bank. I had no such connection to embarrass me, except my own version of what was fair play. At one time whilst planning consent was still being fought for, the Muddymans and their advisers had attempted to reduce the purchase price of the freehold to £3.5 million. My guess is at that time the Bank would have taken around £5 million, but it was not offered.

The board was pressurised to commence legal action against the Royal Bank by the Muddymans and their advisers. I remained against it, which was virtually the end of any relationship with the Muddymans and those who supported them; not, of course, Tom Wilson, who had finally masterminded the so-valuable planning consent, turning a club worth less than £1 million into one worth something approaching £15–20 million. Soon after, Tom and I were asked to resign our positions from the board without delay, but Bill Muddyman, the vice chairman, was persuaded that with only a few games remaining in what was certainly going to be a triumphant promotion season for Fulham, it would not be good public relations to announce that two directors, one of whom was the chairman, were leaving the board at that juncture.

You will appreciate now why neither of us have set foot in the club since. Nevertheless, we follow future developments with extreme interest. For the sake of the club we did not rock the boat at that time. Following the Al Fayed takeover, it no longer matters.

Incidentally, as a leaving present after so many years dedication to Fulham Football Club, the newly formed board very kindly donated four tickets for every home match to Tom and myself, for life. A sad consequence of events also means that the Muddyman family is no longer on our Christmas card list, nor we on theirs.

23

WORLD CUPS

IT's strange the thoughts which remain in my mind from involvement in nine World Cups. Mexico 1970 was joyful whereas West Germany's win in 1974 was brilliant but controversial. There was no doubt in my mind that the two best teams reached the final, but the Dutch style, 'total football' it was called, exemplified by Johan Cruyff's genius, eventually gave way to Beckenbauer's multi-talented and well-organised team. England was represented in the final by referee Jack Taylor, a long-time friend and supporter of good things in the game. Jack gave a penalty to both sides and I'm not all that sure that the Germans didn't get the best of the decisions on that day. Perhaps I leaned that way because of my fondness for Dutch flair, but whether justice was done or not, it was a dramatic, classy final. In England's absence Scotland, by qualifying at least, represented the United Kingdom without disgrace, knocked out only by goal difference. It's worth reflecting that Poland, who history records were fortunate to qualify by drawing with England at Wembley, finished in an honourable third place.

In Argentina in 1978 the performance of six-goal Kempes, Ardiles, Passarella and colleagues, plus home advantage, enabled the host nation deservedly to beat Holland, unlucky again in the final, pushing Brazil into third place. It was Argentina's brilliant players who captured our imagination and stayed in our memories.

It was almost as hot in Spain in 1982 when, in the final, Italy beat the so-consistent West Germans. For the second time Poland finished third, a superb achievement for an unfashionable country.

Scotland's opening match against Brazil was designed to get the nation talking. In Seville our commentary position was unusually not ideal, but that did not seem to matter when at 0–0 Scotland's David Narey broke away at the far end of the ground. As he approached Brazil's penalty area, it seemed as if the ball had run fractionally too far ahead of him. Nevertheless, he shot from well out and scored, sending the Scots and the BBC's summariser into a state of delirium. In describing David's goal I ventured the opinion, 'It might have been a toe poke,' surmising it was the only way in which he could reach the ball to shoot. I went on to say, 'It doesn't matter how he scored, Scotland are ahead of Brazil and perhaps on their way to victory.' No one remembered that phrase when Brazil finally won 4–1. Of course, I was aware that kids not blessed with footballing ability tended to kick with their toe rather than their instep. I wasn't accusing David of that, I merely believed that he couldn't have reached the ball and shot so powerfully in any other way. Crestfallen, disappointed Scots wanted to believe otherwise and have never let me forget it. As they filed past our commentary position on leaving the ground I said, 'Hard luck!' to one lad.

'Have my scarf,' he replied and draped it round my neck.

'Hard luck!' I said to another. He spat, but unlike David Narey, he missed.

In Madrid the BBC rented the balcony of a private house overlooking the corner of the fabulous stadium to install a camera position from which we could stage interviews. In order to get into our balcony position, we had to pass through the family's lounge and dining-room where they assembled to share a sherry before the evening meal. When necessity called, we would excuse ourselves and slip through to use the loo. I don't know about the sherry but the olives always looked irresistible. On the night of the final I nipped out just before kick-off past the smiling family. On the way back I could not resist leaning over the table and helping myself to a juicy olive, popping it into my mouth mumbling, 'Gracias!' They all laughed and before the game began they brought little dishes of olives on to the balcony for us. Even in the excitement of a World Cup final, it's strange how a gesture of kindness makes its mark.

Mexico '86 produced the biggest crowds ever and the biggest profits; 580 million people watched the finals, eight players were sent off, including Ray Wilkins of all people, and 133 yellow cards were awarded. Gary Lineker was top scorer with six goals, and Pat Jennings broke the world record for caps, reaching 119. England was knocked out of the competition by a blatant piece of cheating, Maradona handling the ball for the first goal, but the other talents of that football genius led to Argentina beating Germany in the final. Diego was presented with the Golden Ball as the tournament's outstanding player. With today's retrospective video judgement holding sway in some areas, I wonder what FIFA would do about such a happening now? Justice apart, having seen his second goal one could almost have forgiven him, but in a fair world England did not lose that game but still went home early.

The weather in Mexico was almost uniformly hot. For one match in Puebla between Argentina and Uruguay, John Motson was commentator and I was summariser. As we took our seats among our foreign counterparts, the sky was, as usual, blue. The match was ordinary and much of the drama came towards the end when an enormous cloud began to creep across from one end of the stadium. It hovered for a while and then moved right overhead bringing with it wind and rain of apocalyptic proportions. John and I battened down our notes just in time as a huge gust took every scrap of notepaper away from the poor chap on our left. He was in a real state and what he said for the rest of the game made no sense to us, his language was most strange and I trust it made some sense to his listeners.

The structure of the World Cup in 1990 was unwieldy. The first two weeks were spent in eliminating eight out of the twenty-four qualifying countries. Fear of losing resulted in low scores and penalty shoot-outs deciding far too many games. England, the Republic of Ireland and Holland carefully carved their way through at the expense of Egypt. The Republic lost to Italy 1–0 in the quarter-finals; a David Platt goal and two from Gary Lineker saw England through against unlucky Cameroon.

England's semi-final against West Germany went to penalties and Bobby Robson's reputation for being lucky was in tatters as Chris Waddle, aiming from the spot in Turin, uncharacteristically sent the ball screaming over the bar somewhere in the direction of Naples. Penalties also put Italy out – they later beat England for third place – leaving Germany to beat Argentina with Brehme's solitary penalty goal in an uninspiring final. It was almost a relief when it was all over.

I had my share of fun with Terry Venables and the incomparable Des, who proved himself to be human after all. When looking the nation in the eye he either forgot the name of a team, or a player or even where he was and was lost for words. One slip-up in twenty years – he should be so lucky! On the field it was a lacklustre competition, but the three tenors, Pavarotti, Carreras and Domingo, pitched a tuneful note or two, making a few bob and escalating the popularity of opera in general and our BBC signature tune, 'Nessun Dorma', in particular.

America 1994 had to be different. The story was that FIFA had sanctioned the USA as hosts to popularise soccer there. They were rewarded by our cousins turning out in large numbers, the various European ethnic groups taking the opportunity to turn up and cheer. As a result, it was a commercial success which justified that faith. It didn't change my opinion, based on painful experience, that it will be many, many years if at all, before there is sufficient enthusiasm for the game to prosper professionally in the States. The American male psyche is welded to its indigenous games and is stubbornly insular. We shall see, but I know where my money would be, or rather wouldn't be, second time around.

283

As for the competition, with all the home countries failing to qualify it was Jack Charlton flying the Irish flag who captured the support of most floating islanders, scraping through Group E. It was tight, the four teams finishing with four points. Ireland caused a sensation for 73,000 people in New York, Ray Houghton scoring a single goal to beat Italy; but their luck ran out in Orlando against Mexico, a 2–1 defeat threatening their hopes of qualification. A 0–0 draw put Norway on the rack and out, Ireland going through on goals scored, two in three games.

I derived special pleasure from Saudi Arabia's victories over Belgium and Morocco along the way and some satisfaction from Brazil's final triumph over Italy emanating from a penalty shoot-out. Baggio's flying 'miss' qualifying for a space race, comforted those poor souls, myself included, who had ever missed a penalty. Just think how Charlie Mitten would have felt! Mind you, that comfort couldn't take away the strong feeling that it was an absurd way to end a two-year competition.

24

CHARITY BEGINS AND NEVER ENDS. . .

THERE are advantages to being in the public eye, condemned to being described as a celebrity. Recognition ranges from, 'Are you **the** Jimmy Hill?' to, 'Who's he?' One of the rewarding privileges, though, is to be able to help raise money for charity. Because of the vast army of generous souls who work tirelessly and relentlessly for thousands of worthwhile causes, requests to play a part are plentiful. It's impossible to satisfy all of them, but in my experience the majority of 'stars' are only too ready to help. For some reason the public is happy to turn out and pay to see their favourites make fools of themselves as footballers, cricketers, tennis players and golfers. There are those who even attempt clay pigeon shooting and archery.

It's probably unfair to choose a particular charity when over the years I've enjoyed supporting in different ways the Lord's Taverners, the Variety Club of Great Britain, Riding for the Disabled, the Sports Aid Foundation, Barnardo's, the Injured Jockeys' Fund and many more, mostly through the game of golf which lends itself admirably to raising money. However, two stand out in particular for different reasons: SPARKS (Sport Aiding Research for Kids) and NABS (National Advertisers' Benevolent Society).

When Duncan Guthrie founded SPARKS around 1960, three

285

other sportsmen joined us at the launch: Jim Laker, the cricketer, Dai Rees, the golfer, and Wally Barnes, the footballer. I seem to be the only original supporter left, which is somewhat frightening. . . Since that day whole armies of sportsmen and women have given their time and exploited their skills for the charity's benefit. The money which we raise is used to fund research projects into diseases and medical conditions which happen prior to and immediately after birth and during the early years of life. The ultimate aim is that eventually no child should be born so incapacitated as to be denied the chance to sample the pleasure of playing a game of some kind. Duncan Guthrie's inspirational thought was that those who excelled at sport would be the first to understand how frustrating life would be for a child denied the chance to play games – even badly. So SPARKS was born and countless young ones have benefited from a combination of the support of these sportsmen and women, the skills of surgeons and the generosity of the public at large. Nowadays, it is not only people connected with sport who share in the fun of raising funds for SPARKS; members of the acting and entertainment world make up a long list of celebrities giving their time and energies free.

It was probably an association with Denis Compton and Royds Advertising Agency that led to me being asked to conduct an auction at the annual boxing evening of the National Advertisers' Society way back in 1971. Whatever it was, I agreed to do it that year and with only one exception every year since. Each year the target has been to beat the previous total. In 1981, the auction total had reached a record £97,000. In those days, you may remember, I sported a beard and Ron Miller, long-time chairman of the Society, whispered that if I would shave off my beard in the ring, Gillette would make up the difference to £100,000. Ron thought he was on a loser. My mind raced: BBC technicians were on strike at the time and there could be no 'Match of the Day' for ten days at least, time enough for it to regrow.

'Okay, Ron,' I said. 'I'll do it!' It was easier said than done, but off came the beard and Gillette delivered.

Having celebrated suitably I arrived back at our Notting Hill flat around 2.30 in the morning. Bryony was still just about awake, so I asked her if she would like a cup of Ovaltine to celebrate the hundred grand.

'Yes, please,' she said sleepily. Having made the hot drink I returned and handed her the mug.

'Haven't you noticed anything different?'

'No,' she replied.

'Look, the beard,' I pointed out. 'It's gone!' When she had had a good hard look and regained her composure, her subtle womanly way for not noticing was that, 'We were still at the looking in the eyes stage. . !' Accordingly, I don't think there are many pleasures more enjoyable or rewarding than having fun and raising money for a worthwhile cause.

On the lighter side and in the interest of sanity, charity and getting the odd game of football myself, I joined with a suitably crazy group of celebrities to form the Goaldiggers, an offshoot of the National Playing Fields Association. Our objective was to raise money to create hard-surfaced mini football play areas, in districts where such space was in short supply – a situation which occurs in country areas surprisingly as much as in built-up cities.

His Royal Highness Prince Philip, in view of his connection with the National Playing Fields Association, agreed to become our coach, Eric Morecambe our linesman. We were able also to recruit Brian Mears, then chairman of Chelsea, Elton John, Brian Moore, Willis Hall and Michael Parkinson as members of the council, and Bryan Forbes who took on the task as the first chairman. These valiant souls also made themselves available to play at appropriate times.

We staged our first match at Windsor (where else?) against the local football club with an all-star cast including Malcolm Allison, Jimmy Greaves and Jack Kelsey among others. It was handy for our coach, HRH, who made a wise decision not to follow his first success by taking up the job professionally!

Regular football matches were one way in which we raised money, but the annual Goaldiggers' ball became a social event not to be missed, although Elton did on one occasion, substituting Kiki Dee who was sensational. Another year, a bug confined him to bed and we were left without a star to perform for us. It was a horrific day for me, too, as my franchise of Washington Diplomats had gone into bankruptcy in America and I received the news at the same time as Elton's apology. But the show must go on. . . If, as Sir Winston once said, this was to be our finest hour, as chairman for the evening, I had to get my finger out and my morale back. I braced myself and welcomed our guests, wished them a happy evening and then let drop the news about Elton. I followed it with a rousing message, first that we were there for worthwhile charitable purposes, second that we had fine food, a first-class band and our health. We were often told that during the war people made their own fun when times were hard, why couldn't we do it tonight? I told them my own bad news and how I was determined not to let it affect my enjoyment and asked again for their support.

When the meal was over, we devised a fund-raising sing-song and Trevor Brooking led the chorus of West Ham's 'I'm Forever Blowing Bubbles', Tom Wilson, my old mate from Fulham, surpassed Jolson with 'Bye Bye Blackbird' and Tommy Benfield (London bookmaker) brought the house down with 'Those Barefoot Days', charging £100 for each rendition. It turned into a wonderful knees-up and everyone forgot Elton was missing and all their other cares and woes, too – well, almost everyone.

Another year, before the Goaldiggers' Dorchester ball, we discussed the menu at a council meeting. Such was the forceful nature of the council members, it took all evening. Finally, bangers and mash and apple pie were agreed upon as being cheap, inviting and different from normal fare for a ball, especially for the elegant Dorchester. Once the hotel staff had recovered from the shock, they set to and included a choice of sauces with the meal on the night. Eric Morecambe said afterwards that it was the only time he had eaten the main course in its entirety and licked his plate at such an event – a compliment indeed to the chef and to the lunacy of that talented Goaldiggers' council.

As impresarios they were far from finished. From annual balls and eleven-a-side matches, they launched a pop five-a-side tournament indoors at Wembley, in conjunction with the *Sun* newspaper. The name Wembley is magical and magnetic and so it proved. A full house turned out, attracted by the quality of the groups and their glamorous ex-professionals – each team was allowed one – among them Ron Atkinson, Ralph Coates, Bobby Moore, Stan Bowles and Bobby Charlton. The names of the groups stir some memories, too – The Barron Knights, Status Quo, Uriah Heep, Manfred Mann's Earth Band, Power Plant plus Gonzales and the Electric Light Orchestra who fought out the final.

Although those days are long gone, the annual interest on the money raised, controlled by the Goaldiggers Trust, still goes towards creating more hard-surfaced play areas from derelict sites, and other similar projects.

As if my life wasn't full enough, having been heavily involved in the affairs of the footballers' trade union and less dramatically in the founding of the Cricketers' Association, perhaps I shouldn't have been surprised at receiving a letter from a stable lad in Lambourn asking for help with their problems. They had no individual representation, but some of them were members of the Transport and General Workers' Union. Their working conditions varied from trainer to trainer from being reasonable in some cases to positively Dickensian and unacceptable in many others. I agreed to meet with them one evening in June 1975 at Lambourn and armed myself with Lord John Oaksey and Richard Pitman, two respected and truly knowledgeable friends.

Unfortunately, very few lads turned up for the evening meeting. It was disappointing, but in an hour or so I was able to glean a clear picture from those present of the injustice which was widespread. At the end of the meeting I challenged them: 'I'll come back once more in the autumn and if there aren't a lot more of you here, that will be the end of it.' I should have known better.

September came round and the response in contrast to the earlier meeting was phenomenal. The TGWU turned up, too, with placards and enrolment forms in an attempt to recruit new members for themselves. But the lads wanted their own association and now were determined to get it.

Two further meetings were held at Epsom and Newmarket. Twelve out of the thirteen stables were represented at Epsom and there was equal enthusiasm at Newmarket, although the rump of the TGWU membership existed there.

Not surprisingly the 'opposition' reacted publicly: Sam Horncastle, the TGWU organiser, who had influenced a messy strike at Newmarket some months previously, viewed the new movement as being trainer inspired, with Oaksey and Hill mere puppets. He couldn't have been wider of the mark; the original cry for help came from the Lambourn lad and in the long run, the more ruthless, uncaring trainers began to curse the day I was born, as football's directors and league officials had done nearly twenty years before. Even Jack Logan (Sir David Llewellyn) in the *Sporting Life* described the Oaksey/Hill combination as 'the Primrose League'. Living on his bed of roses, he should have learned more about flowers.

A strong voice of support came from a sturdy Welsh Lambourn committee man, Lyn Burrows.

'I think it's the best thing that's happened to us in the fifteen years I have been in racing,' he said, and history proved him right. As time moved on we established an association with Lord Oaksey, Lord Wyatt and myself as trustees. It soon became evident that we needed a full-time secretary if the organisation was to survive and grow. The income did not lend itself to a full-time experienced employee, but as I'd just moved to a house in Oxford with some acreage, boxes and a cottage or two, I was able to offer Tommy Delaney, who had been head lad at Anthony Johnson's stables and whose brother was head lad at Fred Winter's yard, a house and half a decent salary to look after my horse while the stable lads paid for the other half.

For many years I attended annual negotiating meetings representing the lads and negotiating steady but undramatic increases in their terms and conditions. The majority of current trainers are civilised and fair-minded, although, like all groups of the human race, a scallywag or two does emerge and the SLA is there to see fair play in the stables, for those who underwrite such pleasure for others on the course. Unfortunately, racing finances still do not provide riches for the lads, and nearly always it is their love of the job not the money which binds them to it.

25

THE FOOTBALL LEAGUE AND THE FOOTBALL ASSOCIATION

NOT surprisingly I have often been accused of wearing too many hats, even when it is clear that such hats are not a licence to fill one's pockets with fivers, but represent an obligation to devote one's time, energy, knowledge and experience, albeit a touch masochistically, to the benefit of a cause. This tendency still brings unrest. To be a director of a club, and a television performer, as I mentioned before, needed some acrobatic skill. Add to that the role of a director of the Football League and member of the Football Association Council and you will see what a slender tightrope I trod. I could plead, particularly with regard to the FA Council, that my presence was essential: of the ninety elected representatives from the game of football in this land of ours, I was the only one who had played the game at the highest professional level. There are a few talented amateur gentleman players around, notably Doug Insole, and one or two whose fragile memory reflects illusions of grandeur inaccurately. Once Ron Noades, unselfish statesman that he is, campaigned to replace me on the Football League board, I was no longer in a position to continue as an FA Council member.

Because of my background I had been able to make contributions in a number of different ways on different committees, in particular those closely associated with the professional game. The Technical Control Board, the Referees' Committee, the Instructional Committee and the FA Challenge Cup Committee occupied my time. They sound important and useful, but the real power lies with the ninety council members whose votes allow proposals to flourish or be condemned. The most influential committees are the Executive Committee, the Finance Committee, the International Committee and the Disciplinary Committee.

Those employed by the FA, including their leader, Chief Executive Graham Kelly, and to be fair most of the eleven members of the Executive Committee, recognise that the structure is totally unsuited for the twentieth century, let alone the twenty-first. Yet there is no way the councillors are going to reduce the ultimate power which lies in their hands.

A year or so back an attempt was made towards modernisation by increasing the power of the Chief Executive and his committee to act decisively when necessary. I won't forget it because I was scheduled to speak for the proposition in the afternoon. I was due to have lunch at the Ritz Club sitting alongside Frankie Dettori who was to receive an award. With my passion for riding there was no better place to be. However, I managed only the main course before having to rush back to the meeting. I arrived in time to make my impassioned plea for unselfishness and my fellow councillors' vital proposal for change. The vote was lost, as was my pudding and coffee, but Graham Kelly was kind enough to thank me for trying. The Football Association remains an immovable, self-perpetuating oligarchy, its defence against revolution being FIFA's sanction of its membership of the world game. Without that, the English game would be ostracised.

In contrast, the members of the Football League board were united by one word – survival – all being current directors of clubs not in the Premier League. The then president, Gordon McKeag, had a difficult task in harnessing the talents and ambitions of those at his disposal in an effort to steer the League and many of its clubs through the seas of threatening insolvency.

In such an atmosphere, ranting sometimes replaced reason, but to be fair, the job of running a so-called business with seventy-two opinionated wayward disciples would test a saint. Around ten member clubs were always on the brink of bankruptcy, two or three dangerously so.

Really, it proved to be a nightmare trying to run a national league smack in the public eye in such circumstances. No wonder tempers become frayed off the field at a swifter rate than on it. By now you will understand the problems: fans hungry for promotion pressurise boards to spend money on players in the pursuit of success, or even worse not sell promising players to balance teetering cash books; and sack managers who are not succeeding – numerically that's most of them and it's yet another costly exercise. They stay away if the team loses (which is when they're most needed) and blame directors and managers for everything that goes wrong, when in the very structure of the competitions most clubs are seen to fail, and some disastrously.

It's small wonder that directors look anywhere for respite and someone else to blame. Who better than their elected representatives on the Football League board? I'm describing the environs of a battleground so that you will understand, perhaps even sympathetically, what happened when the current television contract was negotiated, which cost the Football League many millions. Perhaps if it hadn't been for my recurring 'hat' problem, I might have helped to avoid it.

In 1995 it was pretty obvious that the cost of the television rights for the Premier League and the Football League fixtures was going to escalate considerably. Negotiations were not simple because the existing league contract with ITV ran out in 1996, a season earlier than that of the Premier League in 1997. They were separate contracts and deals but each had a bearing on the other. The most significant underlying fact was that ITV, four years previously, had negotiated an option with the Football League to renew its contract on existing terms, or to match any increased offer from another broadcaster.

The BBC's financial power was weakening because its licence

fee was controlled stringently, whereas SKY was free to pick a figure that would make money – loads of it. ITV was unlikely to top SKY's bid, although it maintained aspirations to be part of a deal involving major clubs in Cup competitions, domestic and European. Obviously, Premier League clubs were ITV's main target, not having the space nor the financial inclination to overload its schedules with less than the best. The FA Cup and European matches suited its needs and appetite.

It was an intriguing time for all the participants. As was right and proper, I was not involved in any of the negotiations and unless I was asked, kept a discreet distance. Gordon McKeag, Lee Walker, our television representative, and David Dent, handled various negotiating meetings.

A Football League meeting was held at the Connaught Rooms, London, to examine the options. Representatives of the Premier League, including Rick Parry, Arsenal's David Dein and New-castle's Freddy Fletcher, addressed the meeting asking for patience and cooperation for them to negotiate a formidable joint deal. If their assessment of the potential return was correct, the League could not lose. It sounded too good to be true; previous experience had hardened the audience not to believe in fairies – not yet anyway. The FA through Graham Kelly and Trevor Phillips also promoted a joint venture under their banner.

On the other hand, the time factor and SKY's persistent pressure promising breathtaking sums of money, certainly in comparison with previous contracts, was not easy to resist. The Premier League stated that if we allowed them to negotiate the whole television deal, the League would certainly get twenty per cent of it, maybe even twenty-five per cent. SKY's offer to the Football League was £25 million a year for five years (no linking to the retail price index). It was probably the five years that seemed so attractive to our board. Were it not for SKY and its voracious appetite for any sport, the national game particularly, the Football League could not have dreamed of such a lengthy guarantee.

SKY knew that the majority of its profits had and would be

built from football with some support from rugby, golf and cricket. They needed the national game desperately with three channels to fill, and in addition were anxious to settle with the League before taking on the big boys. A time limit was imposed. When the offer was discussed, I urged the board to insist on more time from SKY. The Premier League were waiting in the bushes; would twenty per cent of their eventual deal top £25 million was the question. If we rejected this offer, could we be sure the Premier League would keep their word? They might offer the money with unpleasant strings attached. Three up and three down increases and prolongs the excitement surrounding promotion and relegation. Most Premier League clubs would rather get in by hook or by crook and then, selfishly, lock the door. I felt we would be able to resist that pressure by harnessing public opinion on one side and the power of the FA on the other to maintain the negotiated terms and conditions of the agreement regarding promotion and relegation reached when the Premier League came into existence.

It's so much easier to say 'of course they would' afterwards than it was at the time. I was ready to gamble, my mates and colleagues weren't! After much deliberation and soul-searching we were asked for approval of SKY's offer by Gordon McKeag. Mine was the only hand which wasn't raised.

It was very near the end of my time with the Football League and I later requested that the vote be registered as unanimous to discourage revolution. Had my colleagues taken the chance, and it wasn't without risk of either SKY or the Premier League moving their ground, the Football League would have had £15 million more to distribute to their members.

There was a mass of clever folk who saw what should have been done in retrospect. I often wonder whether they would really have had the courage to refuse such a plump bird in the hand. . .

Soon after the television fiasco, the League voted to dispose of the services of its president, Gordon McKeag, and reshuffle its hierarchy under the leadership of David Sheepshanks, chairman

296

of Ipswich Town. Regretting the undertakings to remain together arising from the reformation of the League when the Premier League broke away, the hawks in the first division were seething with selfish desire to join them – how much more pleasant it would become to be subsidised from above rather than subsidise those below. It can easily be seen how the original concepts behind the creation of a Football League many years ago no longer had any meaning. In their frustration at not being able unselfishly to compromise and deal with their problems sensibly and fairly from within, the League in its wisdom decided to seek help in restructuring from outside at a cost of an estimated £250,000.

Consequently, after forty years of running football clubs, I joined a number of my third division colleagues at the offices of Deloitte & Touche to meet a charming, businesslike, middle-aged lady for a three-hour session including a buffet lunch, a mini portion of which was a cost to Fulham. Never mind the expense, I'm afraid I was horrified at the idiocy of the situation, although our questioner was not to blame, she was merely doing what she was paid to do. I did not want to be hypocritical and I made it clear from the outset that I felt the exercise was an expensive waste and would lead nowhere. Nevertheless, I was as honestly helpful as I could be.

What ideas I have seen since concerning the reconstruction of the League, embracing alternatives with fancy astral names, leaves me icily cold. Various alternative plans for change were catalogued Earth, Mars, Jupiter, Saturn and Plato. My reaction to it has not changed from the remarks I made to my fellow chairmen at a meeting to discuss, among other matters, whether the management board should consist of six, nine or twelve members. . .

Might I speak to you about harmony, a team spirit among those of us who share the enormous responsibility of running football and trying to keep our own clubs alive. I support, from whatever end of the pitch it comes, a mission for togetherness, collective responsibility and cooperation to make sure that the next fifty years of the League are highly successful and we deal with our enormous problems, whether in the first, second or third divisions. Our difficulties make us bad-tempered with each other, with the public, with referees, and difficult people to live with. In respect of the suggested changes, I do not believe it's going to make the slightest difference whichever of the recommended schemes you choose. Whether it's six, nine or twelve elected board members requesting leagues or regions, there's no special magic in any of them. As a group of people we're unmanageable from within and certainly from without. We have as much knowledge as we could muster from within this organisation – if only in desperation we could harness it, trust it and believe in it. That would be far more valuable than adopting any one of the suggested systems. It is an impossible task to satisfy everyone in this room. What genius or groups of geniuses are there sitting out there who can guarantee to calm the murky waters in which we are presently? As it stands, the League is unmanageable and no professional advisers or structure will change that unless it is done unselfishly from within.

In some ways I'm thankful no longer to be a part of the frustrating mechanism of football government. Gradually, the number of much maligned but unselfish lovers of football in the offices and boardrooms of the professional game was shrinking, those people being replaced by wealthy, self-centred fly-by-nights. Not all their hearts are in the wrong place, but perhaps the challenge has become too fierce for friendship. Perhaps I share some of the blame from 18 January 1961, but in kicking the ball off that goalline, I know sport only reflects society's standards; it doesn't create them. It will be interesting to see how long the Football League embraces seventy-two clubs and how long it is before the first division grabs hold of the Premier League's coat tails in exchange for a bob or two and less promotion and relegation, never mind if it's less exciting for the poor old fans.

Strangely, I've found that I have been more heavily criticised when my judgement has been sound and my instincts correct than otherwise. It can alter a relationship as it did between Alex Ferguson and myself when in an after-match wobbly he called me a 'prat'.

It's not that we had been bosom pals, or anything approaching that closeness. In fact, we had met only once as accidental passing strangers one night in Glasgow after I had presented Alex with a trophy as Manager of the Year. The presentation had taken place in the afternoon, after which we had gone our separate Glaswegian ways. Coincidentally, around midnight, we bumped into one another in the hotel lobby. I forget which one of us suggested a nightcap, but by three o'clock in the morning we had trained the night porter to Olympic standard and he didn't spill a drop of that comforting Scottish liquid. You can guess the substance of the conversation and I found Alex's philosophies on the game and his experiences fascinating, and it became evident that we shared many of the same beliefs. I was impressed.

Move on a year or so and Alex was appointed manager of Manchester United. You'll recall it was some time before he was able to achieve any kind of consistency, let alone success. Tongues were beginning to wag and the pressure was on. During this period I had occasion to telephone Martin Edwards, United's chairman, from time to time. I'm not suggesting that Martin ever lost faith for a moment, but on more than one occasion I emphasised my strong conviction that Alex could turn things around. It sounds silly now that I had such faith, based on three hours' acquaintance over half a bottle of Scotch. Nevertheless, it's true and consequently I rejoiced when eventually things came good for Manchester United and they went on a successful spree that defies belief.

As far as I know, I had done nothing to disturb the original tenor of our short friendship. You can imagine then my shock-horror when he described me as a 'prat' because I had stayed true to my declared and maintained conviction, to condemn any tackle which might prejudice the livelihood of a fellow professional. Eric Cantona's wild and aggressive challenge had put Norwich's John Polston's future at risk.

299

Nevertheless, I've savoured United's achievements under Alex and particularly now because British players form the basis of his teams. Martin Edwards has weathered a few storms during his period as chairman of that majestic club. It's not easy to believe that way back in the late seventies he asked John Camkin and me if a wealthy Saudi football enthusiast might be prepared to invest one million pounds and become a major shareholder; a snip if ever there was one!

26

REFEREES

For many years I have suppressed deeply felt views about one particular aspect of the professional game. If I declared it to be concerning referees you would most probably react with, 'That's nonsense! You've always had a go at them.' In essence, that's not correct. With the aid of television technology, we are mostly in a position to uncover the truth, but far more often than not the outcome supports the decision of the official. Football writers, too, lean towards action replays when available. Believe it or not, those who are most cruel and often wildly inaccurate at the same time are football supporters. They persecute officials relentlessly and unfairly and as often as not incorrectly, as I found out from one mere hour on the touchline at Highbury. Perhaps the most difficult part of a referee's job is to remain a hundred per cent impartial for ninety minutes when, perhaps because of a just, clinical decision against the home team, he is put on a derisive verbal rack for the rest of the game. It's sad, but more than likely true, that the referees who become acceptable – popular is too strong a word – are those who lean sixty forty towards the home team. Before you faint in horror, such a percentage swing does not really notice because there are generally enough fifty fifty decisions which can go either way. So whatever you may think or have thought, I'm not anti-referee. I understand only too well what a tough job it is and how few people have all that it takes to survive, let alone excel.

FIFA do not always assist referees, with some of their campaigns to tamper with the application of the laws. Their instruction pre-1998 World Cup to outlaw the tackle from behind was a dangerous sword unfairly reducing a defender's armament. It is not easy to present a case against the instruction, but there is one. The tackle from behind is both valid and essential to the game's health and future, arising from a fundamental, which enhances its charm and preserves the delicate balance between strength, athleticism and courage on the one hand, and fine skill on the other. The fundamental is that the defender's target is the ball and *not* an opponent. However fierce the tackle, if the ball is reasonably near the ground and contacted first, no foul from the foot has taken place. Providing the ball *is* contacted first, risk of serious injury is almost completely eliminated. FIFA's case is fashioned on the difficult task a defender has in thrusting through an attacker's legs and feet without making any contact except with the ball. In such cases when the feet or legs are contacted first, I fully support a yellow card being shown or, if the thrust is violent enough, a red one. My contention is that if only the ball is contacted and done so cleanly and fairly, it should not matter in the least from which of 360 degrees a tackle arises. Since the modern game developed, a healthy balance between physical strength and skill is a high voltage part of the magnetic attraction of it. In their commendable but misguided endeavour to eradicate unfair and dangerous play, FIFA could well have upset that equilibrium. In seeking to reduce dangerous play, it could disturb the game's inherent balance.

I understand FIFA's desire to eliminate or at least reduce violent and dangerous play from world football. What has happened as a result of that campaign so far is that the punishment meter has moved forward. In far too many cases what was just a foul, e.g. an unintentional trip, has now tended to enter the yellow-card zone and calculated offences, especially involving speed and strength, are candidates for more severe punishment.

If the trend continues there will be no such offence as a simple, old-fashioned foul emanating from an opponent's superior skill. If I am moving towards more refined professional judgement here, I'm not apologising. It's only by going in that direction that football will be able to maintain the fine balance between honest aggression and disguised skulduggery.

It is because of that realisation that I have surreptitiously campaigned, not publicly, but within the corridors of power at the Football Association and the Football League for them to encourage the professional players to train to become referees when they have finished playing. I'm not suggesting that they would all have the necessary qualities, but some among the 2500 of them at any one time would prove exceptional. In addition to the other accomplishments essential for such a demanding role, only a fool would consider that playing experience at the highest level would not help. The adage 'Set a thief to catch a thief' fits; 'a sprat to catch a mackerel' doesn't.

Refereeing players who are chasing huge rewards emotionally or fiscally is never going to be easy and mistakes will always occur. As football spends millions on unearthing and training talent to play at the highest level of the game, it should be an added essential responsibility to ensure that the quality of those officials who control the game's destiny should be impeccable.

For many years professional players, who might have considered becoming referees, were discouraged by an undercurrent of propaganda, the basis of which was that at the end of their playing career it would take many years of training and experience for them to be promoted to the Football League. Even now it's suggested that six years, with a very fair wind, would be the minimum time for qualification, much the same as the training of a doctor. In an effort to circumvent this historic defensive barrier, during the three years I was a member of the FA Council and of the Referees' Committee, I was able, through the PFA and one or two forward-looking county associations, to promote a potential solution. There are thirteen current professional players, mostly in the Lancashire area, who having passed their written examinations, will be given the opportunity in their spare time, midweek and Sundays, to referee junior league matches. So at last there is a stairway to the top for enterprising, intelligent young players who would appreciate staying with the game and even some of the money. By the time they finish playing they will be well equipped for the challenge and ready to spot fouls in contrast to committing them.

There is a fine line between an honest foul, where a player thinks he has a chance of getting the ball and misses, and a calculated sin. It is my view that those who have played the game professionally have a better chance of exercising accurate, often split-second, judgement. If a referee, having been a player or not, is blind to the difference, those who are guilty have as good a chance of getting away with it as the innocent.

So yellow cards, deserved or not, are increasing at the same rate as players lose confidence in the system of justice. Not being able to relieve their frustration by taking it out on the referee, who better than the next opponent in line? As I've said, with all that is at stake in the modern game, it is not easy to referee and players are not saintly. I am proposing most emphatically that because of those inherent truths, the sooner some élite present poachers are trained to be gamekeepers the better it will be for both players and public, if not for all referees.

The reason that I have not trumpeted my belief in the un-doubted benefit of fast-tracking pro players on a whistle non-stop journey is practicality. Until 1997 I had been connected either with Coventry City, Charlton or Fulham at different times. I'm not for one moment suggesting that referees would have fa-voured our opponents because of what could be interpreted as a campaign to make them obsolete. On the other hand, I am aware of their understandable desire to maintain the status quo. I do know that some players looking for an excuse when a penalty had cost them points would have had little difficulty in casting the blame on an outspoken director. Whatever you or I believe, I decided that one way or the other silence on that topic was golden – until now!

Many years ago I was responsible for introducing a scheme through the Football League for all young apprentices to be taught the laws and take an examination – essential anyway you may think, but also sowing seeds. I would recommend the same educational process for one or two of my fellow presenters and pundits, who might wish to avoid embarrassing ignorance catching up with them. . .

I might have anticipated reaching three score years and ten in a mood of calmness, composure and perhaps a touch of self-satisfaction, reflecting on the battles fought and won and ambitions fulfilled. For better or for worse, that's not how I feel, harbouring a feeling of frustration that as a result of their archaic structure the governing football bodies still lack the understanding, the will, the machinery, and thus the capability, to move to better things. Having been a serial campaigner, I suppose I shall never change, although I want others to. I would like to think that because of my background and wide experience, I am still able to view most aspects of the modern game clinically.

Outside its parliaments now, I have little chance of convincing my erstwhile colleagues to tread the paths to logical and exciting progression. Perhaps I have sown a few late twentieth century seeds which will flourish and prosper in the twenty-first. I've had the pleasure of seeing some blossom in this century: no maximum wage, freedom of contract, three points for a win, Coventry City in the Premier League for ever (I trust), Fulham saved and prosperous, and not least, ten grandchildren. I should be satisfied, but I shall always be thinking of ways to repay the simple game which has enriched my life so fully. That was my good fortune.

STOP PRESS – FRANCE '98

Having put my pen away on completing the story of my life so far, I could not resist the temptation to add some thoughts on the events and outcome of France '98, my ninth World Cup. Others will have recorded in detail the drama of those weeks in France and the effect this extraordinary thirty-two team competition might have on football in the future. If you have read this far you will know that I could not emerge from the tournament in any other way than bursting with ideas for harnessing and multiplying the moments of sporting magic which it provided. The domestic ecstasy which boiled over in Paris on the night of the final shook the very foundations of the Arc de Triomphe, so aptly named for the occasion. In a country where the romance of the world game is not quite as firmly embedded in the hearts and souls of the population as is rugby, the pulsating joy that throbbed through the cobbled streets of Paris, and indeed the whole of France, was a delight to behold. The details didn't matter. Brazil had been overwhelmed by three clear goals and France was the country in which the current world champions had been born, as was the idea for the original competition way back in the 1920s. The Almighty unexpectedly provided convenient, consistent rainfall on the following July morning; with some help from the street cleaners, it washed away

306

the legacy of alcoholic celebration of Olympic proportions. 'La Marseillaise' rang out from bars, streets and alleyways, a strident musical expression of a nation's pride. Whatever happens and whoever wins, nothing can produce such a scale of euphoria as a victory for the host country, as it did with England in 1966.

France's glorious exploits on the field of play will grow in magnitude as time passes, only some remembering that the reality was not entirely made of milk and honey. Disposing of South Africa and Saudi Arabia clinically in their group was a formality and Denmark somewhat less so. Blanc's golden goal in extra time overrode a nervous performance against Paraguay, and unexpectedly France's *sang froid* held in a penalty shoot-out with Italy, after a goalless draw in the quarter-finals.

Like a few other teams, they were unable to find strikers who could score against massed and mean defenders. In winning the semi-final against Croatia it was their full-back, Thuram, who won the match with two glorious goals, and again underlined the poor goalscoring record of their strikers. It seemed that for France and other teams the fashionable but boring concentration on a solid, numerically superior defence was dominating the competition. Whether or not it was the effect of the lighter balls, there were noticeably fewer goals scored from shots from outside the penalty area, though the much-maligned David Beckham's successful free kick against Colombia was a gem. By beating Holland for third place, Croatia and their peripatetic players convinced themselves and others that with leading scorer, six-goal Suker, it was within their grasp to have been champions. A brave and entertaining near miss was tarnished in the semi-final against France by Slaven Bilic getting nought out of ten for taking a count of nine!

As for the final, the events leading up to the kick-off were more dramatic than the game itself. The upheaval in the Brazilian camp removed any chance they had of victory. It was apparent even before they conceded the first goal that their morale was batting zero. There was no spark, no fire and positively no cutting edge with Ronaldo, billed as the world's greatest player, giving a passable imitation of Stan Collymore at his most moody. In our Place de la Concorde rooftop studio previous plans evaporated as John Motson, for a change in vision and blossoming, described the staggering events which were taking place behind closed doors in the Brazilian dressing-room.

As I saw it, there were three possibilities – firstly, it was a ruse to confuse the enemy (shades of Glenn Hoddle!); secondly, it was a clerical error on the teamsheet, made by an elderly manager confused through emotion and tension; thirdly, there was doubt over whether or not Ronaldo was fit to play, having not trained for two days. Never mind the theory, there was no way of guessing the truth at that point. At the time of writing, it's still unclear what was at the bottom of it and perhaps we shall never know. As explanations have emerged, they have only blurred the issue.

Whatever the problem was, either mental, physical or commercial, it led to a collective Brazilian attitude which could have brought about defeat by any one of the other thirty-one countries taking part. Certainly they were never in the race against the defensive strength, the midfield creativity, the determined, disciplined teamwork and the fervent patriotism of the doughty Frenchmen. It's probably unfair to select individuals, but Thuram's defensive athleticism stood out, as did Zidane's classic and lethal talent. Petit was quietly superb and Barthez, as befits a goalkeeper, crazily brilliant. But in the final, the massive world audience was denied the competitive, finely balanced game of football it might have been.

From the competition itself, I shall remember Scotland's brave struggle against Brazil, and the silky smoothness of Holland when in the mood and puzzle at what happens to spoil it. I'm sure no one will forget Paraguay's goalkeeper, captain and mother hen, Chilavert, not only for his superb goalkeeping skills, but for the compassion he showed when restoring the morale of his distraught, beaten colleagues.

From the African continent, Oliseh's explosive winning strike for Nigeria against luckless (again) Spain eliminated them from the toughest of the groups, Group D. Multi-skilled Okocha was a player to watch forever, but Moller scored for Denmark after three minutes and the remainder of the game emphasised that Nigeria were better with the ball than without it. They packed their bags, taking with them Africa's chance of glory.

England's match against Argentina was arguably the best and certainly the most dramatic in the tournament. The first half was a classic, blessed by Owen's remarkable, spine-tingling goal, and Argentina's well-rehearsed and precisely performed free kick. Those inspirational moments, one cold-blooded, individual brilliance, the other first rate, inventive teamwork, graced the half despite the injustice of the award of the free kick to Argentina in the first place. Since more than a touch of theatrical talent brought about both penalties and a 1–1 score, it was more than adequate compensation.

The whole nature of the game changed just after the interval when following a brutal tackle from behind by Simeone on David Beckham, the young man was aggrieved enough, while still lying face down, to kick up in the direction of his seasoned opponent. Beckham certainly couldn't have seen Simeone well enough to have taken aim and physically there can be little brute force in such a kick – frustration yes, damaging violence no. The Danish referee, Kim Nielsen, changed the character of a splendid game from an open contest between determined and talented protagonists to an enforced rearguard action; brave, it's true, but eliminating the contest which might have been. Thus England went out on penalties, but with enough honour for Glenn Hoddle to avoid the mauling that previous managers have had to tolerate.

Of course, it's easy to be wise after the event and pick a hole or two. The most obvious criticism was the selection of Teddy Sheringham over Michael Owen in the early games, although perhaps the Argentina game was the perfect time to unleash Owen's talent on the world for the full ninety minutes. The Romanian loss, and with it the easier route to the final, was the result of careless defence more than uninspired forward play. Romania scored once against both Colombia and Tunisia, but twice against England.

What was unfortunate for Hoddle and all of us was that in masterminding the strategy for the second half against Argentina, during which England were denied a penalty kick for a clear handball, Glenn had to replace tiring, artistic players with willing warriors, not necessarily talented spot-kickers. In such excitement and under such pressure, to have expected him to throw his mind forward and consider who would take the penalties was asking a lot. To survive until penalties was the primary target and this his team achieved with some splendour.

There is consolation in that the vast majority of the England squad will still be candidates for the European Championship in the year 2000, and most even for the World Cup in 2002.

I hope it won't be looked upon as sour grapes or in any way unsportsmanlike but in my cold-blooded view England were not knocked out of this World Cup, they were despatched by an inept performance from a referee. Unfortunately, they were not the only country to suffer. I do not suggest for one moment that refereeing is a simple and straightforward exercise. As the rewards become astronomical at the top, the playing skills become more finely honed; running in parallel are the murky arts of deception. Even our decent young eighteen-year-old superstar Michael Owen fell over an invisible foot in the penalty area and earned, gained, cheated, deserved, was awarded, devised a penalty – you choose the verb.

The reason why players both young and old are tempted to deceive is because they succeed more often than not and the rewards for such undeserved success win more games and points than the contemporary punishments lose. They foul or cheat simply because it is profitable. If this World Cup has proved one thing it is that, as matters stand, they are getting away with it. It's strange that FIFA chose as its prime target this time to eradicate the so-called 'tackle from behind'. In retrospect they were encouraging an actors' paradise and that's what the world witnessed. Only FIFA can reverse that trend and I accept that it is no simple matter. The objective quite clearly is to ensure that football crime does not pay. It follows that offenders must be spotted and punished accordingly. It also follows that, unlike in this World Cup, the technology should be used to prove guilt or confirm innocence after a match. Nothing can be done retrospectively to change the result of a game but in other respects a wronged individual should at least be vindicated, being entitled to retrospective justice. Making those judgements in the course of a game is no mean task. The technology exists, as in cricket, for a fourth official to scrutinise the visual evidence and dispense justice with greater accuracy. The problem with football is that it is a non-stop, all-action game to which spectators have grown accustomed, and the danger is that to interfere with that flow would lessen the excitement and reduce the entertainment value. Because of that danger, I believe that the technology should be used sparingly and only when the referee calls for it. He should consult the fourth official when he is in doubt about an incident which could clearly affect the result. Was the ball over the goalline or not? Did the offence take place in the penalty area or outside it? He should also consult when he has not seen an incident himself but suspects extreme violence of any kind. I do not think such limited stoppages would affect the flow, nor reduce the excitement. Such would be the drama and tension in most cases it could increase it.

Sadly, I do not see how the technology can help FIFA eradicate the 'duckers and divers' who were, to some degree, present in every team in France. Unhappily, it's now an international disease of epidemic proportions prevalent on all continents. The task is to make it unprofitable and that would mean a change of attitude and of the laws to apply to such cheating, because that's what it clearly is. As matters stand, a referee is able to show a yellow card for such deception under the heading of 'ungentlemanly conduct'. This is too vague. Additional offences should be added to the existing yellow-card list to clarify matters and to strengthen a referee's hand and his resolution to prevent cheats from prospering. Offences could include attempting to deceive the referee by any action which is designed to suggest an opponent has caused an injury of any kind, such injury not

311

having occurred; attempting to deceive the referee by performing an action or actions which pretend that an offence such as a trip, a push or other offence against the laws of the game has been committed by an opponent; in addition, in World Cup competitions any player receiving two yellow cards for such offences will miss the following two games. FIFA's responsibility is to implement such law changes at the earliest possible moment and to ensure that referees are fully qualified and competent to make the necessary judgements.

I should point out that nothing I saw in the quality of the performances of FIFA's chosen officials caused me to move away from my unshakeable belief expressed in an earlier chapter that the sooner they get the 'poachers' to do the job, the better the best game man has yet invented will be.

INDEX

Photograph Acknowledgements

The author and publisher would like to thank the following for permission to reproduce their copyright photographs: AllSport, Alpha/Sport & General, the BBC, Central Press, Colorsport, *Coventry Evening Telegraph*, Hulton Deutsch, LWT, Popperfoto, Reveille Newspapers Ltd, Rex Features, Bill Smith, Thames Television, A. Wilkes & Son.